The Greening of Antarctica

The Greening of Antarctica

Assembling an International Environment

ALESSANDRO ANTONELLO

OXFORD
UNIVERSITY PRESS

OXFORD
UNIVERSITY PRESS

Oxford University Press is a department of the University of Oxford. It furthers the University's objective of excellence in research, scholarship, and education by publishing worldwide. Oxford is a registered trade mark of Oxford University Press in the UK and certain other countries.

Published in the United States of America by Oxford University Press
198 Madison Avenue, New York, NY 10016, United States of America.

CIP data is on file at the Library of Congress
ISBN 978–0–19–090717–4

1 3 5 7 9 8 6 4 2

Printed by Sheridan Books, Inc., United States of America

Parts of chapter 1 previously appeared in Alessandro Antonello, "Nature Conservation and Antarctic Diplomacy, 1959–1964," *The Polar Journal* 4, no. 2 (2014): 335–53, copyright Taylor and Francis. Parts of chapter 4 previously appeared in Alessandro Antonello, "Protecting the Southern Ocean Ecosystem: The Environmental Protection Agenda of Antarctic Diplomacy and Science," in *International Organizations and Environmental Protection: Conservation and Globalization in the Twentieth Century*, ed. Wolfram Kaiser and Jan-Henrik Meyer (New York and Oxford: Berghahn, 2017), 268–92, copyright Alessandro Antonello.

Contents

Acknowledgments

I AM DEEPLY grateful to the many people and institutions who have made this book possible. Two wonderful friends and mentors have particularly influenced my development as a historian and this book. Tom Griffiths has been unfailingly generous with his time and wisdom. He has always been a sensitive reader and supportive of my aspirations for this work as well as more broadly as a historian. He is the model of a mentor and historian, and his dedication to the scholarly art that is history is an inspiration. Mark Carey took a punt on a distant Australian for a postdoc on his project on the history of humans and their relationship with ice. He was welcoming as both friend and colleague in Eugene, Oregon, and I was sad to leave after my two years were up. He has also been a model to me as a mentor and historian in his care for my personal well-being and career and in his deep engagement with my work.

Most of the work on this book occurred when I was a PhD student in the School of History, Research School of Social Sciences, at the Australian National University. It is a pleasure to recognize the generous financial support of ANU with a vice chancellor's scholarship, which included not only a stipend but also a healthy research budget that allowed extended trips to many archives. In our usual habitats of the Coombs Tea Room and the University House gardens and bar, the school staff and my fellow PhD students were wonderful companions on my journey, and I am thankful to them for reading drafts, listening to and discussing ideas in formation, or generally supporting me in becoming a historian. Thanks to them and others at ANU, including Joan Beaumont, Brett Bennett, Alexis Bergantz, Frank Bongiorno, Nicholas Brown, Murray Chisholm, Doug Craig, Robyn Curtis, Hamish Dalley, Karen Downing, Kim Doyle, Arnold Ellem, Diane Erceg, David Fettling, Niki Francis, Barry Higman, Meggie Hutchinson, John Knott, Cameron McLachlan, Tristan Moss, Cameron Muir, Shannyn

Palmer, Anne Rees, Libby Robin, Blake Singley, Karen Smith, Carolyn Strange, and Angela Woollacott.

This book underwent much revision and refinement while I was a postdoctoral research fellow at the University of Oregon. Here I gratefully note the support of the National Science Foundation under grant number 1253779. In addition to Mark Carey, I found myself in a wonderful community of scholars in the Robert D. Clark Honors College and the wider university. For their engagement with my work, my thanks to Hayley Brazier, M Jackson, Katie Meehan, Olivia Molden, Marsha Weisiger, Tim Williams, members of the Glacier Lab, and the engaged honors students of my Antarctic history seminar. After Eugene, I was very happy to arrive at the University of Melbourne as a McKenzie postdoctoral fellow, where the very final touches to this book happened, and I am thankful to my new colleagues in the School of Historical and Philosophical Studies for welcoming me.

I am thankful to others at various conferences and archives around the world for sharing their knowledge of Antarctica and environmental and international history more generally. A small band of Antarctic historians and other humanities scholars has been a wonderful community to be in, and my thanks especially to Adrian Howkins, Peder Roberts, Lize-Marie van der Watt, Elizabeth Leane, Marcus Haward, and Cornelia Lüdecke. I am grateful to the SCAR History Expert Group and Social Sciences Action Group for a travel grant in 2013. For opportunities to publish elements of my Antarctic research during the work on this book, I am grateful to Klaus Dodds, Alan Hemmings, Peder Roberts, Lize-Marie van der Watt, Adrian Howkins, Wolfram Kaiser, Jan-Henrik Meyer, Marcus Haward, and Tom Griffiths. At Oxford University Press, my thanks to Susan Ferber and Alexandra Dauler as well as the two anonymous reviewers for their crucial input.

My time in archives and libraries has been enhanced by many dedicated and knowledgeable librarians and archivists, and I am grateful to them all. In Australia, to the staff of the National Archives of Australia, especially Christina Beresford and Barrie Paterson of Hobart and Kerry Jeffery of Canberra, as well as to the staff of the National Library of Australia, the Basser Library of the Australian Academy of Science, the Australian Antarctic Division Library, and the Australian National University Library. In New Zealand, to the staff of the National Archives and of the Alexander Turnbull Library and to Neil Robertson of the Ministry of Foreign Affairs and Trade. In the United Kingdom, to Ellen Bazeley-White and Joanna Rae of the British Antarctic Survey; Shirley Sawtell and Naomi Boneham of the Scott Polar Research Institute, University of Cambridge; Renuke Badhe and Rosemary Nash of the Scientific Committee on Antarctic Research Secretariat, Cambridge; and the staff of the Royal Society Library and Archives and the National Archives of the United Kingdom. In the United States, to the staff of the National Archives and Records Administration at College Park, the Library of Congress, the Archives of the National Academies of Science, the Hoover Institution Archives, and Stanford University, as well as to Claire Christian of the Antarctic and Southern Ocean Coalition, Washington, DC.

Many dear friends have also seen this book and me develop over the years and have at various points housed, fed, and endured me. My particular thanks to Madeline Cooper, Danae Paxinos, Lauren Hannan, and Luisa De Liseo. Finally, and most importantly, my deepest thanks are to my family, Fernanda and Peter, Marco and Georgia. While I completed my studies and work in Canberra and Eugene (among other places), they were always there in Melbourne, a wonderful and welcoming home. This work would be impossible without them.

The Greening of Antarctica

Introduction

ORDER, POWER, AUTHORITY AND THE ANTARCTIC ENVIRONMENT

"THE DISTINGUISHED REPRESENTATIVE of the United States has told us that we all know what Antarctica is." These were the arch words of a Soviet diplomat, spoken in the heat of negotiations on the Antarctic Treaty in late October 1959.[1] Gathered in a conference room in Washington, DC, in October and November 1959, representatives of twelve nations were negotiating a treaty for the peaceful uses of, and freedom of scientific investigation in, Antarctica. Following the Second World War, international tensions had been developing in the Antarctic, arising from a contest for territory, geopolitical position, resources, and scientific knowledge. The diplomats from these twelve nations agreed that their treaty had to apply to a specific geographical area; "Antarctica" seemed obvious, but the strictures of international law and diplomacy demanded specificity. The pointed observation, even sly criticism, of the Soviet diplomat—"has *told* us that we all know what Antarctica is"—suggested that the diplomats and scientists of the twelve nations did not, in fact, agree on what Antarctica was. Uncertain knowledge and only incipient environmental sensibilities mapped onto diplomatic disagreement and tension.

The Soviet diplomat—Grigory Ivanovich Tunkin, head of the legal department of the Soviet foreign affairs ministry and one of the leading international lawyers of his day—was not simply dissembling or being contrarian, despite the reality of Cold War competition.[2] On that day the conference discussed the "zone of application" of the potential treaty, a question that touched on the sensitive issue of the freedom of the high seas that had been animating international legal and diplomatic negotiations at the time. Tunkin's point referred to the complexities—indeed, the unknowns—of geographical, scientific, and environmental imagination about Antarctica in the late 1950s and the ways those imaginings and conceptualizations might be codified into a reliable treaty text. It was an issue that threw into relief each nation's distinct historical experience of the Antarctic, those who claimed sovereignty over Antarctic territories, and those who denied that sovereignty could exist there. It was an issue that suggested tensions about how to use Antarctica and how to structure peaceful relations around such uses. It was a question of exactly which parts, which elements of the great and complex, though not entirely known, Antarctic region, were really of concern to these nations.

International legal practice relied on land to set borders and boundaries and to structure relations, so Antarctica, with its ice in various forms and its encircling cold ocean, as well as simple lack of knowledge, challenged textually tidy legalities. Tunkin noted that "in the Russian language Antarctica means the whole area around the South Pole," implying both land and oceans. He added, "The scientists of many countries believe that the boundary of that area is the line of the Antarctic convergence, that is to say, where there is a meeting of the waters of the south regions with those of the temperate regions of the Southern Hemisphere"; this was indeed the geographic area of concern to the newly created Scientific Committee on Antarctic Research (SCAR).[3] Tunkin's Soviet colleague Alexander Afanasiev, a senior polar bureaucrat, noted a few days after the first intervention on the matter: "Until now, the definite boundary of the real Continent of Antarctic which is under the ice has not yet been determined, and in fact the visible boundaries of the Antarctic Continent are more or less everywhere not determined by the coastline."[4] During the ongoing discussion, the Australian delegate—Australian foreign minister Richard Casey, who had a decades-long connection with and interest in the Antarctic—pursued the matter further, offering the point—"not an entirely fantastic one," he thought—that "we do not know yet whether the Antarctic is a Continent. It may well in the course of time by investigation turn out to be an archipelago, a series of islands."[5]

All these words were spoken in a meeting room in Washington, DC, where the Conference on Antarctica, attended by ninety-nine delegates, was gathered. Perhaps only five of those delegates had actually been to Antarctica.[6] Most of the other delegates were acquainted with the region through their official responsibilities as officers in foreign ministries and other bureaucracies, or as diplomats in embassies; they had read reports about scientific efforts there and had dispatched cables and memorandums around the world discussing the various advantages and disadvantages of particular political schemes and scientific plans. Some were clearly more conversant with matters Antarctic than others. This was a drama not of heroic deeds upon the ice or ocean, but of argument and contestation over the negotiating table.

The Antarctica under negotiation at this conference, therefore, was something both real and imagined. As Richard Casey's comment about Antarctica being an "archipelago" suggests, some in the room were conscious of the material reality of the Antarctic, a region of ice, ocean, rock, and animals. The International Geophysical Year (IGY) of 1957–1958, which had in part influenced the geopolitical situation, had profoundly altered and increased knowledge of the region. Yet the material and natural Antarctic was only unevenly present in the words and actions of the negotiators. The preponderance of diplomats, politicians, and international lawyers—as opposed to scientists—around the table is suggestive of the most pressing concern: geopolitical order and stability at a time of tensions to prevent disorder and potential conflict. Antarctica was obviously the place they were concerned with, but the Antarctic they had in mind, which was eventually articulated and codified in the Antarctic Treaty, was a relatively sterile and abiotic continent, with loose and oblique talk of resource prospects. Really, it was a stage for their geopolitical relations and contests. As Casey noted in his diary, "The Treaty in the broad was designed to create stability and a sense of permanence in the Antarctic, so that we would all know where we were."[7] Casey's spatial metaphor here did not refer to the where of the Antarctic region—its wildlife, ice, and seas—but rather to the geopolitical positioning and relationships of the states involved.

Twelve nations did eventually sign the Antarctic Treaty, on December 1, 1959. The treaty was the beginning of what has now become known as the Antarctic Treaty System (ATS), a wide-ranging suite of international law that provides for free scientific research in Antarctica and comprehensive protection of its environment. The twelve original signatories were the only "consultative" members of this regime—that is, members with voting and negotiation rights within the meetings—until 1977, when Poland became the first new consultative party added.[8] If, in 1959, there was disagreement over what exactly Antarctica was, in the decades since, ever-increasing knowledge of the Antarctic, a larger place for scientific voices, profound changes in concepts of the global environment, changes in international political economy, and the continuing reality of national self-interest have meant that the idea of what Antarctica is has changed significantly but has also stabilized in both diplomatic and scientific terms.

Between the signing of the Antarctic Treaty in 1959 and the signing of the landmark Convention on the Conservation of Antarctic Marine Living Resources (CCAMLR) in 1980, a group of states and their diplomats and officials, scientists, and scientific institutions transformed the Antarctic from a cold, abiotic, and sterile wilderness, a lifeless and inert stage for geopolitical competition, into a fragile environment and ecosystem demanding international protection and management. Arising out of a contest for power, control, and authority, this transformation occurred in environmental, scientific, geopolitical, and diplomatic registers and was embedded and codified in international treaties. In successive meetings, in diplomatic cables, and in publications and correspondence, these states and scientists assembled the contemporary Antarctic from an array of ideas, natural entities and bodies, laws and relationships, spatial formations, and temporal conceptions, codifying these to stabilize and make orderly not only interstate relations, but also the human relationship with the Antarctic environment.

Two deeply related developments defined Antarctic history in the 1960s and 1970s.[9] The first was a conceptual transformation from the idea of a sterile and abiotic continent, shaped by geophysical sciences, to a vision of a living, fragile, and pristine Antarctic region that included the Southern Ocean and was shaped by the biological sciences. The second development was the negotiation of a suite of international treaties and associated agreements for the conservation and protection of the Antarctic environment. Together, these two developments constituted the greening of Antarctica and the assembly of an international environment. The term "international environment" encompasses the links developed among the physical environment, the world of ideas and sensibilities attaching to it, and the legal framework articulated through treaties to govern that environment and the people and states who lived with it.[10] Furthermore, the meanings here of the word "environment"—as well as the closely associated and overlapping ideas of conservation, preservation, and protection—must be understood as historically contingent and specific.

The greening of Antarctica was articulated and codified in four major agreements. The first substantial agreement following the Antarctic Treaty was the Agreed Measures for the Conservation of Antarctic Fauna and Flora (AMCAFF) in 1964, negotiations for which began almost immediately after the signing of the treaty. The next major "environmental" agreement the parties made was the Convention for the Conservation of Antarctic Seals (CCAS) in 1972, negotiated after 1964 and partly arising from the limited geographical reach of AMCAFF. The third major environmental agreement and negotiations related to the question of mineral resources and exploitation began in 1969 and culminated in a temporary moratorium agreement in 1977. And the fourth agreement, signed in 1980 following discussions that began mid-decade relating to fisheries and their exploitation, was the legally novel CCAMLR, rooted in the marine ecosystem.[11]

Each of these agreements held the endings and beginnings of long histories of scientific, environmental, cultural, and political engagement with the Antarctic. These texts had many authors, including the twelve states that negotiated and signed them, many individual diplomats and scientists, and other states and individuals besides the treaty parties, who influenced negotiations from outside the regime. These texts, both explicitly and ambiguously, articulated and codified visions of what Antarctica should be, governed legitimate and illegitimate actions, opened up and foreclosed avenues of development, and were inclusive and exclusive of certain actors. Their geographies manifested those that dominated at the time of signing and also normatively inscribed the region for the future, and they suggested histories and futures. These international legal texts were central to the process of knowing the earth. In a way these processes were, as Erik Mueggler has described in the rather different context of botanical collection in China, "putting earth onto paper."[12] Treaties are richer texts than their legal contexts might initially suggest, especially in Antarctica, where they are invoked almost daily, whether rhetorically or legalistically.

As with so many natural environments, there is a tension regarding Antarctica between the environment of the imagination and texts and the material world that people faced and were forced to engage with. There was not, and is not, a straightforward or self-evident relationship among diplomats, scientists, and environments; the nonhuman world, and human relationships with it—whether exploitative or conceptualized in terms of conservation, preservation, or protection—had to be imagined and constituted in various realms of thought.[13] These ideas and bodies of thought were tied, with varying intensities, to the material Antarctic. People's interactions with a material environment are profoundly shaped by their ideas and preconceptions about it. For Antarctica, in addition, not only are states' and scientists' relationships with it mediated by such ideas, but these ideas have the force (weak or strong as it is) of international law and geopolitical reasoning.

The story of the greening of Antarctica in the 1960s and 1970s reveals substantial issues and a time period that are distinct from other, more dominant perspectives on and approaches to Antarctic history, both in social science and humanities scholarship and in more general histories. The image of diplomats, officials, and scientists imagining Antarctica and assembling an international environmental order differs substantially from the well-known stories of the discoveries and researches of the "heroic era" of the early twentieth century, when the likes of Robert Scott, Ernest Shackleton, Roald Amundsen, and Douglas Mawson were exploring—and Scott and Shackleton dying in—an almost completely unknown region, racing for the South Pole, racing for discovery, recognition, and glory.[14] Furthermore, elucidating the competing claims to authority and power in Antarctica during the earliest decades of the treaty shifts attention away from the preoccupations of other scholarship relating to international environmental politics that seeks to evaluate effectiveness, success, or failure in particular regimes, as important as that work is.[15]

Focusing on the 1960s and 1970s also redraws the periodization of Antarctic history and reframes understanding about the origins of conservation and environmental protection in the region. The rejection of the Convention on the Regulation of Antarctic Mineral Resource Activities (CRAMRA)—negotiated between 1982 and 1988—and the subsequent negotiation and signature of the Protocol on Environmental Protection to the Antarctic Treaty (the Madrid Protocol, signed in 1991) are generally portrayed in popular discourse—and to a lesser, though still significant, extent in certain academic literatures—as the turning point of environmental politics and protection in Antarctic history.[16] Though undoubtedly the source of the current environmental regime in Antarctica, the Madrid Protocol's principal concepts and regulations—its specific conceptions of environmental protection, environmental impact, and associated and dependent ecosystems, as well as its rhetoric of environmental stewardship drawing on a closed international system—perpetuated those generated and negotiated in the treaty's first two decades. Even CRAMRA contained ideas and articles that perpetuated the environmental order established up to the signature of CCAMLR in 1980. The diplomats and scientists who rejected CRAMRA and negotiated the Madrid Protocol were working on a stage that had been set, to a significant degree, in the 1960s and 1970s.[17] They obviously could have rejected and reframed the entire environmental and scientific edifice—a radical and perhaps untenable counterfactual act—yet they perpetuated it. It was between the signing of the Antarctic Treaty in 1959 and CCAMLR in 1980 that Antarctica's modern international environmental character was substantially developed and entrenched.[18]

Changing ideas about the Antarctic environment gave the Antarctic Treaty parties new ground—literally and rhetorically, new lands and seas—on which to exercise their powers and attempt to advance their positions. Their geopolitics was not carried out on an unchanging and timeless vision of the Antarctic. The Antarctic environment was reinterpreted, re-envisioned, and invested with new meaning over these two decades, and it was seen and made legible in new ways. By 1980 the Antarctic was a very different assemblage of concepts, ideas, histories, sciences, material things and entities, relationships, spatial formations, and temporal conceptions.[19] The various human and nonhuman, material and imagined elements of the Antarctic were enrolled and assembled in specific ways to advance the competing and overlapping political, environmental, scientific, intellectual, cultural, and commercial projects for Antarctica. By 1980 the Antarctic was not simply, as the historian Stephen Pyne put it, "a white spot on the globe" after its exploration, but a complex region of life with an equally complex human regime engaging with and managing it.[20] By seeing and recognizing the various elements of the whole Antarctic environment—the terrestrial and marine ecosystems, the geological elements—the Antarctic Treaty parties were creating new ground for their politics and relations. States, with scientists attendant, envisaged and created the grounds for their politics as much as simply finding a patch of earth to control.[21]

The modern Antarctic order developed because the political settlement of 1959—limited in intent, tied to geophysical sciences, and articulating an almost inert terrain—could not be maintained in the face of changing conceptions of Antarctica or "the environment" more generally. These changing conceptions—arising from continued scientific inquiry, changing global environmental sensibilities, and new geographies of international law and resource exploitation—disrupted the 1959 settlement, providing an opportunity for the treaty's parties and scientists, both individually and collectively, to advance their interests. The parties assembled an international environment to protect and enhance their own positions; their sense of order; and their stable diplomatic, geopolitical, and environmental relationships.

MODERN ANTARCTIC HISTORY began with the Antarctic Treaty, signed on December 1, 1959.[22] Twelve states signed it: Argentina, Australia, Belgium, Chile, France, Japan, New Zealand, Norway, South Africa, the Soviet Union, the United Kingdom, and the United States. They each had historic ties to the region, with longer or shorter connections through scientific research or whaling and sealing industries; they were also the countries that had participated in the IGY. By signing the treaty they were attempting to ameliorate problems and conflicts that had been troubling their relationships, especially since the end of the Second World War.

Principal among these problems were the explicit disagreements over the character of territorial sovereignty, the foundational tension of Antarctic affairs. Between 1908 and 1943 seven states claimed territory in Antarctica (see figure I.1). The territorial rush began with the United

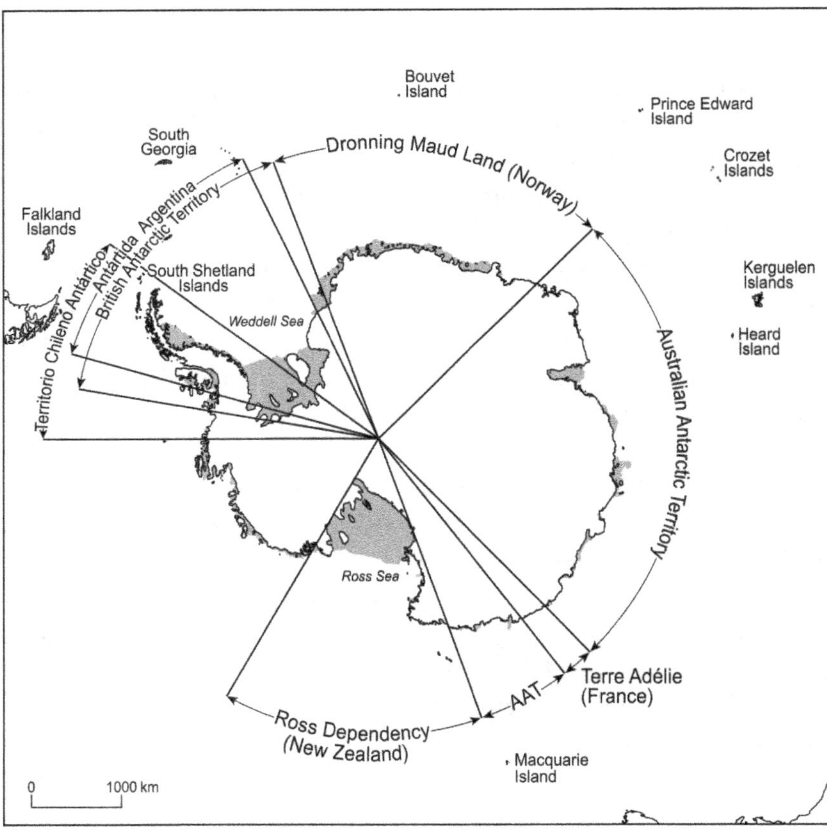

FIGURE I.1 The seven territorial claims to Antarctica. Cartography: Chandra Jayasuriya.

Kingdom's claim to the Antarctic Peninsula in 1908, followed by claims made by New Zealand in 1923, France in 1924, Australia in 1933, Norway in 1939, Chile in 1940, and Argentina in 1943.[23] These claims, however, went generally unrecognized by any other states. Furthermore, the British, Argentine, and Chilean claims to the Antarctic Peninsula region overlapped, and these states lived in a cycle of protest and counterprotest.[24] The United States and the Soviet Union quite explicitly reserved the right to make territorial claims.

The second major problem was the tension and suspicion arising from the conflicts and bipolarity of the Cold War. The main concerns came from the Western bloc countries that had witnessed the projection of the Soviet Union into the region; to be sure, the Antarctic was also enrolled in American Cold War-era nationalism.[25] While Richard Byrd had represented the United States in the south before the Second World War, laying a basis of territorial claim for the nation in the process, the Soviet Union had injected itself into Antarctic affairs in 1950 when it delivered a bold diplomatic missive to the United States stating that any international agreement on the Antarctic must include the USSR. The Soviet Union declared that owing to "the outstanding contributions of Russian seamen in the discovery of Antarctica"—that is, the global circumnavigation voyage of Bellingshausen, which perhaps first sighted the Antarctic continent in 1820—as well as its whaling activities in Antarctic waters, it could not "recognize as legal any decision regarding the regime of the Antarctic taken without its participation."[26]

The third principal challenge was the immense scientific program of the IGY. Occurring between July 1, 1957, and December 31, 1958, the IGY was a worldwide program of scientific research that sought to understand the earth's geophysical phenomena through concentrated, simultaneous, and synoptic observation and data collection. The geophysical sciences had grown in size and importance in the decade following the Second World War, patronized by the American and Soviet militaries, who were both searching for geophysical knowledge on which to build geostrategic superiority and dominance.[27] The IGY brought a significant international scientific program to Antarctica and destabilized traditional geopolitics through the physical activities and presence of scientists from many countries, as well as an ebullient rhetoric of scientific internationalism and the motivating ideals that science and scientists might bring peace and harmony to the world—ironic, given the place of many scientists within national defense and security institutions. The IGY was a transformative event not only for the geophysical sciences, but also because it exacerbated postwar territorial and Cold War tensions. In a general sense, its tenor of international cooperation destabilized the sense of Antarctica as a space that could be claimed by individual nation-states as sovereign territory. In a more specific way, the IGY was seen by Western countries as allowing, even sanctioning, extensive Soviet activities. It also led to the formation of the principal international body of Antarctic scientists, SCAR, which continues to be the main international scientific forum on Antarctica to this day.[28]

These apparently intractable disagreements over territorial sovereignty, the threatening and seemingly immovable presence of the Soviet Union, and the powerful discourse of international cooperation through science led the United States in early 1958 to push for an international agreement for Antarctica. An international agreement had been canvassed in 1948, though it was swiftly dismissed. Australia, Britain, and New Zealand had been in discussions with the Americans from late 1957, trying to convince the United States to make a claim to territory and to push for an international agreement excluding the Soviet Union.[29] After internal considerations in early 1958, US officials decided not to press a claim but instead to invite the eleven other countries participating in the IGY to a diplomatic conference to negotiate a treaty that would guarantee freedom of scientific investigation and ensure Antarctica would be used for peaceful purposes only. All the states accepted the invitation, negotiating the Antarctic Treaty in two stages: first, in a series of sixty preparatory meetings beginning in June 1958 and then in a formal conference in October and November 1959.

The treaty committed the signatories to several basic principles. It stated that "Antarctica shall be used for peaceful purposes only" and that military activities were prohibited (article I). It also established the principle of "freedom of scientific investigation" and committed the parties to promoting international scientific cooperation among themselves (articles II and III). And it prohibited nuclear explosions and the disposal of radioactive waste (article V). Underwriting these guarantees was article IV, a political compromise on territorial sovereignty, which provided that by signing and acting within the treaty, no state was renouncing its territorial sovereignty, renouncing or diminishing its basis of claim to territorial sovereignty, prejudicing its position of recognition or nonrecognition of territorial sovereignty, or doing anything that could be the basis of a future claim or enlarged claim. Without this article, there would not have been an agreement. The treaty applied to the land and ice shelf areas south of 60° south latitude, but not the high seas (article VI). To ensure faithful and effective adherence to the treaty, article VII instituted a system of wide-ranging inspection and exchange of information. Finally, the treaty established periodic meetings—later to be called Antarctic Treaty Consultative Meetings (ATCMs)—"for the purpose of exchanging information, consulting together on matters of common interest pertaining to Antarctica, and formulating and considering, and recommending to their Governments, measures in furtherance of the principles and objectives of the Treaty" (article IX).[30]

The treaty articulated a limited consensus, with some of the parties seeing a productive internationalized future for the Antarctic under the treaty and others hoping for a circumscribed future of limited activities and minimal engagement. In all of this, the Antarctica of the treaty was a stage for their relationships, rather than a meaningful and constitutive part of them. That the natural and living environment would become central to human concerns in the Antarctic over the following decades was not foreseen when the twelve states signed the treaty.

Concentrating on the text of the treaty can suggest that the signatories covered all potential futures and had reached a perfect or robust consensus. Agreeing to the treaty was a substantial achievement that required serious effort and compromise on all parts. Each party had to consider how its Antarctic past and present could articulate into a future characterized by superpower dominance, checks on pretensions to sovereign territory, and freedom for scientific activities. For some this was a desirable future; for others, it was one to enter only out of necessity, perhaps reluctantly. In the process, the parties agreed to a particular disposition of environment, science, and politics.

Yet there were still other Antarcticas and other politics alluded to in the treaty that were maintained and smuggled through the negotiations to emerge on the other side; the treaty had a complex tangle of histories embedded in it. It therefore developed in ways unexpected or not intended by its negotiators. While sophisticated scholarship has critically explored the links between the IGY and the treaty, there is still a tendency to see all the contemporary issues and successes of the ATS as latent in the negotiations and text of the Antarctic Treaty as written and codified in 1959, which many see as a direct outcome of the IGY.[31] This is surely an untenable restriction on critical analyses that might allow a more useful place for history in contemporary Antarctic politics. Understanding Antarctic history during the treaty era requires careful attention to both internal and external dynamics, not just an eye for the treaty's apparent self-perpetuation. The dynamic of Antarctic history after 1959 was not simply one set in motion by the treaty, but rather a complex entanglement of worldwide developments with the particularities of Antarctica, a situation of permanent renegotiation and reinterpretation.

The treaty parties could not maintain their particular agreement in the face of changing circumstances in Antarctica and the wider world. The diplomats representing the treaty parties perceived challenges in the 1960s from scientists pushing for a system of nature conservation and from the prospects of renewed exploitation of seals, and in the 1970s from the potential exploitation of minerals and oil and the expanding extraction of marine living resources, especially in the form of krill. In a growing and developing world with finite resources—as well as an increasing sense of, and global discourses on, those limits and scarcity—these pressures to exploit were profound. But the parties also faced changing global environmental sensibilities, a new sense of fragility and interconnectedness between humanity and the natural environment, and new ideas of preservation and respect for the whole earth system—pressures that were equally profound. The greening of Antarctica was a broad trajectory that encompassed a range of actors looking to keep or gain power in a changing world.

With a large and complex cast of actors—twelve states; a variety of scientific institutions, most especially SCAR; individual scientists; and other actors—there were competing ideas about and aspirations for Antarctica. To grasp and elucidate all of them in a work of this scope—considering especially that there were twelve original signatories to the treaty, speaking six languages—would be untenable. Some signatories and actors were more attached, concerned, influential, and dominant than others. While this book relies on the official archives of the four English-speaking parties—Australia, New Zealand, the United Kingdom, and the United States, who to be sure had independently formed positions of their own—as well as on other smaller personal and institutional collections, I hope it avoids what Klaus Dodds and Alan Hemmings have labeled "polar orientalism," a scholarly and political strategy of delegitimizing the ideas and efforts of non-Western and non-English-speaking states.[32]

Despite the competing ideas, several elements were shared by the actors, both state and nonstate. Following one of the impetuses of the

Antarctic Treaty, each of the treaty parties wanted some version of stability and order. The treaty committed each of the parties to not allow Antarctica to become "a scene of international discord." In a limited reading, this meant principally that the area below 60° south latitude would remain nonmilitarized and without nuclear weapons and waste. In a more capacious reading it meant that the parties had to cooperate and work together in shaping an international region. "Order" here has several more connotations and resonances than simply an absence of disorder. There was also a search—competing and overlapping among the parties—for *an* order, a structure of relations, rights, and obligations. In Antarctica a society of states was seeking stability, good and dependable relations, some measure of power, authority, and benefits with obligations.[33]

In the 1960s and 1970s, the Antarctic states and the community of Antarctic scientists assembled an international environment with particular characteristics. There was an emphasis on the protection of the environment; conservation and sustainable use of natural resources; prevention and mitigation of environmental impacts; the centrality of scientific knowledge and work; an aversion to "discord" and the maximization of "benefit"; and the privileges and centrality of a particular, circumscribed group of actors—all elements that continue to define the contemporary, post-Madrid Antarctic order in various ways. This order was not simply an interstate governance or diplomatic regime; it was made up of a range of environmental, scientific, legal, and geopolitical conceptualizations and ideas relating to Antarctica as much as the codified and formal instruments of international law and diplomacy.[34] Furthermore, the order assembled was not simply among state-actors in a society of states. Their order also consisted of a structure of relations with the natural world and of knowledge and conceptions of the natural world.[35] As a result, stability and order here meant more than simply geopolitical order; they also included stable, dependable, and anticipatory relationships with the physical and material Antarctic itself, which, as a complex assemblage of geophysical bodies and biological communities, was still being scientifically discovered and revealed throughout this period.

Each actor was also seeking some measure of authority and power, both individually and, when necessary, as a collective. Though dominant popular perceptions depicted a howling wilderness without commercial value, industrialists, entrepreneurs, and state officials saw a rather different Antarctica. Beginning with sealing in the early nineteenth century and continuing with whaling in the twentieth century, many officials and scientists held clear visions of a prospective and resource-rich Antarctic.[36] This commercial imagination also stretched to consider potential fisheries and the continual lure of mineral and oil wealth. While exploitation of the Southern Ocean was demonstrably feasible and valuable, the continuing dream of mineral riches, though it seems fantastical, animated a great deal of Antarctic activity in the twentieth century. But the search for power and authority was not simply about gaining wealth through mineral and living resources. For Antarctic scientists, it meant power to speak authoritatively for Antarctic nature, to claim a privileged position for physically occupying the south polar region, and to enhance scientific and institutional standing and esteem.[37] For states, that search for authority and power in Antarctica reflected larger international questions, the most important of which was the law of the sea.

In their search for order and stability, power and authority, the Antarctic Treaty states and their scientists, instead of strictly maintaining their original and limited political agreement to manage their territorial disagreements, found opportunities to advance their own positions, strategically taking opportunities to assemble an international order for the conservation and preservation of the environment, as well as an "exclusive" space for themselves. Some of this politics was old—the continuing contest over the idea of Antarctica as potential sovereign territory and the limits and potentials of sovereignty—and some was new—structures of resource exploitation and issues of environmental impact. These questions, old and new, were not simply Antarctic questions, but issues that each party faced in international relations more generally: power and authority over parts of the earth, amicable and productive relations with others, and structures for peace and order. Furthermore, because these questions so thoroughly involved the natural world—an aggregated entity that was increasingly being called in these decades "the environment," as well as relationships with that natural environment coming under the broad labels of conservation, preservation, or protection—the states, scientists, and others were also thinking in new ways about how "the environment" could or should be included in the broader sphere of international politics and world order.[38]

THE GREENING OF *Antarctica* proceeds chronologically, though with some overlap, through the two decades after the signing of the Antarctic Treaty in 1959. Chapter 1 investigates one of the first major issues dealt with by the treaty parties: the conservation of wildlife. Beginning in 1959, even before the conclusion of the treaty negotiations, biological scientists had observed the effects of human presence on Antarctic wildlife and called for constraints and protections. Within the new SCAR, a group of biologists drew on their scientific knowledge and the worldwide experience of conservation to call for protections of Antarctic animals, especially through protected areas. The parties took up the conservation issue and by 1964 had negotiated AMCAFF. In these early years of the treaty, conservation was a tool of advancement and power both for biologists working in Antarctica (hitherto under the shadow of the physical scientists), who wanted a more explicit place in the new Antarctic structures, and for the diplomats and parties, who recognized the gaps in the Antarctic Treaty and wanted to fill their relationships and regime with meaning and with structures for controlling each other.

Chapter 2 tells the story of scientific and diplomatic debates and negotiations regarding sealing in the Antarctic between 1964 and 1972. AMCAFF was constrained because it only applied to land, not to the oceans in which seals and penguins spent a good deal of their time. This limitation became obvious when it seemed that there might be a resurgence of the sealing industry in the mid-1960s. Despite the specter of sealing quickly passing, the parties persisted in negotiating an agreement, signing CCAS, in 1972. This chapter illuminates these negotiations as a search for authority in Antarctica: for the scientific authority of SCAR and for the political authority of states in a time of emerging global environmentalism.

Chapter 3 analyzes the minerals and hydrocarbon interests that emerged throughout the late 1960s and early 1970s. Though mining activities seemed a far-distant prospect, geopolitical and technological developments made the treaty parties worry that their regime of peace and science might be subsumed again by contestation and anarchy, dredging up the still-sensitive but well-managed question of sovereignty and territorial rights. So they opened discussions on the question of whether Antarctic minerals should be exploited and the forms of a potential regime to control that exploitation. In their negotiations and discussions, the parties' diplomats and scientists articulated ideas of environmental impact and reconceptualized both Antarctic space and time—further enlarging the space and environments over which Antarctic politics occurred and negotiating with visions of the future.

Chapter 4 investigates the other major resource question of the 1970s: Antarctic fisheries and living marine resources. Exploratory fishing research in the 1960s by the Soviets suggested that the foundational element of the Antarctic food web, the super-abundant krill, could be profitably and usefully harvested for human consumption. This chapter looks at the scientific questions arising from these developments, demonstrating the emergence of the ecosystem as the principal object of biological research in the Antarctic and the historically significant step of codifying that ecosystem in an international treaty; CCAMLR was the first treaty to protect a whole ecosystem. The codification of the ecosystem was the result of positioning for authority by scientists with SCAR as well as the dominant Anglo-American conservationist visions of Antarctic space against the Soviet and Japanese visions.

Chapter 5 concentrates on the more political and legal side of the resources questions, tracing how the new conceptions of Antarctic minerals and the marine ecosystem reverberated through the old questions of territorial sovereignty and the international politics of the 1970s. This final chapter shows two contests over boundaries and relationships at the end of the 1970s: the first between the treaty parties and the rest of the world, especially the developing world, and the second a renewed contest between the territorial claimants and the nonclaimants within the treaty. In responding to these developments, the treaty parties tied themselves more closely together, the claimants using the external intrusions to build a stronger, more exclusive regime. The Antarctic order that had been constituted by 1980 was the stage on which the extensive negotiations over mineral resources and debates about global access to Antarctica through such venues as the United Nations were fought in the 1980s; that it continued to provide the foundation of Antarctic affairs into the 1990s and beyond is suggestive of its robustness and durability.

What emerges from this study, then, is a picture of Antarctica not as a clearly defined and delineated region, governed straightforwardly through a frictionless, consensus-based, international regime. Rather, visions of Antarctica were transformed through intellectual and scientific developments, profound changes in the wider world, continuing positioning for power and authority, and a search for order and stability. A particular kind of living, ecosystem-focused, regionally expansive Antarctica was assembled to be the object of international diplomacy, politics, and science. This Antarctica, this international environment, remains in the present, and was fought over in the 1980s especially in the context of a mining debate that eventually led to a comprehensive environmental protection and management regime, whose seeds can be found in the 1960s and 1970s.

I

Principles for "Unprincipled Men"

FILLING THE HOUSEHOLD OF ANTARCTIC NATURE

IN NOVEMBER 1959, as the conference negotiating the Antarctic Treaty was in its final throes in Washington, DC, delegates to another meeting were revealing the newly discovered and refined contours of the Antarctic environment. Fifty-five scientists from the twelve nations participating in the International Geophysical Year (IGY) program in Antarctica met in Buenos Aires at a symposium convened to disseminate and discuss their results. Among the mostly geophysical papers were eighteen on biology and physiology. One of those papers was on the subject of nature conservation; it bore the very straightforward title "Nature Conservation in the Antarctic." That paper's author, Robert Carrick, a biologist and ecologist with Australia's Commonwealth Scientific and Industrial Research Organisation (CSIRO), was not present to deliver his paper, but the official record of the symposium vaguely noted that "the mention of its title gave rise to an interesting exchange of ideas regarding the problem." That problem was one every other part of the earth had experienced and that Antarctica now faced: the negative consequences of human activities for animals, plants, and the environment. At the closing plenary session, the delegates adopted a long and detailed resolution on the subject, opening with the declaration, "The delegates to this Symposium are convinced that the time has come to take positive steps towards the protection and preservation of Antarctic wild life."[1]

Carrick's paper and the symposium's resolution opened the first period of serious and concerted international effort in Antarctic nature conservation, which would conclude with the Agreed Measures for the Conservation of Antarctic Fauna and Flora (AMCAFF) in June 1964. The treaty parties began discussing nature conservation during their earliest meetings following the signing of the treaty in early 1960, even before its ratification. During the four and a half years of negotiation, questions regarding human relationships with the natural environment were linked with those regarding relations among states and the search for authority in guiding the agendas of both the Antarctic Treaty and Antarctic science more generally. Not only was AMCAFF the first international attempt at conservation for the Antarctic continent, but it also signaled the fact that Antarctic diplomacy might address issues not explicitly or extensively covered in the delicately wrought text of the Antarctic Treaty. Though the treaty had envisaged some level of continuing engagement and coordination of the parties, AMCAFF represented the heightened levels of action that were possible with this brand-new treaty—indeed, that were being driven by some parties. The conservation challenge posed by a small group of biological scientists and the Scientific Committee on Antarctic Research (SCAR)—in the hope of protecting their objects of study as well as their aspirations to being considerable actors in the treaty regime—allowed some of the new treaty parties to drive an expansion of the ideas and framework for action underpinning the young treaty regime. These negotiations involved the interplay of an old and diverse body of thinking about nature conservation, in several national contexts as well as at the international level (including Antarctic whaling), and the more recent and continuing political sensitivities surrounding power and control particular to Antarctica. When AMCAFF was finally agreed to at the third consultative meeting, it stood not only as the earliest landmark of international Antarctic nature conservation and environmental protection, but also as part of the drama of scientifically, diplomatically, and conceptually ordering the Antarctic, defining what natural elements of the region mattered and defining the range and force of relationships, rights, and obligations: among the treaty parties, among scientists, diplomats, and states, among humans, animals, and places.

By accepting and codifying conservation as a governing ideal for the Antarctic continent, the treaty parties were not only manifesting a particular moment of developing ecological thinking—as articulated by Rachel Carson's revelatory 1962 book on pesticides, *Silent Spring*—they were also participating in a longer and complex modern history of conservation. As a framework for action, by the mid-twentieth century "conservation" had a range of meanings, especially relating to the use and depletion of natural resources, but also including the protection of wild nature, beautiful landscapes and scenery, and spaces for recreation and scientific research. Conservation policies and actions had both specific national and regional iterations, as well as being circulated and debated transnationally and globally.[2] Conservation was not simply a technocratic response to resource depletion or an apparently rational impulse for species or landscape protection. Rather, it was a way of building and shaping relationships, of cultivating ground to generate a sense, however inchoate, of place and meaningful connection. Conservation did not simply mean recognizing a local ecology and protecting it; conservation entailed filling the household of nature, intervening in nature's economy.

In Antarctica specifically, conservation became significant because it was central to reimagining the icy wastes of the continent, the apparent emptiness, into a more meaningful and vital ground for international contestation and diplomacy. Conservation in Antarctica ordered relationships and the environment in intellectual, scientific, legal, and diplomatic terms. As a project, Antarctic conservation helped to build institutional and individual positions—SCAR and the collective treaty parties—and entangle them in particular relationships of rights and obligations. Issues of extinction or wilderness protection, which were important in other contexts, were not as significant at this moment for the Antarctic continent—certainly not compared with the considerable concern for the potential extinction of whales under the failed conservation attempts of the International Whaling Commission (IWC) at the same time. And without a public being able to visit Antarctica, scenic values and public recreation were also outside consideration.[3] Scientists led the conservation debate and, given their own histories and intellectual lineages, their search for disciplinary and public standing, demanded protections for the quality of their work.[4]

That Antarctic scientists should preempt the signing of the treaty—whose contents were as yet unknown to them—with calls for international action on the issue of conservation, and that the parties should commit themselves to this task so quickly within the treaty regime despite its difficult birth, invites investigation. The treaty was in part a response to the actions of geophysical scientists working within the IGY program. The biologists within SCAR—a distinct group, it must be noted, from the scientists working within the sphere of the IWC—were far fewer in number than the geophysicists of the IGY; though present, they did not yet hold equivalent standing to their geophysical colleagues in the major national Antarctic programs that had arisen in the 1950s. And although penguins and seals were of course part of the public consciousness of Antarctica, the general conception of the region was of a forbidding, physically threatening environment of ice and treacherous climate rather than of a delicately poised and potentially damaged one. Why then did the treaty parties respond so quickly to the demands of this seemingly incidental handful of biologists? And why did they do so specifically in the form of a binding agreement that raised within the first three years of the treaty some of the most difficult diplomatic issues? The answer contains issues of scientific and political leadership and power in the earliest years of the treaty, investigating how scientific and environmental language was deployed, negotiated, and codified in the specific context of the fragile treaty, but also in the broader context of a burgeoning global environmental consciousness and discourse.

Protecting Living Antarctica from "the New Interloper, Man"

As part of a broader geophysical moment in which superpower militaries patronized the geophysical sciences, the IGY had perpetuated the idea of Antarctica as an icy fortress whose ramparts were being broken down by scientists.[5] The "frozen" metaphor predominated, rather unsurprisingly given the scale of the Antarctic ice sheet. As the American biologist Carl Eklund, with coauthor Joan Beckman, wrote after the IGY: "Until the nineteen fifties, the Antarctic continent at the bottom of the world lay in isolated, frozen splendor"—it was a "white and barren land."[6] For Eklund and Beckman, the IGY was an "invasion of [the] icy fortress."[7] The Antarctic was perfect for geophysicists, as it was "an ideal laboratory, a region unspoiled by the clutter of civilization and the complications of trees, plants, and life forms."[8] Eklund was himself an ornithologist and a leading American official in polar matters. The tensions and ironies of this presentation of Antarctica as an isolated and barren land, devoid of the "complications" of life, is immediately apparent in the second chapter of Eklund and Beckman's 1963 book: "Antarctic Life." The Antarctic was undoubtedly associated with certain animals—whales, seals, penguins, and albatrosses—a mixture of the curious and the charismatic. Whales and seals were still objects of economic exploitation at the time. Yet the IGY was so dominant in Antarctic affairs in the 1950s and into the early 1960s that it could not only occlude the biological life of the Antarctic but also suggest weaker connections to the place than were otherwise the case.

In the first place, the impulse for nature conservation in Antarctica at the end of the 1950s had to contend with this dominant, geophysical conception of the region. At the same time, this conservation impulse also built on existing foundations, principally emerging out of the whaling industry. Before the late 1950s, ideas or rules relating to Antarctic nature protection were limited in scope and intent, applying only to whales and seals and framed around the conservation of resources. Specific regulations regarding seals first appeared in the last quarter of the nineteenth century and were applied by Britain over its Falklands territories and by the Australian state of Tasmania over Macquarie Island; the declaration of Macquarie as a sanctuary for fauna and flora in 1933 was actively called for by the Australian explorer and scientist Douglas Mawson, who was notable among the heroic era explorers for his conservation ethic, though he was always committed to seeing productive and controlled use of the region, too.[9] As the Antarctic whaling industry exploded at the beginning of the twentieth century, whales also came to be covered by various regulations. Without whaling licensing and taxation, the British would arguably not have made claims to South Georgia and other islands south of the Falklands. The French, New Zealand, and Norwegian governments all passed similar regulations regarding seals and whales in their Antarctic and subantarctic possessions.[10]

These regulations were not intended as absolute preservation measures. On the one hand, regulations existed most often to tax the profits of sealing and whaling activities; in the British case whaling income began at a time when ideas about colonial development and economic self-sufficiency were taking hold in London.[11] On the other hand, these regulations were also tools of effective occupation and proof of territorial sovereignty under international law. For example, the appointment of officers for animal and bird protection in the Australian Antarctic Territory in the early 1950s was centrally about occupying the territory and perfecting the claims through effective administration.[12]

If Antarctic conservation in the late 1950s had a small and scattered local history to build upon, there was a rich and complex body of thought and action around nature preservation and conservation that it could, and did, draw from for political force and intellectual structure. The late 1950s and early 1960s were a transitional era in conservation and environmental thinking, away from the long-standing resource-focused conservation ideas that had emerged at the turn of the nineteenth and twentieth centuries toward the "age of ecology," with its emphasis on the connections among all elements of the earthly environment and the centrality of the science of ecology. Though environmental politics and conservation thinking may have been more intense in some countries than others, nature protection was a globally interconnected story and had been since its emergence in the modern era. While conservation ideas had specific resonance and trajectories in different nations and localities, they were also developed in dialogue among scientists, government officials, land managers, and other nature-minded individuals and groups across national and cultural boundaries.[13] Protected areas, resource conservation, game management, zones for scientific study, scenic areas, and wilderness areas were all both local and transnational ideas and practices.

Nature conservation was also a burgeoning matter of international diplomacy. The environment—generally conceived in terms of natural resources—first became a diplomatic concern within imperial relations in Africa at the end of the nineteenth century and also within American hemispheric relations at the beginning of the twentieth century. In Africa, the shared concerns of political and scientific elites across the European colonies, especially the British and German ones, in the wake of the "scramble for Africa" of the 1880s generated not only a conservation ethic—as John MacKenzie and, more recently, Bernard Gissibl have shown, rooted in an older European "hunting ethos" combined with late nineteenth-century area protection ideas from America[14]—but also international discussions that led to the first treaty signed, though never ratified, on environmental questions—the Convention for the Preservation of Wild Animals, Birds, and Fish in Africa—in May 1900.[15] Following close behind these actions were negotiations between the United States and Canada on questions of fisheries, sealing, and migratory bird protections between 1908 and 1916—part of the broader progressive era efforts in the United States, and what Kurk Dorsey has described as the "dawn of conservation diplomacy."[16] Scientists and other members of civil society, in parallel with these official developments, also began to cultivate the idea of conservation in Europe and elsewhere.

The First World War interrupted this early international momentum, and it was not until the 1930s that major conservation and preservation agreements were again made. In Africa, several nations signed the Convention for the Protection of Fauna and Flora in Africa in November 1933, marking the slow development from wildlife preservationist approaches to conservationist attitudes that transformed hunting reserves to national parks and further entrenched the separation of wild nature to be comprehensively managed and protected from the outside world.[17] In the Americas, a fruitful combination of the expansive interests of conservationists and biologists and the diplomatic interests of the US government in Latin America led to the bilateral Convention for the Protection of Migratory Birds and Game Mammals with Mexico in 1936 and the Convention on Nature Protection and Wild Life Preservation in the Western Hemisphere in October 1940.[18] The oceans surrounding Antarctica were also part of these international developments. The management of the international whaling industry—led primarily by British and Norwegian companies—became a serious concern in the interwar years, as pelagic industrial whaling exploded in Antarctic waters and with it an early sense of the vulnerability of whale stocks to excessive hunting.[19]

In the years following the Second World War, international conservation work resumed in earnest, still concentrating on a range of issues relating to natural resource conservation, both renewable and nonrenewable, wildlife, and area protection. In the postwar era, though, there was more institution formation than in the prewar period, including the establishment of the United Nations Educational, Scientific and Cultural Organization (UNESCO) and the International Union for the Conservation of Nature and Natural Resources, as well as multilateral conferences and meetings under the aegis of the United Nations.[20]

Simultaneous with the conservation developments within the Antarctic Treaty, biologists working within the IWC were fighting to drastically curtail the whaling industry (still concentrated in Antarctic waters, though the industry was in transition) and the excessive quotas, as well as to address suspicions and explicit knowledge of illegal catching. At the end of the 1950s and beginning of the 1960s there was a distinct sense of crisis within the IWC. In 1959 alone, several states withdrew because of their frustrations, and there was a lack of consensus on what to do to ensure a sustainable industry and resilient stocks. There was only limited success on the part of scientists in curtailing the excessive hunting of the industry, which was clearly leading to profound depletions of whale populations, and injecting scientific research into deliberations on catch quotas; only the decline of the industry as a whole from the mid-1960s would lead to an abatement of the catch.[21]

In the late 1950s, therefore, scientists and diplomats working on Antarctica could draw upon both specific and wider experiences of nature protection and conservation. These resource regulations and approaches were the foundations for the developments regarding Antarctic conservation in the late 1950s. Yet they only went so far, as they did not encompass all of Antarctica's fauna and concentrated mainly on marine resources.

In this regard, the IGY became an inadvertent impulse for the conservation effort between 1959 and 1964. Its program and activities had thoroughly occluded the animal life of the continent in favor of its geophysical elements, bequeathing to the Antarctic Treaty an almost lifeless and inert view of the region, concentrating on the ice sheet, the atmosphere and weather, aurora, and cosmic rays.[22] Yet the continent and its surrounding seas were not lifeless. The troubling reality was that in their search for the hidden forces of the earth and the shape of the continent and ice cap, geophysical scientists were causing harm, if mostly unintended, to Antarctic life. In the eyes of many biologists, the "assault on the unknown"—as the great science journalist Walter Sullivan had described the IGY—actually became an inadvertent assault on the animal life of the Antarctic. As the conservation resolution of the 1959 Antarctic Symposium put it, Antarctic birds and mammals had an "extreme vulnerability to the mischief of unprincipled men and uncontrolled dogs." The resupply operations for scientific expeditions had brought in "persons, members of ships' companies and others, who possess a minimum of interest in the natural life and its conservation and who . . . have made and will continue to cause serious damage to the floral and faunal populations." Modern operations, it was observed, had developed some "careless aspects," such as flying over rookeries and pumping ships' bilges near the shore.[23] Antarctic biologists emerged from the shadow of the geophysical sciences to call for the protection of Antarctic wildlife and areas susceptible to human interference and damage.

Carrick's 1959 paper "Conservation of Nature in the Antarctic" marked the explicit and public beginning of the debate about the issue of conservation.[24] Carrick prepared the paper for the Antarctic Symposium in Buenos Aires in November 1959, but because he could not attend, only the title of the paper was read.[25] Recognizing the importance of the subject, Gordon Robin, the secretary of SCAR and a noted glaciologist in his own right, solicited it for publication in the *SCAR Bulletin* in late 1960.[26] Carrick was a biologist with the Wildlife Division of Australia's CSIRO, and his Antarctic research concentrated on the elephant seals of subantarctic Macquarie Island. For much of the 1950s, during the Australian National Antarctic Research Expedition's early years, he was also de facto head of Antarctic biology in Australia. That research effort was mostly concentrated on Macquarie, an island that had experienced exploitation of both its seal and penguin populations since the early nineteenth century.[27] He was also the first chair of the SCAR Working Group on Biology and a convener of the 1962 Antarctic Biology Symposium in Paris. Born in Scotland and trained in zoology at the universities of Glasgow and Edinburgh, Carrick turned to the behavior and ecology of starlings when he was a lecturer at the University of Leeds before the Second World War. After the war he moved to a senior lectureship at Aberdeen, and in 1952 he joined the recently established Wildlife Survey of the CSIRO in Canberra, where his research became increasingly ecology focused. In Canberra he continued his ornithological work, including establishing the Australian Bird-Banding Scheme and working on the territorial behavior of Australian magpies. In addition to his Antarctic conservation work, he had joined the Royal Australasian Ornithological Union's conservation committee in 1954, and at the end of the decade he also joined the early national conservation efforts of the Australian Academy of Science by convening the Australian Capital Territory subcommittee of the National Parks Committee. Though a reputedly rebarbative character who seemed to have difficulties in his professional relationships, Carrick was certainly a biologist with influence, in both research and policy, in Australia and through his scholarly connections internationally.[28]

The revised and published version of Carrick's paper began with the premise that "man" had an inevitable impact on "his environment." That impact, wrote Carrick, was due to "wasteful over-harvesting, uncontrolled interference, ill-advised introductions of alien forms, destruction of the resources on which flora and fauna depend, and, in general, to lack of well-informed long-term planning during the earlier stages of human occupation." This description of human impact could have been applied to any region of the earth. For Carrick, though, observing this for Antarctica was both "a challenge and an opportunity," because the threat of human activity there could be anticipated and prevented.[29]

Carrick made a threefold case for conservation. First, there were scientific values. The harsh and extreme Antarctic environment had produced "living forms which represent the end-point in structural, physiological and ecological adaptation to extremes of low temperature, high wind and day-length," and knowledge of these adaptations "offers information of fundamental importance on the extent to which anatomical, physiological, and behavioural mechanisms are perfectable."[30] Furthermore, preserving the Antarctic flora and fauna would assist biogeographical studies of the Southern Hemisphere.

Second, there were aesthetic reasons. Carrick felt that "penguins, albatrosses and seals enliven the bleak landscape and open sea"; penguins were particularly attractive for "their upright gait and reciprocal curiosity toward us." There was also psychological succor in these animals as well as visual pleasure. Carrick thought that there was "the mental and spiritual recuperation derived from contact with living nature, especially to those who are becoming introspective, worried and stressed." This was especially important for the Antarctic, as men were isolated, with little outside of their minds. Expeditioners required "pleasant, objective and impersonal thoughts" to help "restore perspective," and for this local wildlife was valuable.[31]

And third, there was the economic value of conservation. Carrick, though hardly an advocate of Antarctic whaling or sealing industries, made the by then commonplace, yet still largely ignored, statement that conservation was necessary to prevent the disastrous extermination of species through over-exploitation. He noted, however, that evaluating the exploitation potential of these animals was a complex ecological problem. He also commented on the household economy, as it were, of the Antarctic, noting that the use of seals, birds, and eggs as food for men and dogs was not without its potential dangers. Given the highly localized character of populations, any excessive use would endanger the local supply.[32]

One of the notable aspects of Carrick's perspective on conservation was its emphasis on the wholeness and totality of the biotic community. In his analysis, one had to look past the "evident losses" of penguins and seals (though certainly not ignore them) to the "more complex problem of conservation of . . . flora and fauna, marine and terrestrial, as a whole."[33] Conservation had to rely on and begin with the "scientific grasp of the ecological and behavioural relationships within the biotic community"—the "intricate interacting system."[34] To be sure, his idea of the whole community was not quite the ecosystem idea with its flows of energy that was increasingly characterizing ecological research at the time. Carrick was an animal ecologist, and his sense of the whole community was of species in aggregate. Carrick's training in Scotland and work in England tied him to the developments there before, during, and immediately after the Second World War, when Arthur Tansley and other leading ecologists were demanding area protection for the purposes of ecological research.[35] Carrick's emphasis on the scope of the conservation effort including the whole community or system was not taken up in AMCAFF, yet it stands as one of the earliest, if inchoate, articulations of the need to protect the ecosystem as a whole, rather than simply parts of it.

Carrick went so far as to argue that the "main threat" to Antarctic wildlife was not the ad hoc, if destructive, intrusions of men, dogs, and bases, but rather a future "food-hungry world" that would "turn to the Antarctic seas for supplies," speculating that the exploitation of "the lower organisms in the food-chains . . . could have profound and permanent effects on higher vertebrates such as whales, seals and birds." For Carrick, the "most important principle of conservation" was "that preservation of the habitat, especially food . . . far outweighs measures to prevent more direct losses, from which all wild populations have a high capacity to recuperate."[36] These perspectives prefigured the serious discussion of Southern Ocean exploitation after the mid-1960s and the ecosystem-level conservation standard of the Convention on the Conservation of Antarctic Marine Living Resources (CCAMLR) in 1980.

Carrick was joined and supported in his position by a formidable group of biologists. They all, notably, shared a scientific research interest and specialty: birds. Carrick, William J. L. Sladen, Robert Falla, Eklund, Jean Prévost, and Robert Cushman Murphy were all important actors in the prosecution of the conservation cause to their own governments and in concert in forming SCAR's position. The bird focus of this group also speaks to the relative emphases of the conservation discussion, in that whales and the whaling industry were not the dominant focus of this debate. The lack of extensive discussion of whales in these developments is especially noteworthy given the (almost existential) problems the IWC faced at the end of the 1950s and early 1960s—still primarily focused, as was the whaling industry, on the Antarctic whaling grounds—in its attempts to make catch numbers and quota allocation more "scientific." Certainly none of these men were ignorant of the industry and its effects on whale populations; it is certainly suggestive of the constrained and divided notions of "Antarctica" at the time, and the sense in this early treaty period of creating relationships and ideas de novo.

Each of these men who joined Carrick was also a highly experienced Antarctic scientist and expeditioner, as well as having deep connections with major conservation efforts in the foregoing decades. The American ornithologist Murphy was an especially significant scientist in this group, being an internationally renowned ornithologist as well as a prominent public figure in the United States. Recently retired from his position at the American Museum of Natural History in New York, Murphy's connection with Antarctica had begun in 1911–1912 when he joined a whaling and sealing voyage to South Georgia. He eventually wrote about his experiences in his 1947 book *Logbook for Grace*, drawing on the logbook he kept at the time, framing his story within the natural history tradition of Charles Darwin on the *Beagle*, and noting the brutality of sealing practices and the flagrant disregard for the future health of seal stocks on the part of the ship's captain; Murphy wrote of his hope "that no sealer from the United States will ever trouble these shores again."[37] That voyage resonated across the decades, and Murphy remained seized by various conservation questions, especially in relation to resource exploitation. The whaling he witnessed in the South Atlantic obviously occurred within this framework, but his connections with the guano industry of Peru in the interwar years, and its anchoveta fishery in the early 1950s, were similarly influential on his thinking. Murphy closely followed Carrick in print, advocating for Antarctic conservation in the pages of *Science* in terms similar to Carrick's, noting at one point: "We need to remember that civilized man can be, and often is, the worst enemy of every other form of life."[38]

Brian Roberts, the lead British Antarctic diplomat, was also a bird man in this mix, as he had been an ornithologist on the British Graham Land Expedition (1934–1937). Another significant voice in this chorus of birds was the International Council for Bird Preservation, which explicitly called for the protection of birds in Antarctica at its May 1960 conference.[39] Not only were they coincidentally all ornithologists, but there were important professional connections among some of these men: Roberts and Sladen had been acquainted from the late 1940s, when Sladen was a member of the Falkland Islands Dependencies Survey; Murphy and Falla had developed a close professional relationship around the years of the Second World War when Murphy traveled to New Zealand, where Falla was head of the Dominion Museum; and Carrick traded off the close relationships of the Australian Antarctic Division and Phillip Law with Roberts and Robin, as well as having worked closely with Falla on biological studies of Macquarie Island.[40] That all the leading scientists in the push for strong conservation measures in Antarctica were ornithologists alerts us to the long trajectory of conservation and the origins of modern wildlife protection in the late nineteenth century. To build their vision for Antarctica and their own disciplinary standing within the Antarctic scientific and diplomatic communities, these ornithologists drew on a venerable vocabulary and sensibility of conservation deeply embedded in the specific practice of ornithology and natural history.[41]

Robin asked Carrick in April 1960 to draft some preliminary recommendations on conservation for discussion at the fourth SCAR meeting in August–September 1960, where it was set as an important agenda item.[42] Carrick responded with a discussion paper outlining general principles, information required from SCAR members for conservation measures, and recommendations for conservation measures. His principles were based on those he had set out in his 1959 paper, though the economic values of Antarctic fauna were played down, and his suggested regulations were narrowly conceived and basically concerned with establishing the idea that species vulnerable to human actions should be protected through a permit system.[43]

When conservation was discussed at the SCAR meeting, there was agreement on its importance as a topic, but there was subtle disagreement about the parameters of SCAR's pursuit of the topic. SCAR had only been established two years previously, and there was not extensive agreement about exactly what part it should play in Antarctica's emerging political architecture. Though science was the privileged human activity in Antarctica by the terms of the treaty—article II guaranteed freedom of scientific investigation and article III provided that parties should exchange information on their scientific activities—SCAR was not specifically mentioned. The negotiators and early interpreters of the treaty assumed SCAR was implicitly covered under the article III subclause stating that the parties would cooperate with international organizations; SCAR was certainly not "given the function of the chief science advisory body" as historian of science Simone Turchetti and colleagues have suggested.[44] In any case, both the diplomatic and scientific sides of the relationship were conscious of the sensitivities; the scientists appreciated the political difficulties, and the diplomats did not want to be seen to influence, either by affirmation or negation, scientific work.[45] In the specific conservation discussions some SCAR delegates, drawing on the IGY tradition of at least superficially excluding politics from its discussions, thought that making specific recommendations about conservation measures would be too political. Robin outlined the problem clearly in a letter to Carrick:

> The use of SCAR as a body making recommendations on nature conservation departs somewhat from our original function of drawing up a programme of antarctic [*sic*] research. Nevertheless I feel confident that SCAR will be willing to take over this type of responsibility and trust that ICSU will also agree to this slight change of function. The idea is certainly getting around that SCAR should

> act as a body to which reference can be made for scientific advice on antarctic problems particularly when requested to do so by the appropriate Working Group of the Antarctic Political Conference.[46]

Despite Robin's hopes, Roberts recorded that some delegates at the August–September 1960 meeting of SCAR did not go along with that position. He noted that "several Delegates expressed fears (not clearly formulated) about involving SCAR in a political matter, since the recommendations can only be put into effect by governments passing appropriate laws and regulations."[47] The situation was even hinted at in the conservation report itself, noting that the SCAR Executive Committee and Working Group on Biology thought the report was "a reasonable compromise between the view that the statements should be confined to setting out general principles and the opinion of those who would prefer more detailed recommendations."[48]

This meeting agreed to distribute Carrick's report on conservation to SCAR's members for comment and agreement by the end of 1960. Most responded with minor amendments and endorsed the general principles. The document was finally conveyed to the governments of the treaty parties in April and May 1961—before the Antarctic Treaty had been ratified, but in the expectation that it would be so and that the first consultative meeting would happen by the end of 1961.[49] By early 1961, therefore, biological scientists working with SCAR had made their position on conservation clear. They hoped the treaty parties would pay attention. Apparently content with this broad-based advice, SCAR and its members did not significantly revisit the conservation question while the parties were negotiating AMCAFF and did not intervene in these negotiations; perhaps the subtle disagreements among scientists on SCAR's place in treaty politics kept them from refining their position or actively participating in negotiations. Though some of those scientists would participate in the consultative meetings, SCAR in some ways exited the stage. If those scientists who had participated in the IGY had the unanticipated pleasure of affecting the course of Antarctic affairs, Carrick and his biologist colleagues were more conscious of their efforts to shape Antarctica's future.

Living Resources in a Lifeless Treaty

Given the speed with which the parties of the soon-to-be-ratified treaty dived into the conservation issue in the early 1960s, one might assume some specific sanction for their actions in the treaty, or at least a broad coverage of the issue and sense of environmental purposes in the recently concluded Washington negotiations. However, the treaty contains only one subparagraph on conservation. Article IX, which establishes the meetings of consultative parties and the subjects for which they should take further action, includes within it the subject of "preservation and conservation of living resources" (article IX(1)(f)); while other parts of the treaty were finely wrought and delicately poised among several national positions, this subparagraph was underdetermined in its conception. While the treaty is concerned with Antarctica as a place for peaceful scientific study, it has a relatively inert and geophysical concept of the environment. This subparagraph is the only one that relates to the living parts of the Antarctic environment. More generally, the treaty envisaged Antarctica through its definition of the "zone of application," which was delimited as "the area south of 60° South Latitude, including all ice shelves," but excluding the high seas.

The IGY had played an important part in this conception of the region, its dominant rhetoric allowing for an evasion of conservation and living resource issues. On the one hand, the IGY had embedded the idea of Antarctica as a relatively lifeless continent (save for scientists and sailors) that was also the observation point for the earth's geophysical phenomena. On the other hand, the IGY also contributed to the view of a continent without a particular kind of economic value. Historian Adrian Howkins has argued that IGY provided proof for the major players—Britain and the United States—that there were no mineral resources in the region, or at least not readily and economically available ones.[50] Persuasive as far as Britain and the United States are concerned, Howkins's argument lends further weight to the continent having become a relatively lifeless and inert region. As a transformative event, the IGY perhaps blinded some actors to the history of seal and whale exploitation in the region, and the Antarctic Treaty doubled down on the sense of historical caesura. The combination of these two conceptions allowed for the treaty to see the Antarctic environment as the neutral stage for international relations.

The Antarctic environment, both its nonliving and living elements, had an uneven presence in the treaty negotiations. For an agreement so tied to a particular and unique place, the treaty has little, if any, sense of place. Part of the problem was that a map of Antarctica in 1959 still had unconfirmed coastlines and unmapped regions. Swaths of the continent had been neither visited on the ground nor flown over. What Paul Siple—a US Antarctic scientist and inaugural scientific leader at the South Pole Station in the 1956–1957 season—had said in 1954 still applied in 1959: Antarctica was "a strange mixture of the unknown and the well known."[51] These great gaps in knowledge did not stop the newly formed SCAR deciding at its first meeting in February 1958 that for its scientific purposes, the Antarctic was "bounded by the Antarctic Convergence" (the oceanographic boundary of the cold waters circulating around the Antarctic continent) and included certain subantarctic islands.[52]

The major reason for the uneven presence of the environment in the treaty was the tension surrounding the question of natural resource rights. The issue of apportioning or recognizing rights to Antarctica's natural resources had a complex history with little resolution. Natural resources featured unevenly in the swirl of plans and potential agreements circulating in late 1957 and early 1958. Some American officials, for example, thought that one of the tasks of an international regime for Antarctica would be the "regulated development and utilization, in the general interest, of the natural resources of the Antarctic region" and the "conservation, in the general interest, of renewable natural resources of the Antarctic region."[53] For others, the very discussion of resources was worrying. Australia bullishly adhered to its position on sovereignty, which meant that it could not countenance any potential regime concerning itself with minerals. Australia's insistent position resulted in the Americans—because they were interested in achieving an international solution, even one without a resources agreement—softening their own position on the question of resources to read: "The establishment of uniform and non-discriminatory rules for any possible development of resources in the future."[54] So thoroughly had Australia insisted on its position regarding resources that Ambassador Paul Daniels did not even include resources within his first scoping document for a treaty in the first preparatory meetings.[55]

The conservation of nature and resources was essentially absent from the preparatory meetings beginning in June 1958, which preceded the main treaty conference. The issue had not, for example, featured in the American aide memoire circulated in March 1958 to canvas the possibility of a treaty conference; at that time its absence was questioned by a Norwegian diplomat in London, who noted the likelihood of discovery of minerals.[56] The first full draft of the treaty was circulated in November 1958 by the United States, but it contained no reference to resources or nature conservation.[57] Except for a couple of reported instances of brief mentions of resources or economic rights—usually the Australian representative insisting that they were not topics for discussion[58]—resources and conservation remained off the table for the remainder of the preparatory meetings. This was not an oversight; rather, the issue was avoided because the desire on the part of some parties to achieve international consensus and agreement outweighed any pre-existing hopes that the agreement needed to be a comprehensive one.[59]

When the treaty conference opened on October 15, 1959, the draft treaty still did not contain any clause relating to conservation or preservation of nature or resources. On the afternoon of October 22, the issue briefly arose when the Chilean delegate stated his country's hope that the treaty might refer "to the preservation of the maritime health and riches in the Antarctic"; it was not seen as a substantial enough comment by the secretariat to include in the summary record.[60] The subject got another brief mention the next day.[61] The Chilean delegate finally expanded on the point at the morning meeting of October 24, when he officially proposed an addition to the article on consultative meetings.[62] On the morning of October 26, he "noted the special concern of the Government of Chile for the preservation and protection of natural resources, especially maritime resources." That "special concern" had animated a great deal of Chile's foreign policy in the 1950s. Given the importance of fisheries to its national economy, Chilean governments had sought significant changes to the international law of the sea, allowing for two-hundred-mile exploitation zones and a general control of the maritime zone, especially to exclude US fishing fleets.[63] In the discussion that ensued, South Africa and Britain explicitly supported the proposal. The British delegate asked whether "natural resources" included minerals and pushed consideration of the question of "wild life." The Chilean delegate replied that Chile was mainly interested in protecting maritime resources, "but had thought it might be useful to use the broader term 'natural resources.'" The New Zealand delegate reported after the conference that the Chilean delegate admitted his country's position was based on making the Antarctic Treaty a possible "backstop" to any future failure of the IWC.[64] Australia, however, thought the Chilean proposal went "beyond the scope of the present treaty."[65] The issue was left in that undetermined state.

The issue arose again the next afternoon, when Daniels, the US delegate, evidently replying to the Australian objection, outlined why, in fact, the issue of conservation was a matter for the treaty parties and consistent with one of the central purposes of the treaty, the encouragement of scientific research. He suggested:

> Certainly one of the objects of scientific investigation in Antarctica is investigation of living things there. And if we don't conserve them, there will be nothing to investigate. I refer to the penguins and the seals and the birds and all other living things. And so it seems to me that it is quite consistent and within the objects and purposes of this treaty that we should conserve those things so the scientists may investigate them.[66]

The Chilean delegate amplified his previous comments by stating that Chile "would have preferred a special article, or at least an annex or protocol" on the issue, but was willing to pursue it in the proposed manner in order not to delay the negotiations. In the continuing discussion, the French and Argentine delegates agreed with the Australian assertion that the issue was outside the treaty's scope.[67] It is evident that different delegations were talking at cross purposes, for the Chileans spoke of maritime resources in an economic register, and the Americans spoke of penguins and seals in a scientific register. The legal adviser on the Australian delegation, Clarence Harders, suggested in his conference report that had the issue of living resources come up after the zone of application question (which had resolved to exclude the high seas), the inclusion of living resources would have been moot and may have been kept out of the treaty—which was very much desirable for Australia's purposes.[68] In spite of the reservations of some delegations and the short and slightly confused discussion, the representatives on Committee II agreed to the inclusion of the clause relating to the "preservation and conservation of living resources." The matter was not discussed again during the conference, and the words agreed upon in the early evening of October 27 remained in the final form of the treaty.[69]

This subparagraph has become one of the most productive of the entire treaty, giving license to major discussions over the following decades on seals, marine living resources, and all environmental concerns. Its expansive reinterpretation has become a hallmark of the treaty era; indeed, nearly all that follows in this book conveys this expansion. That it has become so was through no clear intention of the negotiators in 1959; its inclusion came about through a combination of specific Chilean concerns about fisheries, indeterminate debates about the purpose of the treaty, pockets of insistence, and no determined opposition.

Putting "Living Resources" on the Agenda

The first mention of conservation as a matter for discussion among the treaty signatories occurred in January 1960. At the first interim meeting of the parties following the signing of the treaty (it had not yet been ratified), the US representative and chair, Daniels, suggested that conservation might be an appropriate subject for the agenda of the first consultative meeting, which would meet within two months of the entry into force of the treaty.[70] Since the United States had not internally considered its position, Daniels was evidently hoping either for a general discussion among the parties or for a particular party to take up the issue. Only the British government embraced the conservation issue with any vigor. More specifically, it was Roberts, one of the leading polar figures in Britain, attached since the mid-1940s to both the Foreign Office as a government official and the Scott Polar Research Institute as a researcher, who pursued a full and separate convention for the conservation of Antarctic wild life as part of his broader attempts to force the early agenda of the Antarctic Treaty in his, and Britain's, preferred direction.

The British pursuit of conservation needs to be appreciated within the general context of their Antarctic policy. From the late 1950s, Britain was in the midst of decolonization in Africa and was also facing up to the difficulties of maintaining the South Atlantic and Antarctic outposts of its empire; Britain's new tack within Antarctic affairs was internationalist, hoping to reduce its financial burden there as well as to guarantee peaceful relations.[71] Britain would push for an international approach—British-led, to be sure—to more and more Antarctic issues, even those not countenanced within the treaty. Such a policy, it was hoped, would secure Britain's position and future in the Antarctic, especially against moves by Argentina and Chile.

Within this context, and still in the midst of preparatory meetings in 1960, Roberts articulated the importance of achieving something in the area of conservation as "one of the first real tests of the international cooperation envisaged in the Treaty." Those tests included the potential for cooperation between SCAR and the treaty parties, the harmonization of legislation between parties, and a test of the treaty in the eyes of the public and their "emotional approach to protection of penguins, etc."[72] While

Roberts was enthusiastic about the issue, even the most junior Foreign Office officers had to keep hard political issues in mind. Responding to one of Roberts's minutes, K. G. McInnes wrote: "We must take care however, that by producing too many bright ideas for the Canberra agenda we do not prejudice the Treaty ratifications of Chile, Argentina or the USSR."[73] Conservation was potentially that one bright idea too far.

At the First Consultative Meeting in Canberra in 1961 (see figure 1.1), in the context of the comprehensive advice from SCAR, the parties quickly and readily agreed to a recommendation on the subject of conservation.[74] The recommendation (I-VIII) was extensive if loosely worded. The delegates urged governments to recognize that conservation and protection

FIGURE 1.1 The delegations of the United States and the United Kingdom at the first Antarctic Treaty consultative meeting in Canberra, Australia, July 1961. The American delegate is George Owen (front left), whom the British delegate Brian Roberts (front right) found "antagonistic" and the Australian delegation described as "cold." *Source:* NAA: A6180, AT2.

were needed, that they should promote scientific studies and exchange information, that they should make people aware of protection needs, that they should work toward formal measures for conservation, and that they should accept interim measures. The recommendation also included "general rules of conduct for preservation and conservation of living resources in Antarctica," which closely followed many sections of the SCAR report.[75] The recommendation would therefore only impose the loosest and most general obligations on the parties.

The delegates made their recommendation in the presence of Carrick, who was a member of the Australian delegation. Carrick took his position as a scientific leader in Antarctic conservation seriously, pushing delegates not only to agree on basic conservation measures but also to recognize and act on the need to protect species in their marine environment. He was, however, aware of the difficult nuances of a diplomatic conference. In the midst of the meeting, he wrote to Robin:

> The Conservation of Living Resources item comes up tomorrow. Here's luck to it after the capacity for differences that has been shown over much more innocent-looking items. Most delegations do seem to be in line on it, and the S.C.A.R. recommendations are much appreciated and widely supported. It's the letter rather than the spirit of the law that causes trouble, and I don't think any form of regulation or covenant will emerge this time. Diplomats are too canny, and on occasion the more difficult ones hail from unexpected parts of the globe. It's best to remain a simple scientist.[76]

If Carrick thought his lobbying was wise and necessary and that he was adequately playing the part of a "simple scientist," others were not so sure. Roberts complained in his diary about Carrick's actions, noting that he

> introduced a red herring in the form of a proposal that it is no good protecting Antarctic birds and mammals unless protection is also extended to their food in the sea. Biologically speaking, of course, there is much in this, but he did not seem able to realise that at present this is not a practical issue, and that the complications of attempting any agreement involving territorial waters or high seas would certainly wreck our intention. We wasted two hours clearing this out of the way, and reached no conclusion on the main issue.[77]

With his strong convictions, Carrick frequently bumped heads with his intellectual and professional peers in many situations, and Roberts was simply another to add to that list.

As the recommendation articulated aspirations and involved essentially no obligation beyond goodwill, it was easily agreed to. For the prime mover, the British, the recommendation was an obvious step to a more binding agreement and one step on the road to further internationalization; the British had prepared a full draft convention on the matter, but decided not to circulate it for fear of delaying or preventing the Argentine and Chilean ratifications.[78] For other states, it was a seemingly benign advance.

Following the first consultative meeting, Roberts and the British kept pushing for a detailed and binding conservation agreement. To their disappointment, the 1962 consultative meeting in Buenos Aires was a lackluster gathering, and conservation achieved little progress. It became apparent at this time to Roberts and others that the United States might potentially wreck a robust agreement, particularly on account of the antagonism and conservatism of its principal delegate, George Owen. Roberts wrote of Owen that he was "overbearing and truculent to an extent which leaves me astonished."[79] The other major roadblock—though certainly not opponent—was Chile, which voiced misgivings over the potential form of a conservation agreement. Writing to Robin, Roberts said: "Our project for a wild life conservation Convention was wrecked by the United States and Chile."[80]

To force the pace and further refine the terms of discussion, the British presented to the meeting a full draft convention for consideration. This draft was essentially the same as the one it had prepared, though not circulated, for the 1961 meeting. Britain's suggested provisions closely followed the SCAR recommendations, which was unsurprising, as Roberts had had a hand in drafting both. The draft convention prohibited the killing or disturbance of Antarctic fauna without permission by appropriate authorities within each of the signatories, included mechanisms for designating "absolutely protected species" and "absolute sanctuaries" (and even included a different category of "nature reserves" for those areas needing protection but that had to endure at least some human impact), and included measures for information collection. Notably, the British draft also included provisions, though relatively underdeveloped, relating to commercial activity, which were later silently dropped.[81]

While the 1962 meeting produced another loose recommendation, it was nevertheless clear that all the parties supported negotiating a full conservation agreement. The Chilean government, which maintained its strong position on territorial sovereignty in the early treaty years, took up conservation as a worthwhile pursuit. However, its position frustrated Roberts; the Chileans were not eager for a separate convention, but rather for some agreement within the existing treaty mechanisms. The US delegation made specific complaints that the creation of "absolute sanctuaries" or other kinds of protected areas would hamper actions under the inspection provisions of the treaty, in which it had placed such confidence and importance. Roberts interpreted the US position as contrarianism and part of a broader position to wrest influence in the early treaty years away from the British.

From "Living Resources" to "Fauna and Flora"

Because of most parties' general reluctance to rush to a third consultative meeting, there was now more time for them to grapple with the conservation issue. For fifteen months between March 1963 and June 1964, the consultative parties convened at a series of preparatory meetings in Brussels to discuss the agenda for the third consultative meeting, with a set of meetings dedicated to drafting and thrashing out an agreement on conservation. It is worth noting that despite the recommendations of the first two consultative meetings, some parties appeared not to have given serious attention to the conservation matter before these meetings began. The US State Department had only convened an interagency working group on April 26, 1963 (this was unknown to other parties), and the Argentine representatives to these working groups did not seem to have a full brief.[82]

The parties finally sat down to seriously consider the draft texts on June 6, 1963. There were three papers on the table: the 1962 British draft and the Chilean and Soviet responses to that draft. The Chilean and Soviet papers each supported and offered amplifications of the British draft. The Soviets especially suggested that the agreement should be preceded by a preamble outlining general principles, which, with some stylistic changes, remained at the head of AMCAFF when it was finally agreed upon.[83] The negotiations did not begin auspiciously; the meeting's atmosphere was described by the New Zealand representative as having "deteriorated badly," noting that "some of the exchanges were acrimonious to the point of being embarrassing." More problematically, and adding to the embarrassment, was that, as the New Zealand officer noted, "It was hard to see exactly what crucial points were at issue"—though the "unique display of inconsistency" on the part of the American representative may have had something to do with this.[84] The Australian representative's report suggested that the disagreement was procedural, with the American and Argentinian representatives insisting that the preparatory meeting was no place for substantial discussions, and the British representative countering "with surprising violence and asperity" that it was.[85] The disagreement meant that no particular progress was made, though the evident willingness of most parties to move forward suggested there could be progress in future.

By September 1963, with the meetings showing dwindling momentum, the Belgian chair, Alfred van der Essen, had begun to prepare a composite text of the British, Chilean, and Soviet proposals. It was only at this stage that the Americans indicated that they would circulate their own draft text. Henry Carr, the British representative at this meeting, reported that this "bomb-shell . . . was not well received."[86] The Americans circulated their draft in early November. Their draft took on the Soviet preamble and essentially replicated most aspects of the British draft, but subtly changed the terminology from "absolutely protected species" and "absolute sanctuary" to "specially protected species" and "specially protected areas." Roberts found that the draft was compatible with British intentions, though van der Essen, at a meeting on November 14, was reported as being in a "dark mood" because the Americans had not framed their proposals as amendments to the existing drafts on the table, but rather as a whole new draft.[87]

This negotiating maneuver by the Americans, though it aggravated some parties, did in fact clear the air. The Americans were central to the treaty, in spite of their fitful contributions between 1960 and 1962. It is unimaginable that a conservation agreement would have been finalized without the United States having at least put forward a comprehensive position on the matter, not simply responding to the initiatives of others. This expectation was perhaps intensified because the Soviets had given the matter serious attention. Roberts was annoyed because the Americans had taken so long to come to any position and had then adopted a position so similar to the British one, and van der Essen was annoyed because the American maneuver seemed to undermine his responsibilities as chair of negotiations. But others were evidently pleased; the New Zealand representative reported that "this move served more to resolve the confusion than to add to it, since it forced everyone to accept that a closer examination of the different proposals should now be carried out."[88]

It was this US proposal in November 1963, and the more refined draft of December 12, that framed the discussions firmly around "agreed measures," rather than a convention, as the form of the agreement. Until this point the only full draft on the table was the British draft convention, intended to be a legal instrument separate from the Antarctic Treaty. The only declared opposition was from Chile; other parties acquiesced to the idea of a separate convention. The matter was not only a matter of legal form, but rather one about the operation of the treaty. The United States justified its move toward measures within the treaty as insisting on "the primacy of the Antarctic Treaty and of the authority and procedures it provides for dealing with measures to achieve its objectives."[89] They did not want to risk setting the precedent of dealing with different issues through different instruments and thus creating an unintentional hierarchy of conventions and agreements.[90] Furthermore, though this is not clear in the archival evidence, it is worth considering that as each party had different ratification protocols, American officials (with the onerous constitutional duty of having treaties ratified by the US Senate) wanted to make agreeing to conservation measures as easy as possible. Nevertheless, the British position was firmly in favor of a separate convention (though it softened with time), and the Belgians agreed, making the case for a convention because such an instrument would pass easily through their own constitutional procedures. The matter was resolved in favor of "agreed measures" by February 1964, owing to the immovable US position and the British desire to see something achieved in the area.

A final legal and political issue was related to the geographic area covered by the measures. The treaty applied to all land and ice shelves south of 60°S, but specifically recognized existing international rights relating to the high seas. Many Antarctic species, however, spend most of their lives on pack ice or in the surrounding seas. The question of whether pack ice was covered by the treaty was raised. The Australians in particular pursued this issue with some vigor, for the most part owing to Carrick's influence on Australian policy at this time. Though Carrick did not attend treaty consultative meetings after Canberra in 1961, his ideas had a long purchase; he even managed to aggravate Roberts without being present.[91] In the end, pack ice was not included in the agreed measures, as they were limited to the same zone of application as the treaty, and the issue was only resolved with the Convention for the Conservation of Antarctic Seals in 1972 (discussed in chapter 2).

It was not simply the physical area that mattered, but also how it was labeled. The final measures labeled the whole Antarctic a "Special Conservation Area," but other designations were proposed. In their July 1963 comments, for example, the Soviets referred to the Antarctic as an "International Wildlife Reserve," as did early US drafts.[92] Argentina thoroughly objected to such a designation, as it implied a supranational power over Antarctica rather than of the individual sovereign nations, but the United States put up a fight in its favor.[93]

Other disagreements are suggestive of the state of environmental thinking and its role in intergovernmental agreements and obligations. On the issue of how to label what was being protected (the "fauna and flora"), the disagreement arose principally among the English-speaking parties. Article IX(1)(f) of the treaty in English describes "living resources"—as do the Spanish and Russian versions—but in French it was "la faune" and "la flore." The choice among "living resources," "flora and fauna," and "wild life" was not simply about the appellation for the agreement itself, but a question of tone. "Wild life" was favored by the British for reasons of tradition. On several occasions, Roberts insisted on that term for no other reason than that the English-speaking parties had government agencies dealing with animal and plant management that used "wild life" in their titles; in Australia the CSIRO had a "wild life" survey section, and in the United States there was a Bureau of Wildlife.[94] For the British, "living resources" would be inappropriate because the point of the text was to "conserve not only named species but also certain habitats where it is important to maintain the undisturbed natural balance between species."[95] The Americans disagreed, stating their belief "that the importance of Antarctic flora and fauna lies in the fact that they constitute a 'resource'; that is, something of potential value, whether it be exploited through commerce, scientific study, or simply appreciation of esthetic qualities."[96] This disagreement is also suggestive of the original discussions of October 1959 that resulted in "living resources" being included in the treaty. As we have seen, parties spoke at cross purposes, variously seeing maritime resources or wildlife as the "living resources" intended to be covered by the treaty. The parties finally agreed to "fauna and flora" at the April 2, 1964, meeting, pushed by Australia as a resolution between the US and British positions.[97]

When it finally passed, AMCAFF designated the whole Antarctic a "Special Conservation Area," emphasizing the vulnerability and uniqueness of its fauna and flora and obligating the treaty parties to protect it. The first major aspect of AMCAFF was to protect animals and birds as individuals and as species. In general, it prohibited "the killing, wounding, capturing or molesting of any native mammal or native bird" (article VI, paragraph 1), except with a permit granted by one of the treaty parties for the needs of indispensable food for men or dogs and for specimens for science, museums, zoos, or other similar institutions (VI, 2). The issuing of permits had to take into account the ability of the fauna to "normally be replaced by natural reproduction" (VI, 4a) and for the maintenance of "the variety of species and the balance of the natural ecological systems" within the treaty area (VI, 4b). In addition, the measures obligated governments to "minimize harmful interference" with the living conditions of birds and animals and included restricting the free movement of dogs, aircraft flight, vehicle proximity, explosives, firearm use, and any disturbance during breeding seasons. Polluting water near stations was also prohibited. Some species would be listed as "Specially Protected Species," which could only be taken with a permit under a higher burden of protection insisting on "compelling scientific purpose" (VI, 7).

Combined with the protection of species, AMCAFF also established the category of "Specially Protected Areas," places accorded special protection "in order to preserve their unique natural ecological system." These areas were protected with additional burdens, especially requiring that the collection of specimens could only occur for "a compelling scientific purpose which cannot be served elsewhere" (VIII, 4a). AMCAFF also prohibited the importation of alien species of animals and plants and obligated governments to keep and exchange records of the numbers of animals killed or captured. Nonadherence to these protective provisions was excused by an overriding waiver "in cases of extreme emergency involving possible loss of human life or involving the safety of ships or aircraft" (V).[98]

New Principles, New Possibilities

It was less than five years from Carrick's November 1959 paper being mentioned in Buenos Aires to the passing of AMCAFF in Brussels in June 1964. Yet it would take a further eighteen years for the measures to come into force, when Japan became the final country to accept them, in 1982. The treaty's foundational principle of unanimity meant that recommendations of the consultative meetings had to be accepted by all parties to come into force. For some parties, the complexities of legislative drafting and a lack of political and official will kept the measures off the table.

In spite of the measures not coming into force, the parties behaved as if they had. In AMCAFF they had made their first collective move to impose specific obligations on each other's actions, as well as to create structures for subtly expanding their collective bailiwick. So the parties pursued the inscription of Specially Protected Areas and Species at subsequent consultative meetings. The first fifteen areas were protected at the 1966 consultative meeting in Santiago, as were fur seals and Ross seals. Later, in 1972 and 1975, the idea of Sites of Special Scientific Interest (SSSIs) was brought to Antarctica, and a new category of special area was created to protect areas based on the nature of scientific work being undertaken in them. In 1991 the AMCAFF regime, barely a decade properly in force, was in great measure subsumed into the Madrid Protocol on Environmental Protection, which was more rapidly ratified, with a greater sense of urgency.

AMCAFF subtly articulated developing conceptions of the human place in the Antarctic, taking up the language set out by Carrick and Murphy: man as invader, civilized man as enemy of every other life form, man as an enormous, always threatening, consumer. Scientists were in the invidious position of seeking to study the Antarctic while, in that very pursuit, they were also a destructive alien species—a realization that had progressively occurred to natural historians and biologists from the late nineteenth century onward, though the dilemma had hardly been resolved by the early 1960s. Scientists could not excuse themselves from their own strictures for preserving nature, constituted especially by its animals and birds.[99] In the same rhetorical and imaginative step, the human presence in Antarctica, an almost exclusively scientific presence, was conceived of as interloping, unnatural, impermanent, dangerous, and destructive. This was important for the developing vision of a fragile and precious Antarctica, a movement away from visions of lifeless, inert ice. These conceptions of humanity's relationship with Antarctic nature would have ramifications in the future.

Not all of those who had participated in AMCAFF's negotiation recognized its potential and quality. Carrick, for one, did not seem overly confident of its potential. Writing to an officer of the Australian Department of External Affairs in August 1966, he stated his thought that "the only 'living resources' which . . . really conserved under the Treaty" were "a few mosses, lichens, mites and insects."[100] Carrick could be a prickly character, and perhaps seeing his original ecologically aware proposals watered down for political agreement alienated him from treaty politics and therefore from the science that was intimately tied to it.

By passing AMCAFF, the parties to the Antarctic Treaty were giving principles to "unprincipled men"—to use the words of the biologists' 1959 resolution—and each of the parties (some more than others) was trying to ensure those principles suited its purposes. The Antarctic Treaty was a document whose meanings and purposes arose out of specific antagonisms and frustrations and a peculiar conjunction of events and interests. Its continued existence would rely on it being filled with meaning, principles, and possibilities. That nature conservation was among the first of these lading actions set the treaty regime on a course that it has followed to the present. The next immediate step for the parties was outward into the seas and into the bloody issue of sealing.

2

Arguing with Seals

THE CHANGING TERRAIN OF AUTHORITY

SEALS WERE ON the agenda at the fourth consultative meeting in Santiago in November 1966. More precisely, the topic of *killing* seals was on the agenda. When the treaty parties passed the land-bound Agreed Measures for the Conservation of Antarctic Fauna and Flora (AMCAFF) in June 1964, they explicitly noted that seals were only partially covered. Some species would never touch Antarctic land, and all six species spent much of their lives in Antarctica's frigid seas. By the end of that year, however, the parties' unhurried approach to seals was disrupted by an exploratory Norwegian sealing cruise in the South Atlantic. It was just one cruise, and no others followed the next year; there was no apparent rush. Yet small changes in Antarctica's economic or scientific spheres could generate significant changes in its geopolitics. And so the diplomats and scientists of some parties thought that seals needed real time on the agenda. The commercial-scale killing of seals was the topic of negotiation in 1966, though the short discussion was decidedly pro-seal. If delegates still spoke of an undifferentiated and abstract Antarctic seal as an exploitable resource, they nevertheless pleaded for the seal not to go the way of the near-extinct whales, which were animating diplomatic, scientific, and environmental activities at the same time. After many appeals to preserve the seal, the Soviet delegate in the chair, the affable Antarctic hero and administrator Yevgeny Ivanovich Tolstikov, asked—disarmingly, disingenuously, rhetorically: "Now, who is against seals?"[1]

This 1966 discussion was the first serious step in the direction of a comprehensive agreement on sealing regulation, although the parties were not yet sure what form their agreement would take, whether a consultative meeting recommendation, a protocol to the treaty, or a separate convention. Negotiating an agreement on seals was not some perfunctory and easy filling-in of the seal-shaped void at the center of AMCAFF. Discussions continued for six more years because of suspicions about the motives for a seal or sealing agreement, disagreements over the place of science and scientists in the treaty regime, the flux of environmental sensibilities, and the persistent contest for authority over Antarctica among its various actors, including the first hints of an international public—and, to be sure, a paucity of urgency on the part of some parties at various times. It was only in February 1972 that the Antarctic Treaty parties agreed to the Convention for the Conservation of Antarctic Seals (CCAS). This convention regulated the human relationship with seals in the waters between the Antarctic continent and 60° south latitude. It was fortunate for the seals, however, that by 1972 this convention was perhaps less urgent than it had been only a few years before; public opinion, at least in North America and Western Europe, had decisively shifted against killing marine mammals for commercial reasons, and those commercial reasons were less attractive or compelling than ever.

So why did the parties persist in producing an agreement on seals? Following Tolstikov's injunction, being for or against seals only begins to answer this question. The negotiation on seals became the terrain on which the parties and individuals could articulate their conflicting approaches to Antarctica and claim the authoritative ground; in that moment, seals were good to argue over. It is in the processes and the arguments of the negotiations on seals, more than other treaty matters at the time, that we find important disclosures of competing visions for the Antarctic and the human relationship with it: as something more than the surface of the frozen continent, something with vital and charismatic beings rather than resource-laden bodies, a site for collective scientific work and identity, and a region peacefully renewed for the future in the light of a haunting and bloody history. Agreeing on the CCAS text took so long because these disagreements challenged the implicit roles the parties and scientists thought they played or that others thought they should play.

A central issue of these negotiations was the place of science and scientists in the treaty regime. These tensions were not only about the forms or procedures by which scientists would provide expert advice to diplomats at the consultative meetings, but also about the foundations of the regime. The negotiations disclosed the latent disagreements about who had the capacity and authority to frame and conceptualize Antarctic geography and nature. In a political system for governing interstate relations, was it the parties to the treaty and their diplomats who should claim the principal position in determining what was Antarctic nature, or should it be the scientists in their international committee who would have the decisive position on this matter?

There was also a contest about the content of conceptions of Antarctic nature, which complicated how many sides there were. There were clearly seals at the heart of the negotiations, but what could a seal be? Seals had been commodities and fisheries stocks within the memory of the negotiators, but they were also wild animals that, along with other marine mammals throughout the 1950s and 1960s, were being invested with new meanings informed by new science and changing ideas about the environment. Then there was the question of the seals' habitat. Were Antarctic waters a zone of life of scientific interest or a realm of commercial endeavor? The approaches to these issues were not simply divided down the scientific-political boundary, but also among treaty parties.

This was not simply a battle of wills unaffected by the world in which it was taking place. The ground on which the treaty parties negotiated was not fixed and stable between 1964 and 1972. It was precisely in this period that long-held ideas about the economic potential of whales and seals were dissipating along with many other traditional positions regarding the environment. The diplomats negotiating the question of sealing, many of whom had negotiated the treaty and AMCAFF, were buffeted by these changes, sometimes appreciating the developments in environmental sensibilities around them, yet at other times forging ahead as if little had changed in the world.

The temporalities of the negotiators, their historical sensibilities, in the 1960s were also constitutive. Sealing was the first significant human activity in the Antarctic. Sealers ventured into southern waters at the end of the eighteenth century, acting in the vanguard of Antarctic discovery, but making their greatest mark at the beginning of the 1820s with their catastrophic over-exploitation of fur seals at the South Shetland Islands. They continued to plunder the beaches of sub- and peri-Antarctic islands throughout the nineteenth century and well into the twentieth. By the late 1950s and early 1960s, certain populations of fur seal were notably rebounding, and perhaps even at their late eighteenth-century levels; the extent to which this was aided by excessive whaling was debated at the time.[2] Many of the same negotiators who, with a certain self-satisfied and condescending retrospection, pointed to the depredations of the sealers on the South Shetlands in the 1820s, were themselves directly linked to the Antarctic sealing industry that was finally fading in 1964. The fur seal disaster was easily referred to, yet many, most especially the British, in their positions and interventions distanced themselves as distinct from that same history and tradition. This was in part a diplomatic and intellectual sleight of hand to escape responsibility for the past and seize authority for the present and future.

To illustrate this point in another way, in his landmark text of 1985 on international wildlife law, Simon Lyster suggested that CCAS was significant because it was "the first international conservation agreement to have been concluded prior to any significant commercial exploitation of the resource it is intended to protect."[3] This statement contains some truth as well as a staggering historical oversight. True, at least three of the six species of Antarctic seal had never been taken in any great commercial numbers; one species, the crabeater seal, had apparently only been taken at a commercial scale on one voyage in the late nineteenth century; and one species, the elephant seal, had mainly been taken north of 60° south latitude, outside the CCAS area. But the annihilation of fur seals in the 1820s was, to put it mildly, a "significant commercial exploitation." Lyster's misleading statement in such an authoritative legal text deserves to be dismantled, but it is striking also because it mirrors the curious historical sensibilities of some of the negotiators in the 1960s.

Under the specter of a long and depressing history of sealing and within the newly emerging context of global environmentalism, the negotiations on seal conservation between 1966 and 1972 illustrate the tensions among scientific and diplomatic actors in their contest for authority in Antarctic knowledge and affairs. The British Antarctic diplomat Brian Roberts was central and dominant in these events. While there were other important figures in these negotiations, Roberts stands out for his tenacious pursuit of the seal question over so many meetings; his perspectives on Antarctic politics were all-encompassing in scope and detail, emanating from a driving belief that Antarctica should have a well-ordered sphere of human activities, preferably with British ideas and concerns shaping that order. Within the broader range of diplomatic and scientific efforts regarding seals, Roberts's writings on and interventions in the negotiations articulated part of the continuing contest of vision of the Antarctic in the second half of the 1960s and the first few years of the 1970s. The greening of Antarctica was in part driven by dominating personalities in search of standing and authority. Roberts and his scientific and diplomatic colleagues were not simply talking about seals; they were arguing with them.

The Persistent Lure of Antarctic Sealing

In 1964 Antarctic sealing was not a concern of the distant and forgotten past. Though it was certainly a passing concern, it was in fact still happening in some places. The peri- and sub-Antarctic islands had been ensnared into the great global reach of American and British sealing and whaling in the late eighteenth century, which further intensified in the first decades of the nineteenth century. Sealing was the preponderant form of human activity on peri- and sub-Antarctic islands at that time, eclipsing geographic and scientific exploration.[4] Two of the six Antarctic seals were sought: southern elephant seals (*Mirounga leonine*), for their oil-rich blubber to be sold in the European market, and fur seals (*Arctocephalus gazelle*), for their fur to be sold in the recently opened Chinese market. The hunts for these two seal species were separate but overlapping. The exploitation of elephant seals began in the 1770s and continued, with some hiatuses, into the 1960s, often as a profitable adjunct to the whaling industry, but also sometimes as a separate concern. Although the elephant seal was never made commercially extinct, it did suffer heavy losses in many places. The hunt for the fur seal began shortly after that of the elephant seal, but only extended into the early nineteenth century, owing to the near obliteration of the species throughout much of the Southern Hemisphere.

Sealing was initially concentrated in the islands of the South Atlantic Ocean. Branching out from the Falkland Islands, where a hunt for elephant seals began in the early 1770s, and other areas of South America, sealers made it to South Georgia and the South Shetland Islands. It was in the South Shetlands, a group of Antarctic islands just to the north of the peninsula, that the defining period of Antarctic sealing occurred. Sighted in February 1819 and landed on and claimed for George III in October of the same year, the South Shetlands were home to massive colonies of fur seals. That fact—in addition to the continuing interest generated by the reports of James Cooks's second and third voyages—was publicized in the press and seized upon by ever-searching sealers, and nearly one hundred British and American ships were fitted out for the 1820–1821 season. Only a few years later, the fur seal population had been essentially wiped out; it would only begin to rebuild itself over a century and a half later. In

1953 the British marine biologist Richard Laws suggested that "by 1823 the species was virtually extinct," and that the whole affair "was the most extravagant and wasteful exploitation of biological resources that has ever occurred."[5]

In addition to the islands of the South Atlantic region, sealing affected all subantarctic islands. In the Southern Indian Ocean, the Crozets and Prince Edward and Marion Islands were brought into the sealers' orbit in the 1804–1805 season, where they remained for several decades, into the middle of the century. American elephant sealers moved on to Kerguelen and Heard Islands from 1840 until the end of the century, during which time roughly a quarter of "whaling" vessels leaving New London, Connecticut, went to Kerguelen and Heard.[6]

The scale of the hunt was enormous. Assessing the exact impact of these sealing activities, however, is difficult; the inexact, incomplete, uneven, and estimated quality of the data has been noted by several authors. The historian Briton Cooper Busch estimated that over five million fur seals were killed in the Southern Hemisphere between 1783 and the 1820s, with 250,000 at the South Shetlands; 1,200,000 at South Georgia (using the sealer James Weddell's estimate); 150,000 at Macquarie, Auckland, and Campbell Islands; and 150,000 at Tristan da Cunha, Bouvet, and the French islands of the Indian Ocean. Rhys Richards re-examined Busch's figures in light of commercial evidence and suggested no fewer than seven million furs were sold in the world market. Richards notes that between 1788 and 1833, British and American fur traders sold close to four million southern fur seals to the Chinese through Canton, and over two million southern fur seals were sold on the London market.[7]

For elephant seals, Busch estimated (conservatively in his own opinion) that about one million were taken between the late eighteenth century and 1964. From Kerguelen and Heard Islands 200,000 were taken, 300,000 from Macquarie, and 500,000 from South Georgia. It was at South Georgia that elephant sealing continued well into the twentieth century as a profitable adjunct to the whaling industry there.[8] Unlike fur seals, this harvest over a century and a half did not destroy the species in an irretrievable or drastic sense, though, as Laws noted in 1956, the elephant seal had been "hunted to extinction in many localities."[9]

The cruel irony is that fur seals had been annihilated in their Antarctic habitat before all seal species had even been discovered or properly described by scientists. The leopard seal (*Hydrurga leptonyx*) was known to the sealers hunting the fur seal, but was not taken because it did not possess a good fur; in any case, as a solitary hunter it would not have been seen in concentrated numbers. The Weddell seal (*Leptonychotes weddellii*) was discovered during its namesake's 1822–1824 sealing voyage, which was searching for more seals, having depleted the South Shetlands.[10] Crabeater seals (*Lobodon carcinophagus*) were discovered and described by Dumont D'Urville's expedition in the late 1830s. Crabeaters were exploited by at least one major expedition in the 1892–1893 season, when perhaps 50,000 were taken for skins and blubber in the Weddell Sea.[11] Crabeaters are thought to be not only the most numerous seal species in the world, but perhaps also the most numerous mammal after humans. And finally, Ross seals (*Ommatophoca rossii*) were not described until the 1841 voyage of James Clark Ross. They would remain a mystery well into the late twentieth century; Laws speculated that until 1945, perhaps fewer than fifty Ross seals had ever been seen.[12] Truly Antarctic, these four species live on the edge of the Antarctic pack ice, never touching land and sustaining themselves fully from the sea.

Although it was a bloody business, there was no sense of sealing as a cruel or wasteful endeavor before the 1950s. L. Harrison Matthews, a British zoologist with the *Discovery* Investigations in the 1920s, wrote in 1929 that elephant seals at South Georgia were "of extremely low intelligence, as the survivors take no notice at all of the slaughter of their companions."[13] In 1952, having become scientific director at the Zoological Society of London, he published a popular account of his South Georgia work in 1925 and 1926 that caused a (very) minor and temporary upset in Britain, with questions in the House of Commons and comment in several periodicals.[14] In a more lurid paragraph, Matthews described how, following the dispatch of a large bull elephant seal, one of the Norwegian sealers "knelt down and, putting his mouth to the hole, gulped down the hot blood pumped into his gullet, a stream trickling from each corner of his lips and dripping from his chin," while another commented, "Dat's the stuff to make you strong."[15] The small furor suggested some minor movements in public sentiment, not particularly regarding the killing of seals per se, but about the apparently cruel methods involved. Matthews's 1952 stance remained as unsentimental as his *Discovery* reports.

At the same time that Matthews's lurid descriptions were stirring public opinion in Britain, the government of the Falkland Islands decided to further monitor and manage the elephant seal industry in South Georgia with scientific seal inspectors. It had decided to institute these inspectors based in part on the research and surveys conducted just before that time by Laws, which demonstrated that the South Georgia stocks were being over-exploited.[16] The first seal inspector was Laws himself, followed by Nigel Bonner; both would later become prominent biologists with the British Antarctic Survey (BAS), Laws as director. Through their work and writings, especially their insistence on "rational exploitation," both Laws and Bonner contributed to a sense of the contemporary sealing industry—which they had to some extent helped legitimate—as distinct and better than the early nineteenth-century depredations.[17] It was also clear by the early and mid-1960s that the fur seal populations were bouncing back in places and would be quite a prize for sealers, either sanctioned by the Falklands government with licenses or illegally poached. Both Vivian Fuchs and Martin Holdgate—director and head of biology, respectively, of BAS—feared for the fur seal population when in April 1965 they discovered that there would be few if any funds to employ sealing inspectors and biologists after 1966.[18] Sealing was not a matter of past concern in the mid-1960s, but a real industry of particular interest to the British in respect of the management and government of the Falkland Islands Dependencies.

Elephant sealing in South Georgia withered without much fanfare after the 1964–1965 season. Allied as it was to the whaling industry, the basic reason for its demise was the passing of whaling as a necessary and profitable enterprise; after 1963 more whales were caught outside Antarctic waters. Yet as one sealing industry passed in the Antarctic, another was sought. Though it was recognized as shrinking, Norway had the largest sealing industry at this time, and it was an important element in its economy. Norwegian sealing operators were at this time looking for new fields to compensate for potential new restrictions on sealing in the North Atlantic, following the inclusion of seals in the International Commission for the North-west Atlantic Fisheries (ICNAF).[19] Between August and October 1964 a private Norwegian exploratory voyage operating the MV *Polarhav* worked the pack ice in the western Atlantic sector of the Southern Ocean, around the South Shetland Islands and the South Orkney Islands. This was a novel development, as seals had hitherto been taken from beaches, rather than hunted in the open sea. This voyage caught 1,127 seals, overwhelmingly crabeater seals, with some leopard and Ross seals and incidental elephant and fur seals.[20] Other Norwegian entrepreneurs also investigated the prospects for a new sealing industry.[21] When details of the *Polarhav* cruise were eventually widely publicized in 1968, it was not made clear if it was considered a success or failure. Certainly there was no indication in scientific correspondence, Scientific Committee on Antarctic Research (SCAR) agendas, or diplomatic whispers that a second cruise was planned to follow the first.

The Norwegians were not the only interested parties. George Llano, head of biology at the US Antarctic Program, noted that the Soviets had shown an interest in the mid-1950s in the commercial potential of the crabeater seals—a credible suggestion given their Arctic interests—and speculated that such an interest may not have declined.[22] The Danish shipping company Lauritzen, which provided many icebreakers for Antarctic logistics, hoped to supplement its icebreaking work in the Antarctic with a small sealing concern, having "been forced out of North Atlantic sealing areas."[23] And some Australian officials had intimated their interest in renewing the Macquarie Island elephant seal industry in the 1950s. Though it had ended several decades before with the declaration of Macquarie Island as a nature reserve in 1933, in 1952 the director of the Australian Antarctic Division, Phillip Law, saw the potential economic prospects of Macquarie and Heard Islands. After chartering the Norwegian sealer MV *Tottan* in 1952 and seeing Norwegian sealers pounce on some young elephant seals at Heard Island, Law wrote: "I am convinced that the time is ripe to commence sealing operations at our Islands."[24] Law maintained this position later in 1959 when the prospect of sealing at Macquarie Island generated negative public response.[25]

The year 1964 was eventually one of great consequence for sealing's prospects. In the far south, the Antarctic Treaty parties had, as part of the adoption of AMCAFF, turned their sights firmly on the welfare of living Antarctica and the regulation of human-animal interactions there. In the Northern Hemisphere, the national and international televising of a baby harp seal "skinned alive" by Canadian sealers began an era of close public attention to the practice of sealing and its perceived and actual depredations.[26] Ideas about the conservation of seals (and of cruelty to animals in general) were spreading quickly, ushering in something of a paradigm shift. Prior to the 1960s, seals, like whales, had been viewed as legitimate resources for exploitation, but by the early 1970s they were seen as sentient and feeling animals elevated above the status of mere exploitable resource. By the end of the 1960s, along with so many other changes in perceptions of and engagements with the world environment, marine mammals had become a prominent subject of environmental concern.

The Insistent Authority of Brian Roberts and the Terms of Negotiation

The historical and ongoing experiences of sealing meant that the negotiators of AMCAFF could not but have had seals in mind when they finalized that agreement in June 1964. Yet seals were not well protected by it. AMCAFF was as bound to the land as the treaty was. Article VI states that the "Treaty shall apply to the area south of 60° South Latitude, including all ice shelves, but nothing in the present Treaty shall prejudice or in any way affect the rights, or the exercise of the rights, of any State under international law with regard to the high seas within that area." As discussed in the previous chapter, this physical limitation was noted and remarked upon by several states during the negotiations, especially as penguins and seals spent a great deal of their lives in the "high seas." Though Weddell seals could live on ice shelves and fur seals on land covered by the treaty, crabeater, leopard, and Ross seals as a rule lived on the high seas and on pack ice not covered by the treaty. The parties, aware of these gaps, resolved at Brussels in 1964 to pursue the question of "pelagic sealing or the taking of fauna on pack ice" and to begin regulating sealing activities on a voluntary basis (recommendation III-XI).

Just as the British had been first out of the gate in the AMCAFF negotiations, so too would they attempt to lead on the issue of seals. And by "the British," I mean Brian Roberts. From the mid-1940s to the mid-1970s, Roberts was a particularly potent force in polar affairs (covering exploration, science, and politics) in Britain and internationally. He had studied geography at the University of Cambridge between 1931 and 1934, where he became interested in polar activities through the work of the Scott Polar Research Institute (SPRI). During his undergraduate years he led the Cambridge Expedition to Vatnajökull in Iceland and spent a summer in East Greenland. After graduating he was a member of the British Graham Land Expedition to Antarctica between 1934 and 1937. Upon his return to Cambridge he undertook doctoral work on Antarctic ornithology. During the Second World War he worked at the War Office Intelligence Department and was appointed with Colin Bertram (another prominent Antarctic hand and the same Cambridge generation as Roberts) to prepare a handbook on cold climate equipment. He was subsequently appointed to the SPRI board of management, then to the Admiralty Naval Intelligence Department. In February 1944 he was appointed to the Foreign Office Research Department, with particular responsibility for the

Falkland Islands Dependencies. He would keep a part-time appointment with the Foreign Office until his retirement in 1975; he simultaneously held a part-time research fellowship at SPRI. From his dual position in the Foreign Office and SPRI, he took part in nearly all major developments in Britain's policy on Antarctica. He was centrally involved in administering place-names in the Antarctic, organizing the Norwegian-British-Swedish Expedition of 1949–1951, planning the scientific programs of the Falkland Islands Dependencies Survey and its successor the BAS, and he was a member of the British delegation to the conference that negotiated the Antarctic Treaty in 1959 and each of the treaty consultative meetings until 1975.[27]

Roberts's pen was profuse. He kept a detailed diary of all the treaty consultative meetings he attended, with the express intention of leaving it to SPRI as both justification of and memorial to his own efforts. He tenaciously filled pages of Foreign Office minutes and correspondence, parrying with and informing his colleagues on every aspect of polar affairs. Whether this was welcomed or bemoaned in the Foreign Office (an institution that changed in so many ways over his career) is hard to tell, but it seems that his superiors were content to leave him to his remote bailiwick. Read together, Roberts's diaries and the government archives of Britain and other states attest to his importance, but within a wider context of expertise and attempted leadership in Antarctic matters. Roberts cultivated his extensive international network of polar contacts and could marshal a nearly encyclopedic knowledge of the polar regions. This knowledge was undergirded by the unique polar library classification system he had devised and instituted at SPRI. Roberts did not, of course, have free rein, working within specific bureaucratic structures in Whitehall and, in the context of Antarctic diplomacy, the necessity for unanimity. Roberts was undoubtedly highly esteemed, even if his international colleagues at times found his insistence on (his version of) the proper and effective way forward trying and impolitic in the delicately poised diplomacy of Antarctica. His ideas for Antarctica carried a patina of reasonableness borne of science, a technocratic spirit, and a comprehensive sweep, which made Roberts often paint his proposals as self-evident.

At the beginning of 1966 Roberts, in the hope of framing the terms of negotiation, prepared a major paper outlining the issues and potential scope of an agreement on seals; the paper was in fact cast as being for "an international agreement on the conservation of fauna on Antarctic floating ice, with special reference to pelagic sealing." Roberts saw five "matters of principle." The first presented Antarctic seals as "stocks" forming a "High Seas fishery resource largely located in international waters and hence of potential value to the world community at large." Second was the principle that as a "resource," the seal stocks "should not be needlessly depleted by over-exploitation," and that harvesting should be controlled by international agreement and within the concept of maximum sustainable yield. Third was a recognition of the "imperfect" knowledge of seal populations, and that any controlling regulations should be "interim, cautious, and liable to amendment in the light of later knowledge." Owing to this imperfect knowledge, the fourth principle was that "every effort should be made both to encourage biological research . . . and to gain information from the statistics of commercial operations." The final principle, following points three and four, was that "an appropriately constituted scientific advisory group will be required, able to study research findings and analyse commercial statistics."[28]

Roberts's paper then tried to set out some "practical measures." In addition to the standard elements of a fisheries agreement—such as quotas, protected species, sealing zones, and obligations to keep statistics—there were two noteworthy measures in his proposal. The first was that the area of application should be south of 55° south latitude to take in the area of floating ice, rather than the treaty's 60° south—though Roberts thought it might become more expedient just to use 60° south. The other was the inclusion of rather specific catch limitations. The paper drew on the British marine biologist Richard Laws's estimates to suggest that crabeater and Weddell seals could be taken at a rate of 10 to 15 percent of their populations, while leopard and Ross seals might sustain up to a 10 percent take.[29] Overall, with no sense that sealing would be banned, the paper clearly envisaged a comprehensive regulatory framework for an international sealing industry in Antarctic waters. Seals were to remain primarily resources for use.

The paper was circulated to the other treaty parties. The response of some of America's leading marine mammal biologists illuminates divisions that were emerging between older and newer scientific approaches to seals. On the one hand were those marine mammal scientists whose training and development had gone hand in hand with the exploitation of seals and whales—what the historian Graham Burnett has labeled "hip-booted biologists."[30] Vic Scheffer, who was a preeminent seal scientist and had been closely associated with the fur seal fisheries of North America (especially as regulated by international conventions), represented this mindset when he commended the British paper and suggested that scientific research would very much benefit from commercial operations.[31] In contrast was the sense held by a growing number of biologists that theirs was a science that should not be connected with wasteful and unnecessary animal exploitation; conservation was necessary not for the maintenance of natural resources, but for the purity of scientific knowledge. Where Scheffer was enthusiastic, another American biologist, Carleton Ray, was deeply skeptical. In response to the British paper, Ray scoffed: "Frankly, it looks too much to me like the beginning of another International Whaling Convention with some of the inherent failings attached." He questioned ominously: "Are all those idle whaling ships getting restive?"[32] Notably, several of the American responses interpreted the British paper as the outcome of the long history of British sealing and whaling, and perhaps interests in its future, rather than as a response to the Norwegian investigations.

The paper not only evinced the emerging tensions within marine mammal science, but also brought to the surface the continuing tensions between Britain and America on the way forward in Antarctica. If George Owen, the US delegate to the early treaty meetings, seemed conservative and unwilling to push the treaty into new areas, the leading officers of the Office of Antarctic Programs (OAP) in the National Science Foundation (NSF) were bridling at the British approach to conservation. Philip Smith, deputy director of the OAP, vented his frustration that current approaches to conservation in the Antarctic might not be effective. He felt that, owing largely to British pressures, "discussion of conservation measures relates largely to protection of mammals and birds." He went on to suggest that such "attention to mammals and birds and the related legalistic approach to conservation is not scientifically sound nor administratively practical." He thought that the OAP "should provide some creative leadership which redirects conservation discussion away from the legalistic area toward sound and cooperative programs of scientific investigation and practical field management principles."[33]

The Norwegians welcomed the British paper's focus on exploitation. Torger Øritsland, responding at the invitation of Professor Johan Ruud and the Norwegian Sealing Council, was basically positive about the British approach to the issues. He accepted that a scientific advisory group would be desirable (even if Norway might find it difficult to help fund such a group), and he accepted the rationale for the rotation of closed and open sealing zones. The one major suggestion he advanced was that quotas should, in a manner following the International Whaling Commission (IWC), be set as a whole and then divided proportionally among those countries sending sealing expeditions to Antarctica—a process that would, at least in the beginning, favor Norway.[34] Given their mutually agreeable approaches to the regulation of whale and seal exploitation, the Norwegians and British would be allies from the outset of these negotiations.[35]

The Purity of Science and the Authority of Process

The British paper was an attempt to force the pace and to fix the terms of negotiation. Unfortunately for Roberts, his efforts were frustrated. When the issue of regulating pelagic sealing finally came to be discussed by the SCAR Working Group on Biology, the British position came under further and public challenge. Meeting in Santiago in September 1966, and with the consultative meeting less than two months away, the biology working group had a full agenda. It had to agree to specially protected species and areas to fill the annexes of AMCAFF; it was considering issues of oceanic island conservation, potential Antarctic projects for the International Biological Program, bird-banding, the next SCAR biology symposium, official and scientific relationships with oceanographic sciences, general issues in the biological sciences, and potential future projects; and of course, it had to determine its position on pelagic sealing. All of these substantial subjects had to be discussed in under four days.

Roberts wanted SCAR to quickly grant its imprimatur to his plans—an imprimatur he thought would be little more than perfunctory. The working group did not oblige. Holdgate, the British representative in the group, reported that though he was joined by the delegates from Norway and the Soviet Union (both sealing nations), "a concerted attack was made on it [the British paper] by the members from the United States, Chile, Australia and South Africa."[36] Holdgate complained that instead of developing detailed proposals to control the prospective industry, "the scientists concerned instead took the view that it was quite premature to develop any sealing industry in the Antarctic, unless a great deal more was known about the seal stocks and pressed very strongly for some form of moratorium while new data were collected."[37] The working group did not recommend any specific catch limits, but rather called for "scientific investigations before there is any further exploration of the commercial sealing potential." It did respond positively to many specific proposals from Roberts's February 1966 paper, but its tone rejected any privileging of a potential or imminent sealing industry. It especially shied away from seeing seals solely in resource or stock terms, foregrounding the ecosystem and the "pack ice zone."

Roberts was furious at what he saw as the political naiveté of most of the working group's members. He viewed the papers emanating from the meeting as "disappointing," seeing the sealing paper as "a dog's breakfast compromise which may well torpedo the whole project at this stage," later adding that the recommendations "were adopted in a spirit of a scientific purism wholly unrelated to political realities."[38] Roberts and Holdgate behaved as if the working group had simply asserted that more information was needed. Yet the group did agree, in principle, with the regulation of commercial sealing through quotas, sealing zones, and seasons. The group even recommended that research should be combined with any sealing industry.[39] Holdgate and Roberts painted the working group's discussion as having failed to grapple with the British proposals, but it might be seen from another viewpoint: several delegates did not want the British position, with resource exploitation, substantively and rhetorically at the center, to be countenanced, and tried to push the tone and central consideration more firmly to scientific investigation and conservation. W. J. L. Sladen, who began his career with the Falkland Islands Dependencies Survey but was a long-term member of the American Antarctic community, noted the US position at this meeting, explaining that the relevant US National Academy of Sciences subcommittee thought the British provisional quotas "were in essence founded on extrapolations of extremely sketchy observational data." He continued that the American opinion was that "quotas at this stage of our knowledge were meaningless and did little more than invite harvesting of the animals." Sladen observed that the British paper presented to the working group "barely mentioned" and "omitted reference to research."[40]

Aggrieved by the working group's rejection of his work, Roberts took the implications to an extreme and overwrought position. The instructions to the British delegation for the fourth consultative meeting (written by Roberts to, in effect, instruct himself), read:

> There are signs that international scientific co-operation in the Antarctic is beginning to creak at the joints. SCAR . . . is not operating as effectively as it should. Our impression is that this is due to inanition. . . . The Antarctic scientific work now in progress is more

> routine and less exploratory than it was ten years ago and there is not the same feeling of high endeavour which helped to oil the early complexities of scientific co-operation.[41]

It is difficult to imagine his articulating these sentiments had SCAR more closely matched his exacting standards. One can appreciate why he would have been annoyed by SCAR's actions. If not quite present at its birth, he was omnipresent in the youth of SCAR. He was correct and politically astute in noting that any agreement that completely banned sealing would not be acceptable to the Norwegians and would therefore lack legitimacy. Roberts's thoughts also suggest a latent anxiety about how the treaty regime was moving Antarctic affairs away from the exceptionalism that had formerly characterized human activities in the South—adventurous, groundbreaking, and manly science and exploration—into more regular and perhaps unexceptional rhythms of management and diplomacy, wherein heroic feats with language perhaps counted for more. It is also difficult not to interpret Roberts's pining for unanimity, cohesiveness, and collegiality as emerging from the formative experiences of his own life: expeditioning as experienced in the British Graham Land Expedition and research and collegiality at the SPRI. The homosociality of the conference room replaced that of the hut and the informality of the ties redolent of a Cambridge college or department. And the anxiety must have been as much directed at himself as at his colleagues in treaty affairs. Roberts somehow managed to balance his deep commitment to ordering Antarctic affairs along particular (British) lines with bearing the weight of identity that he had gained in being an expeditioner on the British Graham Land Expedition and part of a generation of Cambridge graduates before the Second World War, inculcated in the culture of exploration and science. Headquartered in the same building as his university department, SCAR seemed a perfect vehicle for Roberts's aspirations, yet it would not allow him the whole stage.

If SCAR's position in September 1966 was too general and too scientifically pure, it was also a little too late to be useful for treaty parties at the consultative meeting in Santiago, which convened on November 3. Seals were not the only item on the agenda. Voting on specially protected areas for AMCAFF and issues of telecommunications and logistics dominated. It was not until November 16—the third to last day of the meeting—that seals were officially discussed. Roberts had primed the most important delegates the previous Friday, November 11, on the all-day bus excursion out of Santiago. After the failure of British influence at the SCAR working group meeting six weeks before, Roberts's efforts at the Santiago consultative meeting were indefatigable. He wrote in his diary that he spent "all day, in the bus" and then until after midnight in the hotel—about "fifteen hours"—principally trying to convince Henry Francis and James Simsarian of the United States of the necessity of regulating sealing. Roberts had to convince Francis and Simsarian to depart from their instructions to advocate for a moratorium, in part following SCAR's position. A difficult task indeed.[42]

When the matter was finally discussed on November 16, the British and Americans had resolved at least some of their differences: the Americans would not insist on a moratorium. The tenor of the meeting, though difficult to retrieve, seems to have settled on the most basic aspect of the issue: the protection of seals. In what he claimed was his longest speech to a consultative meeting to date, Roberts put the protection of seals at the center:

> Mr. Chairman, during the life-time of most of us present in this room, nearly 100 species of animals and birds have become extinct in the world. They have gone for ever because men have killed them unthinkingly. Let us take this unique opportunity provided by the Antarctic Treaty to make sure that the same unfortunate story is not repeated in the Antarctic. We have within our grasp an opportunity not only to save these particular animals for the future benefit and enjoyment of Men, but also to set an example for similar international conservation agreements in other parts of the world.[43]

Roberts's speech was only one of several interventions in the meeting that sought protections, yet perhaps more than other participants, his whole professional and personal identity and history were wrapped up in prevailing on the matter. The pro-seal mood so took the Australian delegate, Ambassador Ralph Harry, that he composed a poem for that evening's dinner—immediately translated into Spanish by Julio Escudero, author of the Escudero standstill plan of 1948—which ended with the call, "Please, please don't be an enemy of the seal."[44]

In the face of SCAR's apparently weak and excessively pure stance, Roberts—now with the backing of the United States and with a little help from the fact that his personal standing on the matter was heightened given that, in the words of the British delegation's report (not written by

Roberts), he was "perhaps the only person present who had actually measured" a seal, and that the "description of a reluctant Roberts wrestling with a recalcitrant seal reduced the Meeting to tears of laughter"[45]—pushed the Santiago consultative meeting to agree to recommendation IV-21, "Interim Guidelines for the Voluntary Regulation of Antarctic Pelagic Sealing."[46] It called on parties not to exceed the maximum sustainable yield of any one species of seal, to take account of the ecological system in localities before taking seals, to observe particular limitations on killing, to rotate sealing among different zones, to not take Ross seals, and to keep statistics of any actions. Roberts suggested to SCAR's executive secretary, David Martin, that some consultative parties were reluctant to act in relation to seals because SCAR had "failed to give any advice on the scientific basis upon which control of pelagic sealing can be based," and so "it was an uphill task to convince the Consultative Meeting that any agreement on this subject was necessary."[47] It was maddening for Roberts that the scientists in SCAR retreated into the position that there was not enough scientific information to support any sealing, seeing that as vacating the field to those who would exploit seals.

The 1966 recommendation called for maximum sustainable yields and sealing zones, but without specifics because the treaty parties called on SCAR to provide those at their next meeting. After 1966, the next opportunity for SCAR scientists to meet was at the July–August 1968 meeting of the Working Group on Biology, which was convened to coincide with the Second SCAR Biology Symposium in Cambridge—a major scientific conference that had been planned for several years. It was fortuitous for Roberts and the British that Cambridge should be the venue and Holdgate the convener of the conference.

The SCAR Working Group on Biology had established the Sub-Committee of Specialists on Seals. This group had nine members: one Chilean, one Australian (Robert Carrick, who had been prominent in the AMCAFF debate), one Norwegian (Øritsland, who had led the Norwegian exploratory sealing voyage), two Americans, and four Britons.[48] This Anglo-American-dominated group (really, Anglo-dominated) contrasted with the more representative composition of the group that had considered sealing in 1966. The brief for the British delegation to the 1968 consultative meeting in Paris (again, written by Roberts) noted that the four US representatives "expressed such divergent views that it is difficult to forecast the policy which may eventuate in Washington."[49] Roberts was clearly disappointed with the group, especially bemoaning the "biological approach" of Carrick, which took "no account whatever of legal realities or political possibilities," and the four "conspicuously differing voices" of the American scientists present. He even threatened Bill Sladen by suggesting that he, Roberts, "would have to make a statement in Plenary Session why I though SCAR could make no useful contribution to this problem." Norway's Professor Ruud, who was present at the meeting in the larger biology group, simply "sat back in detached cynicism."[50]

With the combination of British dominance and the self-reported intervention with Sladen, the Sub-Committee of Specialists agreed that the "Interim guide lines" on sealing passed at Santiago were "an effective basis" for sealing regulation. Very importantly, however, the working group concluded that "scientific knowledge . . . would best be advanced . . . by a properly controlled sealing industry." The working group even engaged in some commercial prognostication, suggesting that even with "the recent severe drop in the price of seal skins," sealing might be profitable again "in the near future."[51] Roberts and Holdgate were more forceful on their home turf.

What in Roberts's eyes SCAR had failed to do in 1966 it finally, though with great difficulty, achieved in 1968: a "reasonable" or politically feasible set of scientific guidelines as the basis for regulation. The treaty parties, when they convened in Paris in November 1968 for their fifth consultative meeting, had before them a scientifically informed document and one that was acceptable to the British and Norwegians. Nevertheless, a set of problems similar to those in 1966 confronted them. The seal question was not pursued by all, nor was it of fundamental interest to all. Only Britain, Norway, the Soviet Union, and the United States sat on what Roberts described as the "sub-working group on seals" at the 1968 consultative meeting.[52] These four states represented the most important sealing industries—the Soviets, for example, still operated a major sealing industry in the North Pacific and Bering Sea[53]—and displayed the most concern about far-reaching conservation. Though there had apparently been agreement on the broadest principle that seals should be protected and managed, all specific issues were unresolved and apparently unresolvable. Roberts noted in his diary that the Norwegian delegate, Øritsland, stormed out of the room, having been provoked to rage by the Soviet delegate, Tolstikov, and Tolstikov himself apparently had been driven mad by every remark uttered by Simsarian. We do not, however, know the exact causes of these antagonisms.[54] By Roberts's reckoning, the problem was that the Soviets were content to exactly and strictly carry over SCAR's language and recommendations to the consultative meeting (a characteristic Soviet position throughout this period), angering both the Norwegians and the British. The major effort at this meeting was therefore to win the Soviets over to a less scientific and more legally appropriate position.[55]

The 1968 consultative meeting in Paris passed recommendation V-8. The recommendation noted that there had been only "a preliminary exchange of views," even though a British draft convention had been on the table—though it had not been circulated in advance.[56] For example, reference to sealing "quotas" was deleted in favor of "permissible catch," on account of the Soviet delegation's insistence that quotas implied that decisions had been based on sound scientific data and reasoning, whereas it was clear—especially given the SCAR paper—that there was little information for such decisions.[57] The major outcome, therefore, of the meeting was the treaty parties' adoption, with some revisions, of SCAR's recommended amendments to the 1966 interim voluntary guidelines. Even this, by Roberts's account, was difficult, given the Soviet delegation's reluctance to amend SCAR's position. The clearest feature of the meeting was that however much the British and Roberts wished to push through an agreement on seals, it would be impossible to do so while the American position remained unstated and unfinalized. This situation mirrored the experience with AMCAFF in 1963–1964.

Though American scientists had been important in SCAR's discussions since at least 1966, its officials had been a brake on rapid development. Roberts had spent a great deal of energy in 1966 convincing the American delegates that something had to be done, then spent much of the 1968 meeting convincing the American delegates to start engaging with the substantive issues of negotiation. It is unclear what prevented the Americans from more seriously addressing the seal issue. One reason was suggested previously: there was disagreement among American scientists about exactly how to respond to the British framing of the issue. In the 1960s North American science and society, in particular, were experiencing a shift in sensibilities regarding marine mammals. They were no longer legitimate resources for use, but animals that could think and feel.[58] Another general reason may have been one that shaped the US approach to the region throughout the 1960s: given the considerable size of its undertakings through the NSF (which dwarfed all other nation's Antarctic programs), the United States was more concerned with its own operations and science than with any particular developments or initiatives within the treaty regime. Given US capacity to do so, a central part of American Antarctic policy was to lead through its scientific program, rather than relying on the treaty regime to achieve its goals. The Antarctic Treaty was not a dominant feature of the 1962 "statement of US Objectives regarding Antarctica," which was still current in 1968, and neither did it have what might be described as an internationalist tone.[59] A further consideration by 1969 was that NSF and State Department officials were preoccupied with a major review of their Antarctic policy and operations following the election of Richard Nixon as president.[60] By June 1970 Nixon had confirmed the new US Antarctic policy, which, in the spirit of Nixon and Henry Kissinger's broader changes in foreign policy, was rather more concerned with the functioning of the treaty regime than the previous policy had been. The Nixon administration's new approach to environmental protection also influenced the new policy.[61]

Resolving the Status of Scientists and of Seals

In late 1970, perhaps because of these new emphases in their Antarctic policy, the Americans began more forcefully to shape negotiations. In preparation for the 1970 consultative meeting in Tokyo, the United States prepared its own draft convention, which was a major redrafting of the 1968 British proposal, though it included the same fundamental points. Although Roberts thought this was "neater and in many ways much more effectively arranged than the draft which emerged from the Paris meeting," he feared it would be seen as a new and competing document, rather than as a complementary development.[62] The major development of this new draft was to carve out issues of detail into an annex to the convention. The draft was approved by the United States, Britain, Norway, and Japan (again, a balance of the major conservationist states and the major sealing and fisheries states) and only then passed to the rest of the parties for agreement.[63]

A full discussion on seals was conducted informally outside of the strict consultative meeting framework under the chairmanship of the conciliatory and experienced Belgian delegate Alfred van der Essen. This was done as a concession to both those who argued that the consultative meeting could not properly discuss issues relating to the high seas and to the Japanese, who had expressed some reservations about discussing a matter of marine resource regulation in Tokyo.[64]

Despite its importance in originally motivating the discussions in 1964 and 1966, by 1970 sealing in the Antarctic seemed more unlikely than ever. No Norwegian company repeated the *Polarhav*'s commercial exploration of 1964, and public opinion in many parts of the world was now firmly on the side of marine mammals. There were therefore subtle shifts in the rationales for the negotiations. At the Tokyo meeting in 1970, the Australian delegation reported that Roberts opened the substantive discussion by referring to the original title of the draft convention—"Draft Convention for the Regulation of Antarctic Pelagic Sealing"—as "an historical accident dating back to 1964 when the primary consideration had been the likelihood of an industry being on the verge of establishment." Roberts continued that "a better title would now be 'a Convention for the Conservation of Seals.' "[65] This was significant, and the eventual convention would bear this title. This development manifested the changing rationale for a convention on seals that emerged at this time. Before 1968–1969, Roberts had most often spoken of the need to regulate the sealing industry to protect the seal as resource from depletion. It was a call for rational resource management combined with his position that the Antarctic needed harmonized international rules. This changed after 1968–1969; though there had only been inklings before 1968, after this time it was clear that major fisheries (for krill and rock cod) were being investigated in the Southern Ocean, and that any convention on seals must include provisions and ideas that could be built upon when these far more promising and worrying developments came to a head.[66]

The 1970 consultative meeting produced a draft convention that would serve as the basis for decisive negotiations. Given that it had been the British and Roberts who had initiated and led the discussion from 1966, it was they who offered to host the final conference in London. Several major issues remained outstanding at this time. Perhaps the most important was the question of independent scientific advice. In late 1971, only a few months before the meeting, Francis, who led international Antarctic affairs in the NSF, pushed Roberts on the issue of an independent scientific committee for the convention: "The principal problem we are considering at the moment is the matter of scientific advice . . . how scientific advice can best be brought to bear on identifying a crisis situation which might develop as a result of commercial sealing activities in the Antarctic or from other causes."[67] An important element in this line of thinking was the haunting specter of the failures of the IWC, which, as was obvious by the late 1960s, had demonstrably failed in its management of whaling and had allowed the further decline of whale stocks.[68] Roberts responded by saying that he and the British had come to the position that the Food and

Agriculture Organization (FAO) would be the appropriate and desirable source of independent scientific advice. Roberts wrote that the prospect of sealing was "a rather small nut" and that the "FAO has the machinery to deal with small nuts of this kind without being paid."[69] But the United States was having none of it, Francis describing the FAO as inappropriate and undesirable as the "ultimate instrument which should be serving governments."[70] The United States foresaw issues of execution in using the FAO, given that not all members of the FAO would be signatories of a convention on seals. If the FAO needed to respond properly to CCAS demands, it might have to go through its own governance structures (which had to account for the views of 125 countries at the time), and the issue of divided mandates could legitimately arise.[71] In articulating this, Francis was expressing the suspicion of treaty outsiders that had characterized the response to India's United Nations push in 1956 and 1958, as well as foreshadowing the rhetoric of treaty exclusivity in response to outsiders' critiques in the later 1970s.

Some parties thought they had a suitable scientific advisory body in the form of SCAR. Yet that prospect was frowned upon by Roberts, who was still driving negotiations. He admitted to Francis that he had "considerable misgivings about SCAR's ability to carry out a task of this nature within reasonable time limits," as well as issues about the membership of such a group—a state could sign the agreement on seals, but not be a member of SCAR, which demanded participation in Antarctic research. As he put it, SCAR scientists were not administrators and were "deplorably bad at answering letters," saying that "scientists often give little evidence that they possess feelings of responsibility" (this coming from a trained scientist!).[72]

The Americans continued to push for a new scientific advisory body. Francis questioned Roberts about Britain's proposed mechanisms:

> Who decides when the data from sealing expeditions shall be requested on a weekly basis? Who decides what conservation measures are needed and should be brought before the Contracting Parties? Who decides when any of the three types of situations in Article 7 [exceeding quotas, having an effect on stocks, or having an effect on systems] exist? The answer to all three questions would probably be "the individual countries," but this would not be adequate for several reasons.[73]

The US draft went so far as to allow the proposed independent scientific body to force meetings of the contracting parties. This position was thoroughly opposed by the British, who, playing to the more entrenched national positions of Argentina, Australia, and Chile, which still remained opposed to any strong international structures for Antarctica, cited the dangers of a new supranational authority for Antarctica.[74]

In the end, neither the British nor the American position won out. The Americans sought a full independent commission and objected to the FAO; the British sought a commission on the cheap with the FAO and certainly not with SCAR; and many of the remaining parties did not want a costly and basically unnecessary structure to regulate an industry that seemed so unlikely. SCAR's appointment in the convention as the independent scientific adviser to the parties was the compromise outcome. That SCAR was appointed represented how far the relationship of the treaty parties and SCAR had come since the late 1950s when the treaty was negotiated. If it was uncertain then exactly what the relationship would be, now that it had been codified in the convention on seals, SCAR was a central part of the treaty regime.

While tensions about the status of scientists and scientific advice had been part of the negotiation on seals since the beginning, another major and potentially destabilizing issue arose in late 1971. When the parties convened in London they were now operating in full view of a world public that, in the foregoing decade or so, had come to see marine mammals not simply as animal resources for human exploitation, but as sentient and feeling beings more valuable to humanity alive than dead. When it was announced that a final conference would be convened in London, a small furor erupted. Environmental groups in the Americas and Europe saw that the conference was about seals and immediately assumed that it was to be a conference about dividing up the spoils of the Antarctic. The ground had shifted so much that the treaty parties could not rely on their own publics to greet the eventual agreement with, if not acclaim, at least benign indifference.

There were unexpected overtures from conservation bodies. The Chilean Comité nacional pro defensa de la fauna y flora worried that the agreement on seals would be "the beginning of the end of the Antarctic fauna," if a pro-sealing convention were adopted "under pressure from the whaling and sealing business interests"; it is notable that the group's memorandum was sent to Peter Scott, son of the famed Antarctic explorer Robert Scott, as chairman of the British World Wildlife Fund.[75] There are records of the committee on seals of the Swiss Comité d'action pour la défense des animaux en peril and the Anglo-American International Society for the Protection of Animals also expressing their concern about the negotiations on Antarctic seals. The British Foreign and Commonwealth Office, as host of the decisive conference, dutifully passed these pleas on to the delegations.[76] One individual (at least) was noted as having rung the Foreign and Commonwealth Office to complain that "the public had not been sufficiently informed" and "blasting off" to the FCO officer that the treaty parties "were conducting 'a bogus conference.' "[77]

The greatest expression of the heightened environmentalist interest in Antarctica was the composition of the American delegation to the 1972 final conference. While most delegations had two or three members—with some only drawing on London-based diplomatic staff—the United States sent a nineteen-person delegation: the usual senior State Department officials, including the special assistant to the secretary of state for fisheries and wildlife and coordinator of ocean affairs, Donald L. McKernan, and NSF and naval representatives, but also two members of the House of Representatives and representatives from several environmental organizations, including the National Parks and Conservation Association, the Friends of the Earth, the Sierra Club, and the Sea Mammal Motivational Institute.[78] But for the presence of the large US contingent, the conference would almost have been attended by only a small group of fisheries bureaucrats and an assortment of professional diplomats.

The Conference for the Conservation of Antarctic Seals convened in London on February 3, 1972. Much of the intellectual work and agreement had already been achieved before the conference convened. The more predictable Cold War political tussle over which states should be allowed to sign the convention—the usual issue of East Germany's potential admittance under an "all states" formula or exclusion under a "United Nations" formula—became quite contentious, but was resolved by the decision that any state could accede to the convention, but with a right of veto by any existing signatory.[79] The conference also became a forum in which to air the diverging perspectives on Antarctic seals: as resources to be scientifically managed and exploited or as wild animals to be protected.

CCAS, as finally agreed, retained many of the elements of the first British draft presented in 1968. Applying to the six species of Antarctic seal in the seas south of 60° south latitude, it regulated the killing and capturing of seals—in the language of the convention, "the conservation, scientific study and rational and humane use of seal resources" (article 3). All measures adopted under the convention were to be "based upon the best scientific and technical evidence available" (article 3, paragraph 2). Parties would have to exchange information with each other and with SCAR, not only on the numbers of seals taken, but also on the methods, time, and place of their being taken. After all the negotiations on an independent scientific body, SCAR was "invited" under article 5 to be that body. SCAR would assess information, encourage the exchange of scientific data, recommend research programs, recommend data to be collected by sealing expeditions, and use all of that collected information to report to the parties on whether seal harvests would have a "significantly harmful effect on the total stocks of such species or on the ecological system in any particular locality" (article 5, paragraph 4b). The convention left the parties significant room to maneuver, establishing mechanisms for the parties to act in the case of future commercial sealing, including the establishment of a permanent commission and the convening of special meetings (article 6). Notably, and distinct from Antarctic Treaty practice, CCAS would not require the unanimity of parties for decisions to amend the annex (article 9).

The bulk of the detail was inscribed in the annex to the convention, and the contents agreed in February 1972 have remained relatively unchanged since. The annex set the permissible catch of crabeater, leopard, and Weddell seals, and completely banned the capture or killing of Ross, elephant, and fur seals. It established closed and sealing seasons and sealing zones that would be open or closed to sealing in sequence, and established three seal reserves—near the South Orkneys, in the southwest Ross Sea, and an inlet near Cape Hallett. It required the exchange of information relating to the size of sealing ships; their days and positions of operation; and the number of adult and pup seals taken, their sex, reproductive condition, and age. Finally, it detailed appropriate sealing methods, prohibiting the taking of seals in the water (that is, they could only be taken on sea ice) and calling on SCAR to investigate "quick, painless and efficient" (7a) sealing methods.

Authority and the Pelagic Terrain

At noon on June 9, 1972, the monocle-wearing Anthony Kershaw, the British parliamentary under-secretary of state for the Foreign and Commonwealth Office, drew ink from a magnificent well on and led the signing of the convention. In the glory of the India Office Council Chamber at the Foreign and Commonwealth Office (slightly faded in the postcolonial era), representatives of only seven of the twelve countries that had agreed to the convention in February turned up to sign the document; most spurned the inkwell. As further demonstration that many of the conference participants were in no rush to give effect to their agreement on seals, the convention did not come into force until 1978—though it still managed to do so before AMCAFF did in 1982.

How distant seals were from these and the foregoing proceedings. The convention was an achievement of uncertain value, and it was unevenly valued. It was clear to the negotiators in February 1972 that a major renewal of the sealing industry was not likely. The elephant seal operations in South Georgia had petered out by the mid-1960s and had been managed scientifically since 1952. Whale and seal oil were increasingly marginal commodities. Even if economics had allowed seals' continued exploitation, public opinion generally would not. The exploratory Norwegian cruise of 1964 had not led to any plans, let alone actions, toward a new lease on sealing, and the Soviets and the Japanese—the other two likely sealing candidates—had been testing the capacity of the potentially greater Antarctic krill fishery. For the Norwegians and Soviets, there were enough seals for the market in the Arctic, closer to home.

What, then, were the parties really doing? The convention pushed some boundaries for Antarctica in particular, both physical and conceptual, but was in many ways a reflection of existing changes in broader environmental sensibilities and economic realities than an instrument of further change. More significantly, it is in the processes and the arguments of its negotiation that we find important disclosures of competing visions for the Antarctic—both of the relative authority of science and diplomacy in engaging with Antarctic issues and in relation to the differing views about the Antarctic's capacity to be simultaneously a scientific and commercial space. If the sealing agreement suffered from bad timing (in many senses), the discussions kept the idea of Antarctica as a resource-laden environment central and was part of the groundwork for the discussions on minerals that soon followed.

There was also clearly a quest for personal authority and standing in these negotiations. While all Antarctic agreements had many authors, both implicit and explicit, for CCAS one person above all others might be given credit and be recognized as the driving force. It is difficult to contemplate the convention on seals occurring without Brian Roberts.[80] "I have worked hard to rally support," he wrote in his diary toward the end of the 1970 consultative meeting in Tokyo. He wrote of the negotiations as unique in their difficulty: "No diplomatic subject in my personal experience has required so much sustained lobbying over so many years." He bemoaned the effort required "to put across such a relatively simple idea and to secure the agreement of twelve governments in the face of indifference." Roberts was perhaps overstating how "simple" the idea actually was, or how coherent or sustained it was, for even he had subtly shifted his position over the period, from a more resource-oriented to a more protection- and species-oriented approach. And the "indifference" was more a different range of intensities and opinions about whether there was a real issue to deal with in the first place. Roberts continued in his diary, recounting all the places in which he had pursued his task: in plenary sessions, in working groups, on buses, and in "many midnight sessions in hotel bedrooms." Yet he felt he was the only one truly committed to the cause: "But I am still left holding the baby." He reflected, "There is a real danger, I suppose, that I shall be thought to have become a fanatic about the PROTECTION OF SEALS."[81] Roberts's evaluation of himself and the seal issue was a mix of his usual political acuity and slightly unreflective self-regard. With his initial leadership of the fauna and flora conservation measures from 1960, Roberts marked himself and the British position out for its audacious initiative in pushing (perhaps even forcing) particular outcomes from the treaty parties-in-concert. That concerted effort—behaving as a collective in relation to third parties—was subtly and slowly becoming entrenched in treaty politics.

If the signing and ratification of CCAS were lackluster, they marked the beginnings of a new and more expansive geography emerging from the treaty regime. By staking a claim to the high seas and some of its denizens, the treaty parties were reclaiming, in part, the pelagic heritage and history of the Antarctic. Kept out of the seas by traditional international law, the international whaling regime, and their own treaty, the treaty parties were excluded from the longest and most consequential part of Antarctic history. And since it was in the seas that the bulk of Antarctica's limited ecosystem and biodiversity was to be found, this pelagic expansion was the first in a series of moves that allowed the Antarctic Treaty parties to encompass a larger region, connect more comprehensively with biogeographic reality, and populate the Antarctic "environment" with more nonhuman subjects to govern.

3

Mining the Deep South

EXPLOITATION, ENVIRONMENTAL IMPACT, AND CONTESTED FUTURES

IN AUGUST 1969 the representative of a small Australian mining firm wrote to the prime minister of New Zealand to apply for "the exclusive rights to explore, prospect and develop" areas in "New Zealand Antarctica" for "Petroleum, Coals and all Minerals." This brisk letter of only nine short lines, along with two other inquiries in the same month, found the New Zealand government rather unprepared; it was not the only country to receive such inquiries, with British and Australian officials also fielding questions.[1] More publicly in the same year, an American think tank called Resources for the Future, Incorporated, in association with the American Geographical Society, began a study entitled "Economic Potentials of the Antarctic." Its first published report in the *Antarctic Journal of the United States*—the official Antarctic journal of the National Science Foundation (NSF)—specifically asked: "What are the chances that this 'new' continent or its surrounding seas may be economically exploited?" The report's answer was mostly equivocal, and on the subject of minerals—both metals and hydrocarbons—the author felt that "the Eldorado of rich minerals may never be found," seeing other resources such as marine living resources and tourism as more important.[2] Mining and drilling were now firmly part of the conversation about Antarctica.

From discoveries of coal in the heroic era to hopes for uranium in the postwar era, minerals had been a persistent lure for exploration in Antarctic history. The new burst of minerals talk in 1969 thus took up earlier hopes and prospects. Yet in this new era there were fresh anxieties, new structures for deliberation and action, and new ideas to contend with.

In the context of seeming global scarcity of resources and ever-growing world demands, these new ideas about and explorations for minerals hung ominously over the delicately poised diplomacy and politics of the Antarctic Treaty. Many of the treaty parties took this matter seriously because it had implications for the status of their territorial claims, the status of their working relationships, and the potential payoffs. Yet it was only the New Zealanders who insisted that the sixth consultative meeting in Tokyo in 1970 should consider the issue. The other consultative parties were not eager to discuss it, and the United States was the only other party that wanted the matter aired. When the American delegate to a preparatory meeting conveyed his government's opinion that the matter should be officially placed on the agenda, the New Zealand representative noted that "a horrified silence fell on the room."[3]

No commercial mining activity would eventuate by the end of the 1970s, but the consultative parties decided that the absence of a structure for governing mineral exploration and exploitation was potentially destabilizing, perhaps fatally so, for the Antarctic Treaty. The initial resolution to the minerals talk begun in 1969 occurred at the treaty consultative meeting in 1977, when the consultative parties agreed to refrain from mineral exploration and exploitation activities while they were in negotiations and temporarily put the matter on hiatus to negotiate and conclude a separate resources agreement on the subject of Antarctic marine living resources (discussed in chapters 4 and 5). This was the first phase of the Antarctic minerals debate.

While the parties did not agree on a comprehensive minerals regime before the end of the 1970s, they nevertheless deployed great time and energy to thinking about the issue. In this first phase of the minerals debate, scientists and diplomats began to create an international environmental and economic order that conceived of Antarctica as an exploitable and working region, full of resources. In their negotiations, they began to deploy and flex the idea of "environmental impact," questioned and extended the idea of "resources" in Antarctica, continued to modulate and morph the region's geographies, and turned their collective sights firmly toward a future Antarctic in place of a past Antarctic.

The second phase—more remembered and more analyzed—of minerals negotiations occurred after 1982, and the first phase provided the intellectual foundations and geopolitical stage on which those negotiations played out. After 1982 the treaty parties negotiated the Convention on the Regulation of Antarctic Mineral Resource Activities (CRAMRA), which they signed in 1988. This agreement created a structure for assessing and authorizing potential mineral activities in Antarctica, including with environmental management and protection safeguards. Despite signing CRAMRA, Australia and France subsequently rejected it, owing in great measure to environmentalist pressures both domestically and internationally. Breaking the foundational treaty principle of unanimity, the Franco-Australian rejection killed CRAMRA, but the negotiating and environmental energies of the Antarctic Treaty System were directed toward negotiating an agreement on environmental protection, including a ban on mining, which eventuated with the Protocol on Environmental Protection to the Antarctic Treaty (the Madrid Protocol) in 1991. The Madrid Protocol in great measure recapitulated the concepts and structures embedded in the treaty between 1959 and 1980.[4]

Unlike the negotiations on seals—which began because the rejuvenation of an existing industry seemed possible—the parties began discussions on minerals even when the exploitation of those minerals seemed improbable in the short term and only vaguely possible in the distant future. Scientists and diplomats could only imagine what minerals Antarctica had. By the mid-1970s there had been no major studies of mineral prospectivity, though several leading geological and geophysical programs that began in the early 1970s implicitly involved prospecting of a kind. Core drilling had commenced in the McMurdo Dry Valleys to understand Antarctica's geological history, and deep-sea drilling by the *Glomar Challenger* in the Ross Sea in the summer of 1972–1973—also directed toward enormous questions of the earth's geological and climate history, including testing and elucidating the theory of plate tectonics—uncovered evidence of natural gas, a fact emphasized in press coverage at the time and in the years following.[5] Minerals had not been discovered in anything near commercial quantities and had barely been seen, and those maps that depicted mineral deposits were fictions. The figures bandied about, or taken as indicative, were mere speculation; sometimes that speculation was admitted and framed as best scientific inference, while at other times it was rhetorically buried. Geological and geophysical scientists did not even seem particularly keen to assess Antarctica's mineral prospectivity at the time; two lists of "problems" for geological research submitted to the 1970 Scientific Committee on Antarctic Research (SCAR) meeting by the Soviet geologist Mikhail Grigorevich Ravich and the American geologist Campbell Craddock contained only brief mention of "economic geology" among many other pressing research problems.[6]

Although there was no mining in this period—there was only thinking and talking about, and tentative and implicit prospecting for, minerals—there were three other major developments. First was the growing prominence of the question of whether or not to exploit Antarctica's resources and the related expansiveness of what, in fact, constituted the Antarctic's resources. The novelty of the minerals debate was that, in a concerted way, it moved discussion away from the older, and at the time passing, exploitative industries of whaling and sealing toward exploitative activities that involved more than furs and fats. A part of this shifting debate was a new approach to the question of Antarctica's value, beyond simply a crude account of the economic value of certain resources to broader conceptions of scientific and other intangible values. Talk of mineral resources was therefore in part about resources and usefulness in general. In a larger global moment when scarcity of natural resources, especially oil and food, seemed pressing and was pervasive in public and professional discourses, Antarctica was a site of abundance, however potential, rather than of scarcity.[7]

If Antarctica did seem a region of abundance, an outlet for the industrial world's (slightly) frustrated cornucopianism, it was, however, a region increasingly laden with a sense of fragility and preciousness. As a result, a second major development of this era was the deployment and debate of the idea of environmental impact. The 1970s was the first decade of environmental impact assessment procedures and regulations, spurred by the passing in 1969 of the National Environmental Policy Act in the United States and the spread of the practice internationally. This was an important element in the shift from older conceptions of nature, wildlife conservation, and natural resource management to ideas of *environmental* protection and the prediction and prevention of the damaging effects of human actions. For Antarctica this led to consultative meetings considering "man's impact on the Antarctic environment" and the assessment of the environmental impact of scientific activities and potential mineral exploitation. These ideas and practices still had humans and communities at their core; as they negotiated the place of mining in the Antarctic environment, the treaty parties were also assessing the impacts of mining on their interstate relationships. Furthermore, environmental impact assessments were significant not simply because they focused on potentially bad outcomes, but for instituting processes that, in theory at least if not in practice, were about consultation, deliberation, and inclusive processes. Thus, the "horrified silence" that greeted New Zealand's proposal for a discussion on minerals in 1970 was increasingly filled in successive meetings with talk of the environment; the process-oriented imperatives of environmental impact assessment, which in other contexts unleashed controversy and dissent, helped sustain the Antarctic Treaty through uncertainty.[8]

The treaty parties also turned toward the future. This new orientation was distinct from the treaty's temporalities in its first decade, which generally focused on and wrestled with the implications and hangovers of the past, whether in sealing or territorial claims, or with maintaining the delicate balance and goodwill of the treaty or arbitrating expertise and authority in the present. In turning toward the future, Antarctic affairs participated in the larger hopes and anxieties about the future that preoccupied global politics and culture in the 1970s. The historian Matthew Connelly has suggested that, especially in America, "people became extraordinarily focused on the future," in part because of a deep dissatisfaction with experts and politicians who had not predicted the great crises of 1968 (social unrest), 1973 (the Arab oil embargo), and finally 1979 (further energy crisis).[9] Environmental questions were prominent in this future-mindedness and its anxieties. Indeed, Timothy Mitchell has suggested that "the environment" became an "alternative project to that of 'the economy,'" a particular "set of forces and calculations that rival groups attempted to mobilise" in the political field.[10] Moving away from the "flora and fauna," "wildlife," and "nature" of earlier treaty diplomacy, the consultative parties and scientists also mobilized "the environment" in Antarctic politics, constituting an increasingly general and encompassing "environment" with a range of ideas, "resources," and biophysical elements, and appealing to that "Antarctic environment" in their quest to shape and control the future of the regime and the region.

Prospects from the Heroic Era to the Treaty

Before the systematic discussions of the 1970s and 1980s, mineral resources had an important if fitful place in thinking about Antarctica from at least the heroic era of the early twentieth century. Just as the Antarctic seas had been exploited from the late eighteenth century, so too was there hope that the Antarctic might provide minerals. Along with drawing the contours of the world map, the leaders of heroic era and interwar expeditions—Robert Scott, Ernest Shackleton, Douglas Mawson, and Richard Byrd, among others—searched for useful resources. The same can be said for the major national postwar expeditions, which went to the Antarctic with more in mind than collecting new scientific data.

Although the presence of coal was part of the reports of Scott's and Shackleton's expeditions, it is in the rhetoric of exploration of Mawson and Byrd that one finds some of the strongest statements regarding Antarctic minerals. Following his work on Shackleton's 1907–1909 *Nimrod* expedition, Mawson frequently referred to the potential mineral wealth of Antarctica; those references continued from the 1910s, when he organized and led the Australasian Antarctic Expedition, until the 1950s, when he was a central voice in advising Australia's national expeditions.[11] He advocated "economic exploration" of both minerals and fisheries, and this was as much a part of his postwar vision for a "permanent connection between Antarctica and Australia" as of science.[12] In the years following the First World War, Mawson was joined in proclaiming possible mineral riches by the publicly revered geologist Edgeworth David, who had predicted massive coalfields.[13] In the context of Mawson's Antarctic ideology—that there was an "Australian quadrant" of Antarctica, and that it "seems to belong to Australia"—Antarctica's minerals were, by this same logic, Australian.[14] Because mineral riches were central to Mawson's vision of Antarctica, they also became central to Australia's Antarctic imaginary, in both public and official minds.

The American explorer Byrd was similarly optimistic about potential mineral wealth. The subject became increasingly important in his public statements at the end of the 1930s. The question of economic value arose in 1938 and 1939 when the US government was considering whether to send its first official expedition since Charles Wilkes's in the early nineteenth century. Byrd, as the foremost American Antarctic explorer, was central to planning this expedition. In testimony before Congress at that time he claimed that many types of minerals were likely to be found in the South, but notably did not comment on their quantity or quality.[15] As the Second World War was drawing to a close, Byrd again began his campaign for an official US presence in the South. Apart from strategic interests, he wrote of the "folly" of assuming that Antarctica had no value.[16] Not of the heroic era, Byrd's technological approach to the continent, such as through airplanes and communications, perhaps heightened his sense that exploiting Antarctic minerals was, at least theoretically, possible. His was a spirit of technological domination of the polar regions.

In the years after the Second World War, new hopes about minerals emerged. With the development of nuclear weapons, world uranium supplies came under intense scrutiny, and their possible presence in Antarctica had to be assessed. During the planning for the Norwegian-British-Swedish Antarctic Expedition in 1949, Larry Kirwan, secretary of the Royal Geographical Society, invoked the potential of minerals in Queen Maud Land, specifically referring to uranium.[17] One of the first great discoveries of Australia's continental research program in 1954, the Prince Charles Mountains, was also framed in press coverage and by Minister for External Affairs Richard Casey as heralding new and potentially significant mineral wealth.[18] Even the presence of a Geiger counter in the hands of an Australian geologist in an early cut of the 1954 publicity film *Blue Ice* was deleted because of what it might imply to the world about Australia's activities.[19]

Despite a half-century and more of commentary on the potential value of Antarctic minerals, the subject did not appear in the Antarctic Treaty. It did, however, feature as an important part of the negotiations, and its absence in the final document was conspicuous. Adrian Howkins suggests that while British and American officials were skeptical of the potential for mineral riches, other states regarded the significant presence of minerals as rather more likely.[20] Australia and New Zealand were particularly open and clear about minerals. If the presence of a living resources clause in the treaty was not overly determined (as discussed in chapter 1), the absence of a minerals clause related more to the sensitivities of those territorial claimants who had not given up on the frozen El Dorado. Australia's objection to any mention of economic exploitation in the treaty was closely linked to its opposition to any broad or comprehensive internationalization of Antarctic affairs. Governed by strict, cabinet-level instructions, Australian negotiators at every step tried to minimize the range of activities of which the eventual treaty mechanisms might take charge.[21] Moreover, the central pillars of Australia's approach concerned demilitarization and the recognition, in some way, of its territorial claim and interests. Australian diplomats narrowly pursued the latter and saw other developments and designs for the treaty as asking too much of the Australian position.[22] Even when clauses of a generic nature were proposed—such as one in the June 1959 draft that allowed for parties to pass administrative measures on "other matters not inconsistent with the purposes of the present Treaty"—Australia opposed them, first because they might allow for slow movement toward international administration of Antarctica, and second because they might be used to bring economic issues into treaty affairs.[23]

New Zealand's Labour government after the end of 1957 was active in Antarctic matters, having a particularly internationalist tone. Its leader, Walter Nash, held the controversial position that any treaty should deal with economic exploitation and rights, specifically calling for some international authority for the region.[24] The New Zealand delegation's brief for the 1959 treaty conference noted that traces of many minerals, though no major deposits, had been found. Reflecting the technical optimism of the time, the brief noted: "It is not inconceivable that some time in the future, in order to render these minerals accessible, portions of the ice cap could be melted away by nuclear heat. The cost of mining on the continent would undoubtedly be high, but nuclear advances may cut this cost." It also saw parallels with Norway in Spitsbergen and Denmark in Greenland, the obvious suggestion being that Arctic mining activities were clear examples that exploitation in harsh conditions was more than possible.[25]

In the end the treaty contained no reference to minerals specifically or economic rights more generally. With the aim of achieving consensus, Australia's position on economic rights was acquiesced to, and the treaty gained a far more circumscribed character than others—especially Britain, New Zealand, and the United States—had hoped for. Partly as a result of this, Antarctic affairs in the 1960s saw very little activity in and consideration of the subject of minerals, until the fateful approaches of 1969. Not even then was there scientific and technical consensus on the short- or medium-term prospects for mining. Whereas in 1964 the American geologist Duncan Stewart stated that Antarctica might supply commercially valuable minerals "in a hundred or more years," the leader of Australia's Antarctic expeditions, Phillip Law, confidently predicted subterranean Antarctic mines and townships powered by nuclear reactors and nuclear families.[26]

The presence of minerals in Antarctic discourse in the first half of the twentieth century should not be overstated. Minerals were a small if very alluring element of engagement with Antarctica, and if they loomed large in the minds of Mawson and Byrd, they did not so loom in the imaginations of others. Explorers and scientists could use mineral potential as a claim on the public's imagination, from which they could claim funds and support for their expeditions. The specter of Antarctica's "value" frequently reared its head at moments of competition, moments when the possibility of territory and sovereignty seemed perfectible and imminent.

Renewing Prospects and the Promise of Easy Abundance

Renewing Antarctica's mineral prospects within the treaty regime and in an age of rapid technological and geopolitical change in relation to minerals and energy was a fraught task. In the previous age of explicit national rivalries in Antarctica, the public pronouncements of potential riches in the South by heroic explorers or government ministers were par for the course; such speculations drummed up interest in the Antarctic and cemented official recognition of, or funding for, science. Under the treaty there were now good working relations among the twelve parties, and any idle speculation about commercial activities, with related questions of profit, in the Antarctic might destabilize those relationships. Unfortunately, the treaty parties could not control private mining interests; with ever-growing global demands for consumer goods and a certain way of life—concentrated in the industrialized West—companies had to continually look for new reserves, and this was so even before the energy crises of the early 1970s.

When the parties first sat down at the 1970 consultative meeting in Tokyo to talk about minerals—hidden in the agenda under "other business"—they were not sure what to expect, but knew that this was only the very beginning of discussions. New Zealand started off the talks and posed four questions: Was there a distinction between prospecting and extraction? If there was a distinction, was prospecting a scientific activity and therefore covered by article III of the treaty, and would parties have to circulate the results of that prospecting? What reply should be given to organizations applying for prospecting rights? What should the parties do about controlling commercial mining by organizations from nonsignatories?[27] The New Zealand delegate insisted that he and his government had no answers to these questions, but thought it necessary to begin a discussion on them. All the parties contributed to the discussion, but only, it seems, with basic affirmations that the treaty was an important regime worth preserving and that the mineral question should not be allowed to destroy that.[28] The meeting did not produce any decisions; there was little expectation that it would.

Even at this early stage, no party even hinted at an outright and permanent ban on mineral activities. Perhaps such a position was aided by the fact that exploitation might be many years in the future. Discussions were difficult and sensitive because of issues relating to sovereignty and jurisdiction, which pitted claimant states against nonclaimant states. Who would approve exploration or exploitation activities? Who would grant licenses? Who would set the conditions of exploration and exploitation? Would there be royalties, and to whom would they flow? Furthermore, the treaty parties had devoted much energy in their first decade to environmental matters, so the potential environmental impact on the Antarctic and its ecosystems was also an early and pervasive matter of discussion.

When the parties reconvened in Wellington in October 1972 for their sixth consultative meeting, though these questions remained pressing, a different diplomatic issue arose. All the parties seemed to believe that they would slowly work toward a comprehensive regime, but in the meantime there were differing opinions on whether there should be a temporary moratorium on mining exploration. The to and fro of the meeting came down to the question of how long a temporary moratorium should be. The United States would only agree to a moratorium lasting until the next consultative meeting, yet the Chileans wanted one of at least ten or fifteen years.[29] The American delegation seemed to be the only one advocating exploitation, so its call for a short moratorium—or one tied to the schedule of meetings—may have been read by other delegations as presaging a rapid entry on its part into prospecting. The American delegation certainly felt that the other parties were "strongly of [the] opinion that commercial exploration in Antarctica must be discouraged."[30] These two extreme positions did not meet, and the eventual recommendation contained no moratorium; coming to an agreement would not be easy. So the moratorium became one of the major issues of the early mineral debate among the parties, combined with the initiatives of gathering scientific and environmental data on the potential effects of mining.

These negotiations were inescapably bound up with the global geopolitics and economics of minerals and oil and the dominant and demanding place of the United States within that system. The two and a half decades following the Second World War saw an astonishing growth in demand for oil and a continued growth in the demand for other minerals. Between 1949 and 1972 world energy consumption more than tripled, and the demand for oil increased more than five and a half times. Oil in particular fueled postwar growth; it was the age, in Daniel Yergin's words, of "hydrocarbon man."[31] Within this growth, the United States was a leader. By 1970 it had become the greatest consumer of energy in world history, and compared to other highly industrialized countries at the time, it relied disproportionately on oil.

The optimism of this seemingly unstoppable growth began to diminish from about 1970 and was fully challenged and questioned in 1973. First, in 1970–1971 US production was at its lowest levels in decades, and policy makers became acutely aware that perhaps US production had reached capacity; the words "energy crisis" entered public discourse and the United States became a net importer of oil and more reliant on an integrating world economy. If the facts of 1970 suggested a gentle and slow decline, events beginning in October 1973 were a fundamental shock. In that month the Organization of Arab Petroleum Exporting Countries (OAPEC) instituted an oil embargo against the United States for its material support of Israel following Egypt and Syria's surprise Yom Kippur invasion. This watershed moment had been preceded by worries about disruptions to the Middle East oil supply; when the disruption finally came, its economic and mental effects were significant.[32]

Though the embargo shocked those oil-reliant publics into appreciating the limits of resources, the response was not to focus on demand for oil but rather on supplies. David Nye has suggested that the American public "demanded from politicians both a return to easy abundance and independence from foreign energy suppliers."[33] New fields in the Antarctic did not feature in this rhetoric, but new Arctic fields did, with newspaper advertisements run by Atlantic Richfield, the company leading Arctic drilling, showing the North as an important part of the solution to the energy crisis.[34] Even if the Antarctic did not count as "easy abundance," it was nevertheless a part of some future abundance. Nye has suggested that "the energy systems a society adopts create the structures that underlie personal expectations and assumptions about what is normal and possible."[35] In this case, America's "energy world" allowed official policy positions to see the exploitation of Antarctic oil and minerals as normal and possible. In the minds of energy policy makers and planners, Antarctica, like the Arctic or the deep sea bed, was an abstract place bearing oil resources, where natural barriers were simply impediments to be overcome. Given the pressing realities, Antarctica came to be seen as part of future US energy systems, which in turn powered the world economy.

If actual mining in the Antarctic seemed remote to the treaty parties, the desire to mine and drill was present and real. The willingness and capacity to drill and mine in remote and difficult situations was developing with greater intensity in the 1960s and early 1970s. Offshore drilling for oil had been a reality for decades in the Gulf of Mexico, and wells were increasingly drilled to greater depths.[36] In some minds, a naïve comparison between the Gulf of Mexico and the Southern Ocean might have seemed straightforward; the Gulf endured destructive hurricanes, so nature was potentially destructive and fatal even in the most promising oil field. At least two other sites of new exploitation were being planned or were coming on line in the late 1960s and early 1970s. The first was the commencement of drilling at Prudhoe Bay in Alaska in 1968. Although this was land-based drilling, these Alaskan fields were still subject to extreme environmental conditions.[37] The other major development at this time was of the gas and oil fields of the North Sea between Britain and Norway, which involved Dutch, Danish, and German interests. These fields also faced hazardous and capricious weather conditions and deep wells.[38]

In addition to the technological triumphs of offshore drilling, the intellectual breakthroughs in earth sciences spurred mineral imaginaries about Antarctica. The theory of plate tectonics was widely accepted by the late 1960s, and the reconstructions of the Gondwanaland supercontinent by decade's end provided tantalizing mineral links between the continents. New research attempted more accurate reconstructions of exactly where the modern continents had once joined, and these reconstructions—which appeared in both the public and scientific press—had Antarctica at their very heart. The frequent inference was that Antarctica must possess minerals in some considerable quantities because the neighboring continents did (see figure 3.1).[39]

During the late 1960s and early 1970s continental shelves and the ocean floor were central sites of resource development and central issues for international politics. Talk of manganese nodules on the sea floor sparked a hope that there were new sites of mineral reserves. But those same nodules raised issues in international politics and law; they existed on the seabed outside of areas of national jurisdiction. Questions of ownership and benefits arose, and nations began discussing how those resources might be the "common heritage of mankind" and how the use of and profits from those resources might be equitably divided among nations.[40] A comprehensive law of the sea became the subject of a massive diplomatic effort beginning in 1973 (discussed at length in chapter 5).

If, at the close of the 1950s, minerals in Antarctica seemed a far-off if hoped-for prospect that could safely be ignored, at the opening of the 1970s the pressure of world events made a diplomatic and legal vacuum potentially destructive of goodwill and peaceful relations. Though the broader world situation appeared unevenly in the records of parties' discussions,

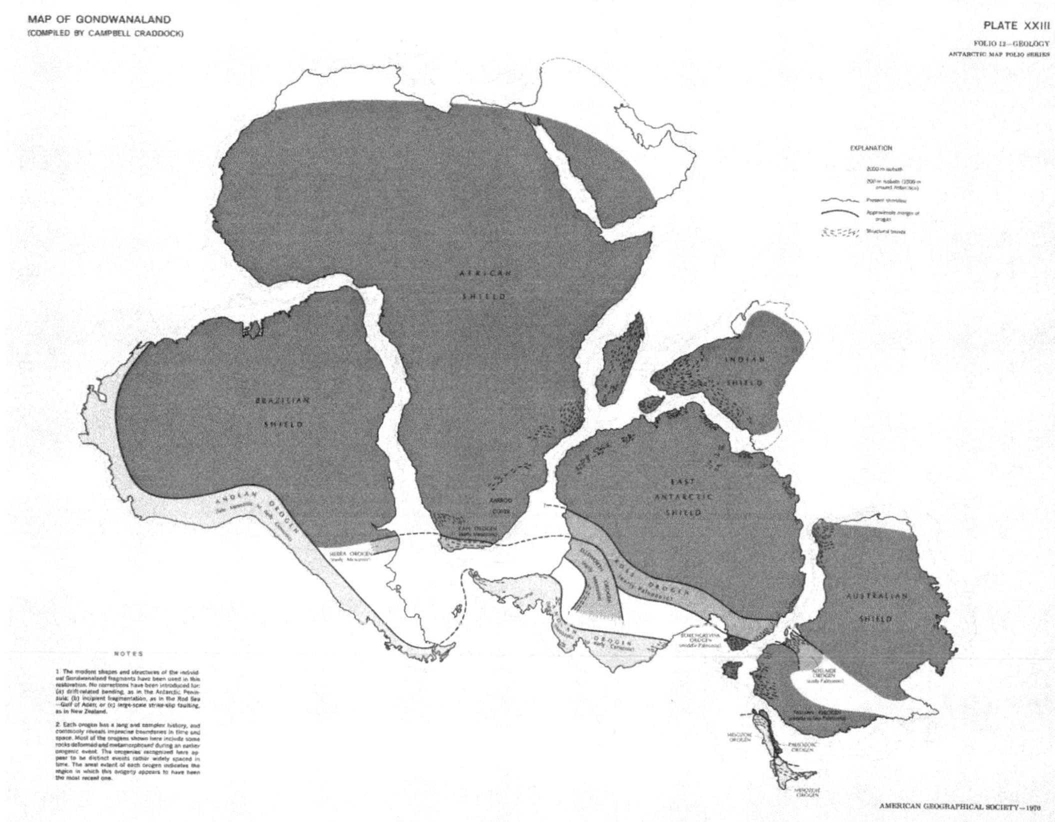

FIGURE 3.1 Antarctica at the center of Gondwanaland. In the late 1960s and early 1970s, new reconstructions of the Gondwanaland supercontinent had Antarctica at their heart. Antarctica's connections to other continents with proven mineral reserves suggested that it too might share in the earth's mineral wealth. *Source:* Campbell Craddock et al., *Geologic Maps of Antarctica*, Antarctic Map Folio Series, folio 12 (New York: American Geographical Society, 1969–1970).

the linkages of scientists and officials and ideas brought the question of Antarctic resources clearly onto the agenda.

Uncertain Pressures, Assessment, and Reassessment

Despite discussions at two consultative meetings in 1970 and 1972, progress on the mineral questions seemed to be exceedingly tentative and going nowhere. The Nansen Foundation in Oslo, led by its director and former Norwegian diplomat Finn Sollie, intervened in this stagnant situation and invited scientists and legal experts from the treaty parties in their individual capacities to discuss the current scientific, technical, and legal matters relating to Antarctic mineral exploration and exploitation. The conference convened between May 30 and June 8, 1973, a few months after the news broke that the Deep Sea Drilling Project—a major American offshore scientific program, using the ship the *Glomar Challenger*—had discovered gas in the Ross Sea, but a few months before the shock of the Arab oil embargo, though still under the shadow of an expansionary global oil and mineral economy.[41] The conference did not live up to its hopes for a free and frank exchange of ideas—it was certainly never intended to resolve any particular issues—but it nevertheless aired many issues that the parties had not broached at the 1972 consultative meeting.

The Scientific and Technical Working Group—chaired by the Norwegian geologist Tore Gjelsvik, with the director of the New Zealand Geological Survey, Richard Willett, as rapporteur—considered five topics: known mineral deposits and occurrences, Arctic experience and its relevance to Antarctica, how to distinguish commercial exploration from scientific exploration, the environmental effects of exploration and exploitation, and the question of urgency. Willett's draft report dutifully conveyed the substance of the discussions, though it appears a final report was never finalized.[42] The draft report suggested that the scientists could agree that known mineral occurrences were unlikely to be commercially attractive, though they admitted that there were significant gaps in their knowledge. They also agreed that there would be environmental disturbances during both exploration and exploitation.[43]

Yet on two of the topics there was apparently dissension. When considering whether the Arctic experience might guide the Antarctic experience, some thought that sea ice and iceberg conditions in the Antarctic were more severe and prevented a meaningful comparison. On the question of urgency there was also no unanimity. The draft report does not specify which members took which positions, but some members "argued that while minerals on the Antarctic continent were unlikely to be commercially attractive in the foreseeable future there would be a steady, and possibly rapid, increase in demand to explore and assess the hydrocarbon potential of the Antarctic continental shelf." Furthermore, some members more than others recognized that there was "heavy pressure" on the oil industry "to discover more and more resources of oil and gas world wide," and that exploration and prospecting were likely in the short term, if eventual exploitation might not be. Even if companies would not proceed with exploration in the short term, some members of the working group thought that companies would be willing in the following five to ten years to pay for exploration rights.[44] Some scientists protested that "the world's scientific capacity would be better applied to the development of alternative energy sources" than chasing after potentially small and difficult reserves of oil and gas. Overall, there were mixed messages about urgency.

If the pressure of assessment emerging from the Nansen Conference was too diffuse given the lack of unanimity and uneven energies, other pressures were more singular and expected. It is clear that most, if not all, of the consultative parties awaited a clear sense of the American stance on minerals and a regime to govern exploitation. In 1972 there were two issues: the large and long-term one, which was the whole question of mining and the form and substance of a comprehensive regime, and the smaller and more immediate one, the question of a temporary ban or moratorium while negotiations on the larger question were advancing. The United States, alone among the parties, led the charge for nondiscriminatory access to the region for mineral prospecting, as well as opposing any barriers to mining. This position kept it from agreeing to a temporary policy of restraint until 1977. That the United States held such a position in the negotiations stemmed principally from its clear position as the leading mining nation in the world; its companies were the most capable of mining the Antarctic as well as the most willing to do so. The additional problem was that internal disagreements within the US bureaucracy hampered its outward stance. Longtime Belgian Antarctic diplomat and international lawyer Alfred van der Essen "pointedly" told a US diplomat in October 1974 that "everyone was looking to the U.S. to assert leadership in this matter."[45]

American policy makers were thinking about Antarctic minerals even before the fateful New Zealand agenda suggestion of 1969. In addition to Neal Potter's 1969 study "Economic Potentials of the Antarctic," economic resources had also been part of the US Antarctic policy review of 1969 and 1970. In March 1970 the NSF's leading Antarctic policy official, Henry Francis, found that tourism, mining, and fisheries were "all feasible given the appropriate circumstances." He specifically invoked the experience of the American Arctic, which "dramatize[d] the very rapid change which can occur with a sudden discovery of an economic resource"; he cautioned that this was not likely "in the immediate future" for Antarctica, though "not outside the realm of possibility."[46] Francis's statement contained the fascinating interplay of hopeful speculation and realistic expectation. All Antarctic resources might feasibly be exploited "given the appropriate circumstances," but not in the immediate future. Yet because of the dramatic and relatively quick changes occurring in the Alaskan Arctic, nothing could be discounted.

In the wake of the 1972 consultative meeting, officers of the US State Department initiated a study of minerals within the Antarctic Policy Group—whose three members were from the State Department, the NSF, and the Defense Department—with the addition of a representative from each of the Departments of the Interior and Commerce.[47] This study proved to be a protracted affair, principally because two approaches to the problem emerged. On one side were the State Department and the NSF's Office of Polar Programs, which owing to their historical attachment to the regime were supporters of the Antarctic Treaty and the international approach it enshrined. On the other side was the Department of the Interior, which, given its decades of globally projected extractive resource ideology and activity, was a strong advocate of keeping options open for US exploitation of the Antarctic.[48] State Department officials were especially wary of Interior's approach, assuming that it would wish to influence a US policy position that was not based on an international approach to the problem through the Antarctic Treaty.[49]

The recommendations based on this review made their way through the US hierarchy, finally being put to the president in April 1974 by the Under-Secretaries Committee of the National Security Council.[50] In July 1974 President Richard Nixon approved National Security Decision Memorandum 263, which outlined three objectives for a mineral regime. First, commercial exploration and exploitation should "not disrupt the implementation of the Antarctic Treaty as long as it is in effect, and does not become a cause for significant international discord." Second, "any exploitation of Antarctic mineral resources is compatible with environmental considerations and with United States obligations under the Antarctic Treaty." Third, the United States should get other parties to come to the position that there should be an international agreement on the subject of minerals, and such an agreement should "permit free access . . . to any part of the Antarctic Treaty area except those areas specifically designated for other uses," be compatible with US law of the sea interests (which insisted on "worldwide access to fossil fuels and hard minerals"[51]), protect the Antarctic environment, and preserve the rights of scientific research. As a temporary measure, however, the United States held that while an international agreement was being negotiated, it would oppose exploration and exploitation.[52]

It was also in 1974 that one of the most comprehensive assessments of Antarctic minerals to date was released by the US Geological Survey (see figures 3.2a–b). The report's vague title, *Mineral Resources of Antarctica*, perhaps stoked the fires of speculation; however, the abstract of the report was quite clear: "Although the existence of mineral deposits in Antarctica is highly probable, the chances of finding them are quite small."[53]

By the time of the 1975 consultative meeting in Oslo—the third meeting at which minerals were discussed—the US position was still internally divided, despite the policy direction from the president in 1974. The US delegation to this consultative meeting could not even contain its disarray, being outwardly clear in its discord. Dixy Lee Ray, the assistant secretary of state for oceans and international environmental and scientific affairs, thought that the resource agencies could not agree on one delegate, and there was "acrimony and recrimination, discord and indecision."[54] This situation of internal politicking was known to both other treaty party delegations and the media. Brian Roberts noted in his diary that the minerals working group in Oslo was disrupted because of the late night "disarray, discussing and telephoning to Washington" of the US delegation.[55] The leading journal *Science* reported on "internecine warfare among agencies" and suggested that it was "still a tossup in government circles as to whether political pressure generated by the energy crisis will succeed in reshaping American policy toward the icy, almost deserted, South Pole continent." The desire to exploit Antarctica may have seemed understandable, as that same article also reported a US government report that estimated there were 45 billion barrels of oil and 115 trillion cubic feet of natural gas in the continental shelf.[56]

(a)

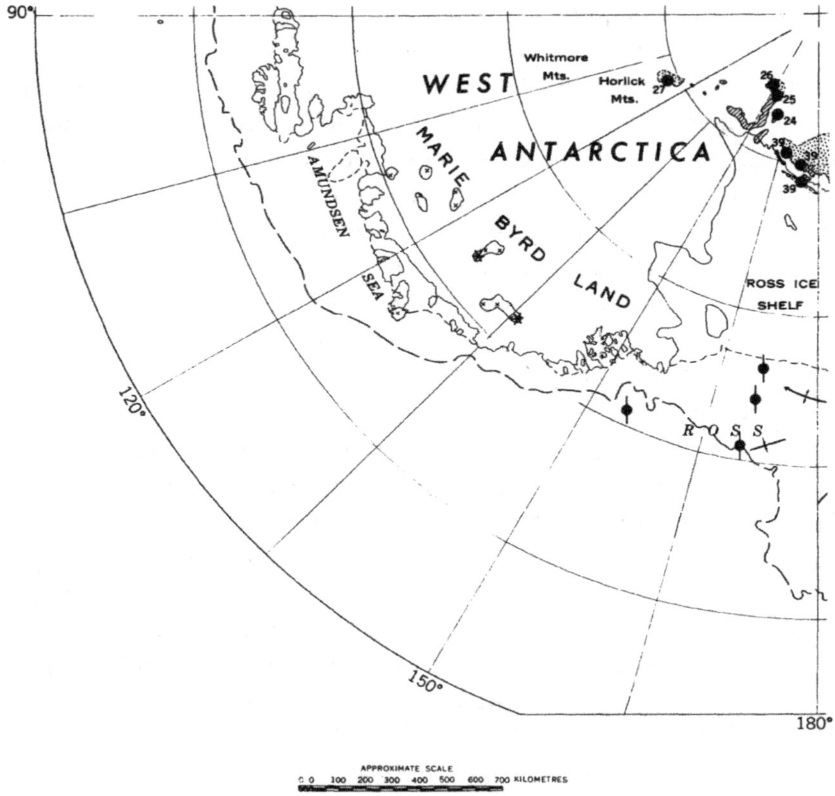

FIGURE 2.—Known occurrences of potentially valuable minerals in Antarctica—Continued.

FIGURE 3.2 The potential sites of minerals extraction in Antarctica. Though a 1974 assessment of Antarctic mineral resources by the US Geological Survey was mostly pessimistic about finding economically-viable reserves, by representing the locations of known mineral occurrences and future drilling sites of the *Glomar Challenger* it stoked visions of a potentially prospective Antarctic. *Source:* N. A. Wright and P. L. Williams, eds., *Mineral Resources of Antarctica,* Geological Survey Circular 705 (Reston, VA: US Geological Survey, 1974).

(b)

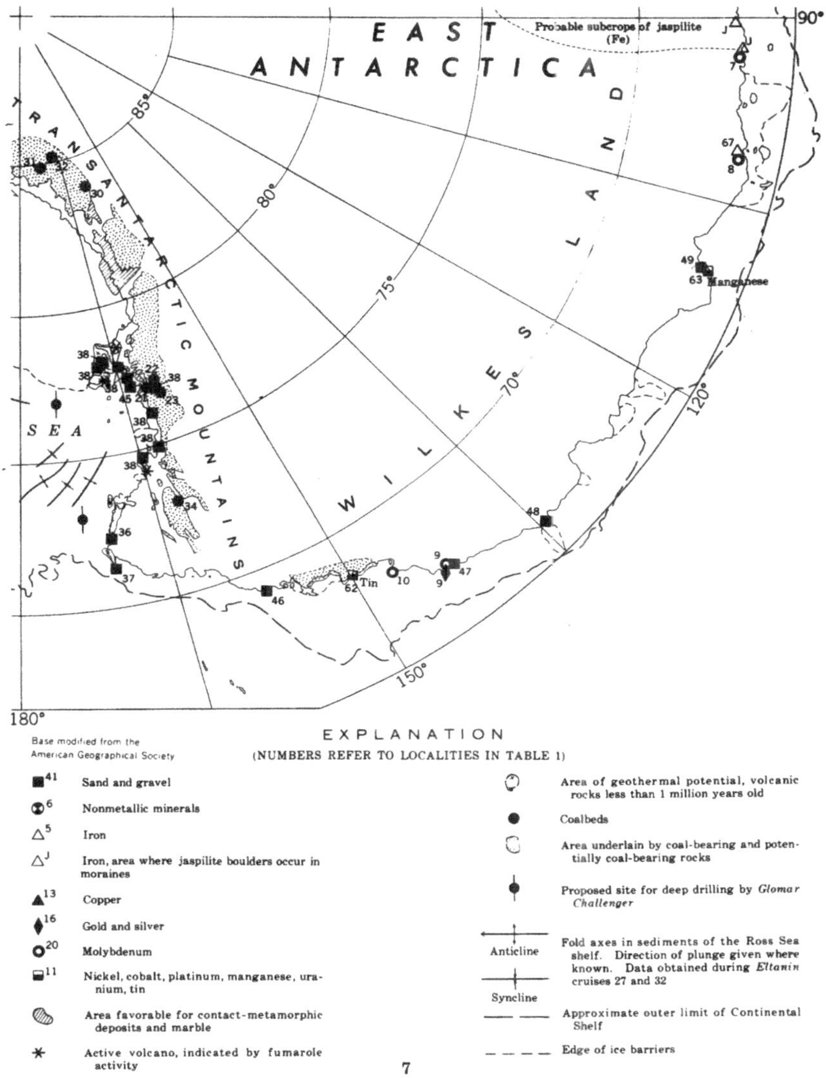

FIGURE 3.2 continued

The lack of unity in the American delegation deeply affected the Oslo consultative meeting. One element of the problem was that some parties saw a lack of good faith on the Americans' part. At the second preparatory meeting for Oslo in February 1975, Argentina and Chile were open about their mistrust of America's motives. In conversation with the New Zealand representative, the Chilean representative, Fernando Zegers, divulged his suspicions, stating that the Americans had to "come clean about the nature and the extent of the resources already known."[57] Though the US delegation was not in possession of some secret source regarding mineral extent, they were specifically instructed not "to support any regime which discourages the finding and development of new sources of energy and other raw materials."[58] By the time of the consultative meeting in June 1975, suspicions had not abated. The New Zealand delegation noted that once again, the United States could not accept a "full restraint clause," and speculated that it held this position because of the "mineral lobby" back in Washington. The New Zealand delegation also noted "some dickering on the part of the British," who seemed to backtrack on their previous strong support for a temporary moratorium. Perhaps, the delegation reported, the British were "greedy for more than North Sea oil."[59]

In spite of all the intellectual and policy efforts, the outcome of the 1975 consultative meeting was not a great advance on the 1972 recommendation, for it contained no temporary prohibition on exploration or exploitation. The New Zealand delegation thought that the meeting "came very close to breaking down on the question of Antarctic minerals exploitation," although the US delegation happily reported that its hard-line negotiating stance against a moratorium was capitulated to in the last moments of the meeting.[60] The two major outcomes were the call for a specific meeting on minerals in 1976—an "uneasy compromise" according to the New Zealand delegation[61]—and a call on SCAR to prepare an environmental impact statement (recommendation VIII-14). With the American position lacking internal unity and the different national positions seemingly antagonizing rather than accommodating each other, handing the matter over to the "experts" was an exercise in displacing tensions.

SCAR and the Geographies of Impact

SCAR remained formally outside the minerals discussion until the treaty parties called upon it at the 1975 consultative meeting to assess the possible environmental impact of mineral exploration and exploitation.[62] As more complex environmental and scientific issues were appearing on the treaty agenda, SCAR was further entrenched as the central, even sole, source of definitive and authoritative scientific information and advice. Its scientific response to this call for an assessment of environmental impact brought forth disagreements, both explicit and implicit, about the nature and extent of Antarctica's resources, geographies of environmental impact and regional knowledge, and the place of scientists in an international political system.

Though scientists had been contributing to the minerals debate from the late 1960s, the treaty parties' request to SCAR was of a different order. SCAR, of course, had been an important actor preceding the Agreed Measures for the Conservation of Antarctic Fauna and Flora (AMCAFF) negotiations and during the negotiations on the convention on seals. It was also simultaneously, in the mid-1970s, becoming increasingly central to the debate on marine living resources (discussed further in chapter 4). If the treaty parties thought they flattered SCAR by calling on it for advice, some within the organization were cautious and aware of the perhaps invidious position in which they found themselves. Gjelsvik—the Norwegian geologist, president of SCAR, and director of the Norwegian Polar Institute—suggested that "the diplomats of the Treaty parties are trying to get the scientists to solve the political questions which the diplomats are not able to solve at the Consultative Meetings." He went on to note, however, that "the future of SCAR to a great extent depends on the success of the operation of the Treaty," and so "political and scientific matters are certainly interrelated in Antarctica."[63] Gjelsvik, though a geologist, felt that his position as president of SCAR was "to ensure that all pertinent information and a broadest possible exchange of views is forthcoming, rather than to express my views as an 'expert.'"[64]

Whatever their misgivings about the position they were in, the SCAR executive did respond to the parties' request. They appointed two leading British scientists, well known to each other, who were clear leaders of the small Antarctic establishment with outstanding international reputations and could be expected to provide an assessment efficiently and within moderate bounds. One was the ecologist Martin Holdgate, who had conducted field research in Antarctica, had led the biology unit of the British Antarctic Survey, and had moved into larger ecology and conservation roles in the British government by the mid-1970s. The other was the preeminent glaciologist Gordon Robin, who had been director of the Scott Polar Research Institute at the University of Cambridge since 1958, had recently completed a four-year term as president of SCAR, and had led the massive aerial radio-echo sounding effort that was progressively mapping the depths of the Antarctic ice sheet.[65]

Ready for the 1976 special preparatory meeting in Paris, Holdgate and Robin's paper, "Antarctic Resources—Effects of Mineral Exploration," was a statement with an imprimatur of authority, though with an overall equivocal position on the effects of exploitation. "Mineral exploration or exploitation would be attended by various environmental effects," the paper stated, but the severity of those effects "would be governed by a variety of factors such as location, type of product and techniques used."[66] The paper concentrated on offshore resources as the most likely to be sought or exploited in the "foreseeable future," rather than on the "improbable" extraction from ice-covered land areas. Generally, the paper stated that "the sheer size of the Antarctic region should, however, permit the development of a pattern of exploitation which would allow reasonable access to minerals which the world may need without endangering either the major living resources or the value of the Antarctic as a study and research area."[67] In addition to environmental impacts, the paper also briefly mentioned the potential impact of mining on scientific activities. It suggested: "Even relatively minor widespread pollution of the ice sheet from airborne effluents is likely to affect significantly the unique usefulness of the Antarctic ice sheet for providing baseline data on global pollution levels and climatic conditions."[68] The paper concluded by suggesting future "research requirements" necessary for providing adequate impact assessments.

This final paper was the outcome of limited consultation within SCAR. Though Holdgate and Robin were both tasked with drafting SCAR's position, it was Holdgate's draft that dominated and was sent to a handful of leading SCAR scientists. Each engaged with the paper, some suggesting minor amendments or changes of tone, while others were more fundamentally critical. A particularly negative response came from Uwe Radok, a leading Antarctic meteorologist and glaciologist at the University of Melbourne, who had been a scientific adviser to the US Office of Polar Programs between late 1973 and early 1975. He wrote of the "total resources of Antarctica." His critique conveyed a sense that the Antarctic could only bear a limited range of activities and that certain activities had a value beyond money. He thought it was

> highly probable that [the total resources of Antarctica] would suffer some, if not even major, damage and neglect from a change in

> Antarctica's present role as the international science continent. The use of the ice sheet in monitoring global pollution levels and climatic trends, the study of complex geophysical phenomena near the rotational and magnetic poles, the programs of Antarctic biology, all are incompatible with intensive mineral exploitation claiming more and more of the limited logistic resources available. A more intangible resource, the present international harmony and collaboration would suffer irreparable damage in a diversion of emphasis from scientific objectives to the exploitation of mineral resources.[69]

These intangible social and scientific resources were, in Radok's view, "the true major resources of the region which SCAR holds in scientific trust."[70] Few responses to Holdgate's draft paper were so extensive and broad in their view of resources and Antarctica's value, though several made strong statements about the needs of scientific research. Radok's particular articulation also represents how pervasive the philosophy of Antarctica as an "international" and "scientific" continent was and suggests how participants in SCAR during the 1970s who had been there at its foundation in the late 1950s took the boundaries between science and politics very much for granted. Taking on Radok's position in full would have demanded SCAR make a far more active and interventionist statement on the subject of minerals than most scientists within it could have accepted.

In analyzing and discussing environmental impacts and resources, Robin, Holdgate, and their colleagues were crafting and articulating new Antarctic geographies. When calculating the possible effects of an oil spill, Robin noted: "For 1% of the area of the Southern Ocean to be covered by oil would require, at a thickness of 1mm, a total of around 500 billion tons of oil." He thought such a large amount of escaped oil "unlikely," trusting that a well blowout would be attended to before it reached this size. He concluded: "It seems unlikely that spillage of vast amounts of oil would have much effect on the climate." He immediately went on to say that an oil spill's "ecological effect on the life of the Southern Ocean may be very serious but again this is perhaps open to question."[71] In pursuing this logic, Robin was obviously trying to emphasize the environmental impact on the Antarctic region as a whole, disentangling some parts of the Antarctic environment from others. Perhaps, with his glaciological and climatological preoccupations, Robin was slightly blind to ecological considerations; by his calculations and presentations, an oil spill seemed almost innocuous. Not all of Robin's colleagues appreciated this particular appraisal of the matter. The American geologist James Zumberge, at the time president of Southern Methodist University in Texas, suggested: "The idea that the very size of Antarctica protects it from accidental release of oil . . . is suspect and should be examined closely."[72]

Another intervention that played with Antarctic geographies came from the Australian government geologist and secretary of the SCAR geology working group, Ian McLeod. He insisted that it was only by investigating the geology of a specific locality that any mineral occurrences could really be known to exist; this was also a self-reinforcing process whereby further refinement in the size of particular regions went hand in hand with continuing research. As he said in response to Holdgate's and Robin's drafts: "Until someone wants to explore in a particular place or a mineral deposit is discovered, any discussion of environmental effects of mineral exploration must be in general terms, or purely hypothetical." Interestingly, McLeod suggested a reverse approach to the situation. He thought that, owing to the "impossibility at present of identifying particular places which will be affected by mineral exploration, perhaps biological work should be directed to identifying the various types of biological systems or ecological groups and their likely distribution." Overall, McLeod thought that SCAR's advice should "be in a continental context rather than for particular regions."[73]

Each of these interventions contained particular conceptions of Antarctica, some complementary and some contradictory. On the one hand was a view of the Antarctic as a whole geophysical and biological region, a continent and continental shelves in tight connection with the ecosystem. On the other hand was a more disaggregated and subregional geography of the Antarctic, which saw detail and variation. Each of these perspectives had a particular history, yet with the International Geophysical Year and the Antarctic Treaty, the continental and regional conception of the Antarctic had become rather dominant.[74] The SCAR scientists were doing two things by framing discussions of environmental impact on a regional or continental scale at such a tentative stage in the development of the minerals issue. First, they were rearticulating one of the dominant geographical conceptions of the Antarctic, which had been embedded in the 1950s. Second, they were recognizing that totality as having within it a sensitive natural environment. This continental view was important to both SCAR and the treaty parties, for it emphasized a totality that demanded specific forms of diplomatic and scientific governance.

Refining the Idea of Environmental Impact

SCAR's initial response to the treaty parties was tabled at the special preparatory meeting in Paris, held between June 28 and July 10, 1976. Rather problematically, not all the delegations had even received the SCAR report, so its use was immediately diminished.[75] As previous meetings had been, the Paris negotiations were divided into scientific-technical and legal-political discussions, and in a similar way to the 1973 Nansen meeting, many parties saw the meeting as purely an opportunity for discussion, delimiting the agreements and disagreements among the parties. The parties addressed the same set of scientific-technical questions that they had in previous meetings and studies: what was known about mineral occurrences and reserves, what effect mining would have on Antarctic ecological systems, what the state of technology was and whether it was suited for Antarctic conditions, and what the economic aspects were. Their answers to these questions were also very much the same as their previous answers: very little was known about Antarctic minerals, and there were no proven reserves; mining activities would certainly have an effect on the Antarctic environment, but at an unknown level of severity; technological development was allowing hydrocarbon exploitation in deep water and under adverse conditions, but its transferability to the Antarctic was unknown; and the economic aspects of the question were avoided because of the "absence of background documentation."[76]

Though the meeting went over well-trodden ground, it had some new features. John Heap, the British Antarctic diplomat and successor to Brian Roberts, particularly observed an interesting shift in attitudes toward the urgency of exploitation.[77] Prior to 1976, he remarked, the parties had been working under the assumption "that the exploitation of these minerals was necessary in order to satisfy a world demand." This was not apparent at the Paris meeting, with Heap noting the significance "that no delegation at the meeting—not even the US—based its position on the need to exploit such resources in the near future for its national benefit."[78] Perhaps Heap was grasping to find any new developments arising from the meeting. In the end, the most the meeting seemed to achieve in scientific terms was to call for yet more SCAR work.

SCAR responded in October 1976 by forming the Group of Specialists on the Environmental Impact Assessment of Mineral Exploration/Exploitation in Antarctica (EAMREA).[79] Chaired by Zumberge, the EAMREA Group had twelve other members. The group had less than a year to produce a report in time for the 1977 consultative meeting in London. The report was a much longer and more detailed document than Holdgate's initial paper, including a more detailed assessment of the level of geological knowledge in the mid-1970s. The report was also more explicitly an environmental impact assessment, devoting significant space to considering the impact of mineral exploitation on the exploitable species of the Southern Ocean. By 1977 krill and the Antarctic marine ecosystem were at the center of treaty politics and scientific interests, and a potential fishery seemed imminent, compared to far-distant mining and drilling. Such references to marine living resources therefore continued to suggest the many resources and values that the Antarctic possessed, rather than privileging minerals. The report's assessment of prospects was short and sharp: "No mineral deposits which are likely to be of economic value in the foreseeable future are known in Antarctica." However, it continued, "given the right economic conditions, there is hardly a place on earth that will not be the site of some exploratory activities for mineral resources sooner or later."[80]

The EAMREA report also turned away from the geographies articulated in Holdgate and Robin's SCAR paper. Zumberge had disagreed with Robin's suggestion that even a massive oil spill would have only a small impact; the EAMREA report therefore emphasized highly localized impacts of mineral activities. In fact, the latter parts of the report read as an incessant litany of localized impacts, of potential contamination and pollution of the environment at every stage of the mining process, affecting both natural systems and scenery.

Yet there were still tensions between local effects and problems for the whole ecosystem. The report suggested that "the greatest environmental concern is aroused by those activities that most hold the prospect of persistent and extensive effects on natural processes in the Southern Ocean."[81] It was in these years, as emphasized in chapter 4, that talk of interconnected, dependent communities and ecosystems of the Antarctic was developing. The spatial tensions here were complex and sometimes contradictory. By emphasizing highly localized impacts, Zumberge and the EAMREA Group were perhaps guided by the notion that any single impact might have ramifications for the whole Antarctic. This contrasted with the view that emphasized the "continental" Antarctic as a whole—held, as we have seen, mainly by geologists—and with the implications of that view that small or localized impacts might be tolerable.

A central part of SCAR's two assessments between 1975 and 1977 was the idea of environmental impact. The 1970s was the first decade of the environmental impact assessment, the practice having been planted in the regulatory landscape by the US Congress in its 1969 National Environmental Policy Act (NEPA), which came into force at the beginning of 1970. In the context of NEPA, the impact assessment (and its associated public statement) was intended as an essential regulatory tool—an "action-forcing device"[82]—that would actually give "teeth" to environmental protection and the bodies set up to advance that goal, especially the US Environmental Protection Agency.[83] The historian Samuel Hays has also suggested that EIAs were developed to allow for a consideration of effects on communities that were not easily accounted for in traditional monetary terms.[84] The practice of assessing environmental impact spread rapidly throughout many polities and scientific organizations, becoming an essential regulatory element of the ecological age. Environmental nongovernmental organizations (NGOs) in the United States also used NEPA to force agencies working overseas—such as the Department of State and the Agency for International Development (AID)—to undertake environmental impact assessments for their activities abroad; after a great deal of internal bureaucratic argument, this became standard by 1977 and 1978.[85]

At the heart of an environmental impact assessment was not the environment per se, but humans. One of the definitive statements on EIAs came from the Scientific Committee on Problems of the Environment (SCOPE) and its Commission on Simulation Modelling. Scientists at the 1974 Workshop on Impact Studies in the Environment (WISE) defined an environmental impact assessment as "an activity designed to identify, predict, interpret and communicate information about the impact of an *action*, on man's health and well-being (including the well-being of ecosystems on which man's survival depends)."[86] The centrality of human health and well-being to this definition is inescapable, as is the parenthetical appendage of impact on ecosystems. Impacts on human health were equal to impacts on the environment.

The EAMREA report was quite explicit about assessing impacts on human activities. In addition to considering ecological impacts, it considered the potential impact of mining on other economic activities in the Antarctic and on scientific research, and the impact of mining activities on the exploitation of marine living resources was specifically noted. The report was not just about impacts on economic activities, though, but also about human relationships. An essential element of the mineral debate was the consideration of the impact of mining on the treaty regime itself and the interstate relations it embodied. A consistent feature of the discussion on minerals from 1970 onward was a concern about the continuing vitality of the Antarctic Treaty under the strains of talk on minerals. The report of the Australian delegation at the 1976 Paris meeting is indicative: "There was a widespread perception at the meeting . . . that the resource issue posed a threat to the survival of the Treaty."[87] The minerals question was challenging the parties to consider whether they wanted to keep their treaty relationships or dissolve them, and which parts of the Antarctic environment should be considerable elements of their regime. If an environmental impact assessment was intended, in part, to assess the impact of activities on humans, then carrying out the process was another instance in which the Antarctic became a peopled and human place. As the diplomatic discourse about Antarctica became more and more explicitly about environmental protection, it also became more and more implicitly about the humans at the center of that environment.

Though prepared in under a year, the EAMREA report was a major statement on the potential environmental impact of mineral activities, if for no other reason than that there was no competing document of its type in the field—although, as I've suggested, it also manifested a set of tensions relating to the place of science in the minerals debate and with respect to Antarctic geographies. Disappointingly for its authors and for other SCAR officers, the report was effectively sidelined at the 1977 consultative meeting. Perhaps the treaty parties (or at least some of them) just did not want to listen. In EAMREA's place, yet another group of experts, chaired by Holdgate, produced a new report. This new group, which met at the London consultative meeting, had thirty-six members, compared to the thirteen of the EAMREA Group, with only two members overlapping between the groups.[88] The Holdgate group's remit was not to produce an environmental impact assessment, as had the EAMREA Group, but a much broader consideration of mineral issues, including details of available and potential technology, suggested "guidelines on appropriate methods for mineral exploration and exploitation," and thinking through the required infrastructure for the Antarctic context as comprehensively as possible.[89]

The apparent rejection by the consultative parties at London of the EAMREA report was troubling to SCAR officers. Gjelsvik complained to

Heap that the poor reception had "caused surprise and hard feelings by members of SCAR." Gjelsvik was particularly pessimistic, feeling that "the role of SCAR as an adviser to the Treaty" would have to be examined, though he felt that it would "be very difficult to find people of high scientific qualities willing in the future to use time and effort to advise the treaty on scientific questions related to difficult political problems."[90] Heap tried to assuage Gjelsvik's concerns by suggesting that blame could be laid at the feet of the Soviet delegation, and particularly its geologist, Mikhail Gregorovich Ravich.[91] The Soviet delegations at the 1975 and 1976 meetings had protested that what was required in the minerals debate was more basic scientific research—an argument they also trotted out in relation to marine living resources. More specifically, Heap speculated at second hand from Holdgate's reports that Ravich was being personally obstructive of the EAMREA efforts. Heap would not venture to say in writing why this was the case.[92]

By the end of the London consultative meeting, and eight years after the New Zealand agenda proposal of 1969, the treaty parties and SCAR had explored quite thoroughly the science and technology of potential Antarctic mining activities, yet the meeting did not see a definitive settlement on minerals. One of its achievements, though, was that for the first time the parties could agree on a recommendation (IX-1) with a clause calling for restraint on mineral activities. The parties urged "their nationals and other States to refrain from all exploration and exploitation"; it also recommended that the parties should ensure that "no activity shall be conducted to explore or exploit such resources" while they were negotiating an agreement. This was far from the moratorium several parties wanted, but was a concession to the United States, which demanded no restraints.

Mining Words, Valuing Antarctica

The London consultative meeting in 1977 was the end of the first phase of the Antarctic minerals debate. The parties had finally agreed to a temporary freeze on mining activities while they negotiated a comprehensive minerals regime, and in the following three years they directed their diplomatic energies to negotiating the marine living resources agreement. While the voluntary restraint recommendation of 1977 seemed anemic, even anticlimactic after so many years of talk, and still only in its foundational phase, the minerals negotiations were highly productive. The meanderings and explorations in all the assessments and reassessments had continued the refinement and delimitation of the contested question of what Antarctica was. Antarctica here was a total and all-encompassing region as well as a collection of specific and highly localized places; it was real and abstract, with some places more valuable than others; and it was a region full of resources, a working and workable human landscape, deeply peopled.

At the heart of the minerals debate was the question—sometimes implicit and sometimes explicit—of Antarctica's value, of what constituted Antarctica's resources. What emerged by 1977 was a vision of broad utility and workability. Scientists, both individually and collectively through SCAR, emphasized the value of the Antarctic as a source of scientific knowledge for the world. In their hands, as well, environmental impact assessments concentrated on the many potential uses of Antarctica and therefore on the complex ways that mineral exploitation could damage the Antarctic. By engaging in all of these assessments—of environmental impacts, mineral reserves, and values—the scientists and diplomats within the treaty regime also did a thorough job of peopling and humanizing the region.

The narrative difficulty with the decade at hand is that we are trading in abstractions and futures: a minerals industry of the imagination, mineral reserves of sheer speculation. It is not the abstractness per se that we should note, but rather that the minerals abstraction was competing with another abstraction that, owing to the forces of history, would dominate because it was resolved first: the idea of an Antarctic region filled by an extensive and fragile ecosystem. This view of the ecosystem was supported by extensive scientific research and the presence of real and tangible things (the animals within it), and it was germane within a broader field of environmental politicking and thinking in that moment. If the related issue of the exploitation of marine living resources had not arisen, perhaps a minerals agreement would have emerged more quickly and with a very different spatiality and field of concern.

The Antarctic Treaty's life after 1959 was one of greening: the treaty parties and other Antarctic actors, ever searching for power and authority, enrolled new nonhuman entities and new relationships to cultivate a living, dynamic, and fragile region to displace the inert geophysical continent. Coming in the midst of the foundation and strengthening of an environmentalist way of thinking among both scientists and the public, this minerals debate could perhaps only be resolved according to the discourses and terrains of the "age of ecology," which was distinct from saying that it should be banned or allowed. There is a dramatic irony in this, for the actors felt themselves to have agency in an ordered process, yet it was an emerging environmental order that was slowly circumscribing their options just as they were fashioning it. The foundations that kept Antarctica from being mined in this ecological age were already hardening.

4

Seeing the Southern Ocean Ecosystem

ENLARGING THE ANTARCTIC COMMUNITY

ON THE MORNING of March 1, 1978, a group of Antarctic Treaty party diplomats and scientists assembled for a scientific lecture. They were gathered in Canberra to negotiate a regime governing the conservation and exploitation of Antarctic marine living resources (see figure 4.1). Their terms of negotiation had been set at the 1977 consultative meeting in London. One of their central, self-imposed obligations was to shape a regime that "should provide for the effective conservation of the marine living resources of the Antarctic ecosystem as a whole."[1] "Ecosystem" might have tripped easily off the tongues of those diplomats, but as Sir Donald Logan, the British delegation head who chaired the scientific working group they were gathered as, put it: "It would be useful to know from the scientists what that term implies."[2] If Logan hoped to learn more about what "ecosystem" meant, he did not simply want a scientific lecture, but a specification of scientific ideas that might "illuminate" the treaty parties' political discussions and help them to agree on what they were intending to conserve. Was it the Antarctic marine living resources, the Antarctic marine ecosystem, or some combination of both?[3]

The scientist at the lectern was Richard Laws. A marine mammal biologist and ecologist and a preeminent scientist of the Southern Ocean, Laws had begun his work there in the late 1940s and had risen to become director of the British Antarctic Survey (BAS) in 1973. Over the course of his career, he had become the leading authority on elephant seals, had helped manage the sealing industry of South Georgia, had been an inspector on whaling ships in the Southern Ocean, and had spent time studying and managing elephants and other large mammals in Ugandan and Kenyan

FIGURE 4.1 The Australian minister for foreign affairs, Andrew Peacock, addresses the opening session of the special consultative meeting for Antarctic marine living resources in Canberra, February 27, 1978. It was here that Richard Laws delivered his lecture on the Antarctic marine ecosystem on March 1, 1978. *Source:* NAA: A6180, 28/2/78/2.

national parks.[4] He was not strictly speaking an ecosystem ecologist, yet with a confident voice and a measured and assured pace, he opened his half-hour lecture by defining the Antarctic marine ecosystem as "a volume of ocean with unique physical and chemical properties and all the living organisms within it, the structure of the communities they form, the dynamic functions and the biomass of the organisms and different trophic levels, and the complex interactions of species with each other and the environment, are all part of the description of the Antarctic marine ecosystem."[5] He then conveyed details on all the trophic levels of the ecosystem, describing, among other things, the phytoplankton, zooplankton, squids and fish, whales, seals, penguins, albatrosses, and petrels. He suggested that there were two central characteristics of an ecosystem: its diversity and its stability. Maintaining both was a central objective of management. He concluded by posing the following question: "What kind of an ecosystem do we wish to conserve?" Though he did not offer a specific answer to guide the negotiations, he pointed out that if, for example, all the whales were removed, there would still be an ecosystem. His challenge in making this observation was that a part of the negotiations must be "to decide what the limit of variations that can be accepted is."[6] Laws's lecture was a forceful centering of the ecosystem and a rhetorical preemption of more exploitation-focused approaches to the negotiations.

The problem that had brought the Antarctic Treaty parties to Canberra was the seemingly rapid development since the late 1960s of a fishing industry in the Southern Ocean (especially for krill), concerns about overexploitation in the context of a particularly simple and sensitive ecosystem already damaged by whaling, and the changing foundations of international law in relation to the oceans. Most of the treaty parties felt that, combined with the question of mineral resources, the lack of a regime to govern the exploitation of marine living resources might become a problem, leading perhaps to renewed discord among them and perhaps even to the loss of their status as the countries with almost exclusive control of Antarctic affairs (and therefore of Antarctic resources).

On regulating exploitation in the Southern Ocean, science, industry, and international resources law presented the treaty parties with two main options for their potential conservation regime—or more fundamentally, they presented two visions of the Southern Ocean and the living organisms within it. On the one hand, the treaty parties could view the krill and other fisheries stocks as resources to be exploited, whose exploitation could be managed, most likely through a traditional fisheries management regime, based on the principle of maximum sustainable yield.[7] On the other hand, the consultative parties could look into the Southern Ocean and see an ecosystem—a relatively simple and fragile ecosystem at that—drawing upon emerging concepts of resource conservation and an increasing tendency to see environmental problems through the lens of ecological sciences. Laws's lecture that March morning was noteworthy, for there was no similar lecture from a fisheries official.

In just over two years, the parties successfully concluded their negotiations, in May 1980, with the signing of the Convention on the Conservation of Antarctic Marine Living Resources (CCAMLR). The convention created a permanent international commission and codified principles to protect the whole ecosystem, manage its exploitation, and facilitate and promote scientific research. To protect the ecosystem, the conventions's boundaries closely followed the natural oceanographic boundary known as the Antarctic Convergence (in more recent times known as the Antarctic Polar Front; see figure 4.2); this meant the convention had a larger area of application than the Antarctic Treaty, which applied to all land and ice shelf areas south of 60° south latitude. Importantly for the signatories, CCAMLR also embedded the centrality of the Antarctic Treaty of 1959, and the parties to that treaty, in the management of Antarctic affairs. Article II of the convention was among the most important and pathbreaking provisions because it provided for the conservation of the whole Antarctic

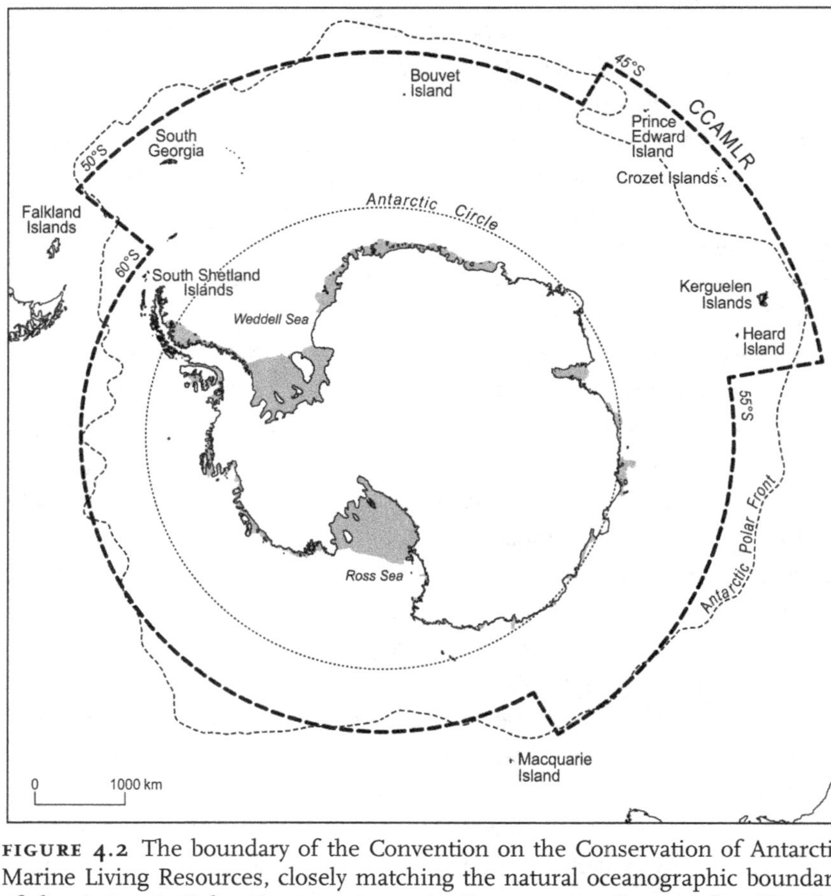

FIGURE 4.2 The boundary of the Convention on the Conservation of Antarctic Marine Living Resources, closely matching the natural oceanographic boundary of the Antarctic Polar Front or Antarctic Convergence. Cartography: Chandra Jayasuriya.

marine ecosystem, the first fisheries or environmental treaty to do so.[8] Yet the conceptual boundaries and contents of the ecosystem idea deployed in the convention and in related diplomatic discourse remained flexible and did not fully overlap with scientific meanings and definitions; in its Antarctic geopolitical register at that moment, "ecosystem" lost some of its associations with energy flow, biogeochemical cycles, and the sense of ecology as the study of organisms *and* their physical environments.

The process of seeing the Southern Ocean as an ecosystem required marginalizing a vision of the ocean and its inhabitants as resources to be exploited. Some of the treaty parties and an international community of scientists bound themselves in new ways with the story of the ocean to generate new fields of power and status (the more geopolitical aspects of the negotiations and developments are discussed in chapter 5). That was no easy task, because both the resource and ecosystem visions of the Antarctic oceans were present and strongly held into the mid-1970s. Most consequentially, in seeing the Southern Ocean ecosystem, the consultative parties were envisioning an enlarged and interconnected region over which they could be masters; in addition to the trophic relationships, the consultative parties were tightening the allowable diplomatic and geopolitical relationships. Indeed, they saw an ecosystem that they were part of, so Laws's main question—"What kind of an ecosystem do we wish to conserve?"—took on a double meaning. Admittance to the region and that ecosystem would be based on the acceptance of the obligations set out in CCAMLR and an acceptance of the geographies that emerged in the process of its negotiation.[9]

This chapter begins by describing the immediate driver of diplomatic action, the Soviet—and later Japanese, Polish, West German, and South Korean—investigations of the potential Antarctic krill fishery. It also discusses the longer interaction with the Southern Ocean based on visions of its resource value, especially through the interwar *Discovery* Investigations. It then discusses the major developments in scientific engagement with the Southern Ocean beginning in the 1960s. It particularly emphasizes the efforts of American and British scientists who undertook the research, then used their positions within their respective national bureaucracies to entrench the idea that the Antarctic marine ecosystem demanded strong protection. This section brings in the longer history of the ecosystem concept and draws out some of the specific developments the concept experienced during the 1970s and the "age of ecology." A discussion of the efforts of the Scientific Committee on Antarctic Research (SCAR) to control and guide Southern Ocean ecosystem research and its establishment of the BIOMASS program follows. The final section examines how the treaty parties, when they began discussing the issue at their consultative meetings, thrashed out the issue. It demonstrates that the acceptance of the ecosystem as the object of conservation was not a foregone conclusion simply because it was the most "scientific" and therefore best outcome. Nor was the acceptance of the ecosystem a total victory, for the convention (in its title and articles) was still directed toward "Antarctic marine living resources."

Krill, the "Gift of the Ocean"

In 1962 the Soviet fishing research ship *Muksun* trawled the Atlantic sector of the Southern Ocean for krill. It was part of a continuing investigation of the Southern Ocean's biology and stocks, and it was the beginning of a study to see if the Antarctic krill could be caught and consumed, as well as what fishing gear was needed for that task.[10] The Soviets embarked on these exploratory fishing expeditions in Antarctic waters because their commercial fleets had slowly been expanding throughout the world's oceans as part of a massive enlargement of their fishing capacity. Paul Josephson has described these years as the third stage of modernization of the Soviet fishing industry. From the mid-1950s, the Soviets used advances in shipbuilding and other technologies that emerged from the Second World War and the early Cold War to enlarge an industry that could materially contribute to the Soviet economy—not to fill demand per se, but to generate economic activity.[11] The *Muksun* was part of the fleet of the Soviet Atlantic Research Institute for Marine Fisheries and Oceanography, one of several Soviet research institutes allotted a section of the world's oceans to exploit. Krill, some scientists and fisheries boosters supposed, might in fact stand up to a greater fishing effort given the fact that their main predator, whales, had been so diminished through whaling.

The quarry in question for these fishermen was the Antarctic krill, *Euphausia superba*. A small crustacean that grows to a length of about six centimeters (quite a bit larger than most other krill species), the krill lives in great swarms, sometimes tens of kilometers long and wide and tens to hundreds of meters deep. Krill is fundamental to the life of the Southern Ocean and Antarctic ecosystems, as it is the food of whales, seals, penguins, and fish; whales, most spectacularly, consume tons upon tons of krill each day. The ubiquity and importance of krill in the Antarctic food chain can be expressed in its species biomass, the combined weight of all individual krill, which, though estimates have varied significantly over the years from hundreds of millions to billions of tons, nevertheless have the largest biomass of any animal on earth.[12]

Krill—the name comes from the Norwegian word for small fish—as individual organisms have received sympathetic and almost doting attention from writers through the years; the travel and nature writer F. D. Ommanney discerned their "delicate and feathery beauty" in the 1930s, and biologist David Campbell poignantly described his gentle, though in the end lethal, probing of a single virgin female krill under the microscope in the 1980s.[13] Their individuality has generally been subsumed to their massive collectivity, for in their abundance they are central to the life of the Southern Ocean; they are "one short link" between the phytoplankton and the whales, seals, and penguins.[14]

The earliest major krill research was conducted within the *Discovery* Investigations, the research undertaken by the British *Discovery* Committee in the 1920s and 1930s in the Antarctic seas of the South Atlantic Ocean, around the Falkland Islands Dependencies. Funded by the proceeds of whaling, this research program was mainly concerned with whales, principally as an exploitable resource. In this context, krill was merely "whale food."[15] However, even if krill were a subordinate or derivative part of these investigations, Graham Burnett has suggested that some of the *Discovery* work contributed to later ecological approaches to the ocean.[16] These investigations lead to fundamentally important scholarship on krill. Rather coincidentally with the *Muksun*'s voyage, 1962 was also the year in which the British biologist James Marr's enormous and foundational study on krill was finally released after many years of preparation.[17]

One of the major participants in these voyages, the British marine biologist Alister Hardy, became a public proponent of the exploitation of krill in the 1960s. In 1964 and 1965 he made public statements in *New Scientist* about the potential of krill as a food resource. He enthused about "almost unbelievable quantities" of krill: "Can we not save the starving children of the world with krill?," he asked, and suggested that, if blue whales could rear their young on krill, why not we humans as fellow mammals. He even envisaged "huge steam, or diesel (or perhaps nuclear) 'artificial whales,' gathering the krill by the shipload to add to the larder of the world."[18] Hardy's call was part of a broader international trend that invoked marine living resources, in the form of fish meal or fish protein concentrate rather than identifiable fish species, as a source of protein for starving and nutritionally poor communities worldwide.[19] Hardy's call was also partly nationalistic; he was proud of the achievements of the *Discovery* Investigations (in his view too long ignored by the scientific world) and the long history of British oceanography stretching back to the *Challenger* expeditions of the nineteenth century.[20] In a world ever searching for food, Hardy's was a fascinating speculation, though perhaps fantastical.

Though Britain's long tradition of scientific engagement with the Southern Ocean continued after the Second World War, the efforts of the Soviet Union and the United States surpassed all others, especially from the mid-1950s. In physical and biological oceanography and marine biology, both the United States and Soviet Union deployed great efforts in studying all the world's oceans and seas. Driven by the countervailing, though linked, demands of Cold War competition and international cooperation, the 1950s and 1960s saw enormous growth in the scale of oceanographic research. Even though often dedicated to military ends, this research contributed in particular to the resolution of the question of continental drift and the subsequent plate tectonics revolution. But the two superpowers launched upon the waves with different perspectives and different questions.[21] In Antarctica, while the Americans were interested in the scientific problems of ecological productivity and the movement of the sea floor, the Soviets wanted to survey fish stocks, bathymetry, and hydrography.[22]

Knowledge of the Soviet efforts reached Western scientists. Alan Waterman, who had been the first director of the National Science Foundation (NSF), communicated the concern of some of his colleagues as early as 1965 that both Soviet and Japanese fishing in Antarctic waters was "highly organised, efficient and destructive."[23] A year later Vivian Fuchs, director of BAS, passed on information to a British fisheries civil servant about Soviet vessel visits to the South Orkneys in the 1964–1965 season, Japanese interests around South Georgia, and the visit of an East German vessel to Port Stanley in late 1966.[24] The first results of the Soviet research were presented at a major Antarctic oceanography conference in September 1966. The Soviets were not the only ones exploring the exploitation of krill at that symposium, with Alister Hardy and the Japanese marine biologist Takahisa Nemoto also presenting papers partially covering the subject.[25] In the context mainly of physical oceanography, these papers perhaps did not get the attention they warranted. It was at the 1968 SCAR Biology Symposium in Cambridge that Soviet efforts finally seemed to gain the attention of Western biologists.[26] Several accounts suggest that many scientists present were astonished. Though they were aware of the Soviet efforts and research, they were at the same time unaware of their advanced state and the Soviets' dedication.[27]

By the early 1970s interest and concern were uniformly aroused. Henry Francis, the main US Antarctic policy official within the NSF, recorded the changes, and the State Department was collecting intelligence from overseas posts.[28] The British conscientiously took note of all Soviet ships visiting Port Stanley or anchoring around South Georgia[29]; Charles Swithinbank, a glaciologist with BAS, after a tour of the *Akademik Knipovich* in November 1971, observed that the laboratories on-board were "small, dirty, and very unsophisticated."[30] The French were sensitive to Soviet ships fishing on the banks off Kerguelen and Crozet islands that were taking considerable amounts of the *Notothenia* genus of cod.[31] And Ray Adie, the principal geologist with BAS, could not escape one fisheries consultant on a plane from Aberdeen who "quizzed" him "carefully" about fishing potential around South Georgia.[32] In the summer of 1972–1973 the first Japanese exploratory fishing voyage joined the Soviet efforts. The scale and importance of this situation surprised many Antarctic powers.

The purpose of this significant effort was to acquire krill for human consumption, directly as food or indirectly as animal food and fertilizer.[33] Krill paste or mash was the product most often associated with these activities throughout the 1970s. A British fisheries officer noted that its "flavour was similar to a mild brown crab meat and the texture was similar to processed cod roe in that it was initially rubbery but this soon disappeared leaving a fibreless paste in the mouth."[34] The Soviets marketed it aggressively under the title "ocean paste"; they had to be aggressive, for even the captive Soviet consumers were wary of eating the miscellaneous fish that the Soviet fleets insisted on indiscriminately scooping out of the ocean.[35] In an advertising supplement to the newspaper *Evening Moscow*, ocean paste was heralded as the "gift of the ocean." It read: "The ocean gave this paste its life—the native element krill from which it is prepared. 'Ocean' paste has another name also—protein." It continued, "'Ocean' paste gives dishes a crab aroma and mixes well with cheese, eggs, mayonnaise, sour cream and vegetables" and suggested several recipes, including salads, various pastes, pâté, and krill sausages with fish. The advertisement, bordered in a lurid pink, with images of supermarket shelves full to bursting and smiling young women—yet without a hint of ice, seals, or whales—encouraged Soviet citizens to partake of the fruits of the Southern Ocean.[36] In Chile, where such pastes or other fish derivatives could not be foisted onto a captive market, krill was minced and crumbed to form frozen krill sticks, which even officers of the British embassy in Santiago were willing to try.[37]

These krill products, however, did not easily find a market. Japan's leading fishing companies found them difficult to sell, with one report from the New Zealand embassy in Tokyo stating "that while they have developed an efficient catching technology for krill they are faced with difficulties over its end uses. In broad terms, it does not suit the Japanese taste; it has an unpleasant appearance, and also it does not keep well." Notwithstanding the difficulties in marketing, the report continued, a large part of the 1975–1976 catch was used commercially, and frozen krill was available in supermarkets for ¥150 for 200 grams.[38] Rejected by human consumers, krill was redeployed as animal feed, but it seems that pigs had the same poor opinion of the product.[39] Only heavy subsidies from the Japanese Marine Resources Research Centre kept the endeavor going.[40]

Despite great hopes and intentions, by the middle of the 1970s krill fishing had not yet taken off, with technical factors constraining the industry in addition to lack of consumer demand. Environmental factors were important; in addition to the already treacherous waves and weather of the Southern Ocean, the Antarctic summer and the known habits of the krill limited the season to sixty to ninety days between December and February.[41] Other factors were technical and economic: because of the short season and the initial consumer reticence, the expense of dispatching a fleet to the Southern Ocean was high and without certainty of a good return.[42] Krill also had to be rapidly processed at sea, as the highly active enzymes in their organs lead to autolysis, or decomposition. In spite of all these obstacles there was still an outward optimism about the potential of a krill fishery. "With fishermen's optimism no doubt," the New Zealand embassy in Tokyo reported, the Japanese company Nippon Suisan expected that the annual yield of krill could be up to seventy million tonnes out of a total resource of two thousand million tonnes.[43]

There were major inducements for the expansion of fishing into the Southern Ocean. One was the continuing growth of all the world's fisheries to meet demand. Associated with this was the supply side, with many countries seeking to bolster and expand their fishing industries so as to support employment and economic activity—a situation that continues to exist in the present.[44] Another was the introduction of two-hundred-mile exclusive economic zones in the seas of most countries in 1977. This latter factor was specifically mentioned by Japanese officials to a New

Zealand diplomat in November 1977; they stated that a mother-ship operation in the Southern Ocean had been dispatched under "'pressure from fishermen's associations and politicians' to find alternative employment for vessels and fishermen displaced from fishing grounds now within the Russian zone."[45]

In moving to krill in the 1960s and 1970s, the idea that the Antarctic was a legitimate place for human resource exploitation was maintained in spite of the continuing exceptionalism the continent itself seemed to hold in the popular imagination. With the near extinction of several species of whale, the Southern Ocean had in fact been fundamentally affected by human exploitation. The loss of whales was used by some pro-exploitation parties to claim that krill were ready for harvest, as the elimination of a major predator had opened up tons of krill to be exploited without harming the ecosystem. Portraying the Southern Ocean as abundant and untapped was an essential move in the CCAMLR story, for it allowed the renewal of the Southern Ocean's exploitation. Yet it also allowed the parties who negotiated the convention, or at least some of them, to portray themselves as actively protecting the Antarctic environment.

Thinking about the Southern Ocean Ecosystem

From the edges of the Antarctic continent to the dynamic zone of the Antarctic Convergence, where the cold waters of the Antarctic seas abruptly end, there exists a biomassive but also relatively simple ecosystem. It was only in the 1960s that major scientific research began to pursue questions about the ecology and ecosystem of the Southern Ocean. That early research was done principally by American and British scientists.

Emerging in the young discipline of ecology—which only began to coalesce and emerge beginning in the very late nineteenth century—the word "ecosystem" was first used in a 1935 article by the British ecologist and botanist Arthur Tansley. As a discipline, ecology encompassed several approaches to plant and animal life, including research on individual organisms and species in their environments, as well as communities of organisms; ecology also came to have close ties to practices of land management. Though there had certainly been concepts of ecological communities before Tansley's article, his was a specific physical and mechanistic response to, and rejection of, climax community concepts, which saw ecosystems as whole, complex organisms—an influential idea most notably put forth by the American ecologist Frederic Clements in the early twentieth century. The shift that Tansley's concept suggested, and was the foundation for, was from the practice of ecology inspired by natural history to a more quantitative, mathematical, and physical approach, with a mechanistic view of nature. While Tansley's article was well received, the ecosystem concept only gained greater use and recognition after the American ecologist Eugene Odum made it central to his 1953 textbook *Fundamentals of Ecology*, which remained influential for decades.[46] The discipline of ecology rapidly grew as a result of its participation in, among other developments, the scientific demands of the American Cold War state and its nuclear and energy research programs. In addition, the ecosystem gained greater traction from the mid-1960s onward within the broader cultural moment in both the United States and the Western world in general, when environmental concerns gained a greater place in public discourse.[47]

The specifics and highly detailed elements of the scientific research on the Southern Ocean ecosystem were not enrolled into the CCAMLR negotiations, nor were they central to the discussions of the treaty parties' diplomats and officials tasked with negotiating the convention, so they are not discussed here. However, the general outcomes of the research of the 1960s and 1970s were of great importance. Representations of the system, pared- back and generally diagrammatic, were presented to diplomats, and descriptions of the ecosystem in a more traditional "natural history" mode by the likes of Laws were the scientific hub of the discussions.[48]

The American Antarctic community—its scientists and officials—was central to understanding the Southern Ocean ecosystem in the 1960s and 1970s. The accretion of American experience with the Southern Ocean, together with major developments in regulatory approaches to ecosystems, meant that American scientists and policy were perhaps most capable—in intellectual and institutional terms—of engaging with its ecosystem and disseminating research and ideas about it. These years were also a time of intense government thinking about all elements of ocean policy, in line with both the developments in the UN Law of the Sea negotiations and broader trends based on intellectual and technological changes.[49] The strength of vision of a Southern Ocean ecosystem benefited from American administrative and regulatory developments of the 1970s, which focused on the complexity of environments and human actions within them, both in America and abroad where Americans were operating.

The most important body of US research in this area was conducted aboard the USNS *Eltanin*. The *Eltanin* was commissioned by the NSF in 1961 as a floating laboratory for Antarctic marine research, covering physical and biological oceanography. Between 1962 and 1972 it completed fifty-five cruises throughout all areas of the Southern Ocean, contributing fundamental knowledge on the ocean and to the oceanographic disciplines.[50] Important leaders in its biological work were Sayed El-Sayed and Mary Alice McWhinnie.

Sayed El-Sayed was a major figure in the science of the Southern Ocean ecosystem, in the leadership of SCAR's Working Group on Biology that studied it, and in leading the development of BIOMASS. His research experience working on phytoplankton and primary productivity shaped his whole academic career and outlook on potential governmental actions in relation to ecosystems. By 1971 he was advocating that there should be conservation efforts covering the whole ecosystem. At a 1971 conference on Antarctic conservation with other American scientists, his concern was primarily with the effects of marine pollution. The ecosystem was "simple and unstable" and therefore susceptible to even minor disturbances.[51] After this time, El-Sayed's interventions on the subject of conservation always insisted on the ecosystem, and his statements also increasingly emphasized the potential damage to its predators of exploiting krill to excess.[52] In December 1976, writing in response to questions from Robert Rutford, head of the Office of Polar Programs, El-Sayed was explicit: "There is no doubt in my mind that if we are interested in establishing a regime for the Antarctic marine living resources that it should be approached as an *ecosystem problem*. Ecosystem approach is now central in ecological thinking, and has completely superseded the single-factor approach which dominated ecological literature during the past 20–30 years."[53] He emphasized that the "simplicity" of the Antarctic marine ecosystem made it "more vulnerable to outside disturbances." He described a single-species approach as "myopic."[54] He was also certain that the United States could take a leading role in the conservation effort. During preparations for the Oslo consultative meeting of 1975, he stressed that the question was not whether krill would be exploited, but whether US scientists would play a leading role "in planning how they will be exploited and the sort of international control which can be effective."[55]

El-Sayed's influence also included the training of graduate students at Texas A&M University. A particularly important student there was

Katherine Green. When, in late 1975, the NSF was preparing papers to support discussions on resource issues, the "Krill Position Paper," circulated in October 1975, featured all the hallmarks of thinking by El-Sayed and Green.[56] Green's work in modeling the Southern Ocean ecosystem—a necessary step in understanding and speculating about its dynamics—was also influential (see figure 4.3).[57] In 1977 Green's reports to the Marine Mammal Commission (MMC) and to the State Department hammered home the point. She rejected the fisheries concept of maximum sustainable yield in favor of the optimum sustainable yield concept that had found expression in the MMC's work.[58] Green also prepared the environmental impact statement on the potential regime for the Department of State in 1978.[59]

Mary Alice McWhinnie was a similarly vociferous voice for krill and Southern Ocean ecosystem conservation. McWhinnie began her research on krill, primarily in physiology, in the early 1960s, around the same time as El-Sayed. She was the first woman to participate in a US Antarctic

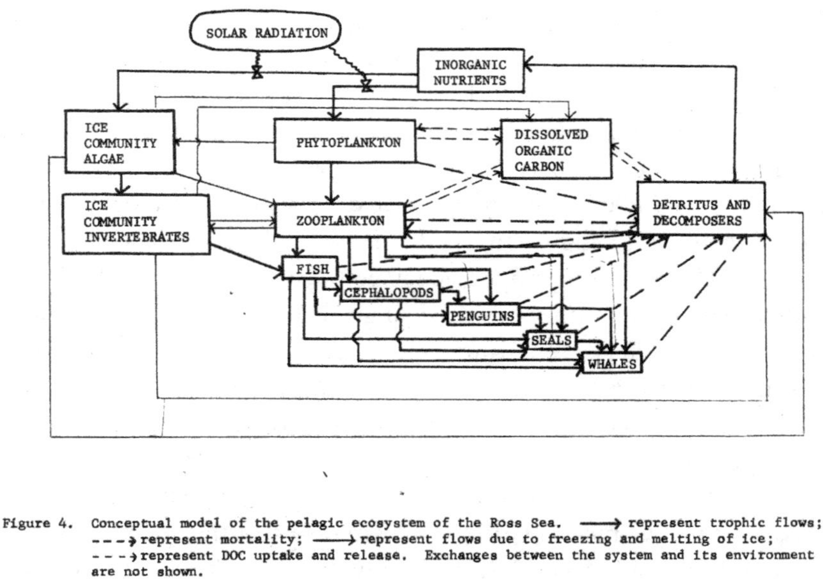

FIGURE 4.3 Katherine Green's conceptual model of the Antarctic marine ecosystem. Green's doctoral research on the Ross Sea under the supervision of Sayed El-Sayed led to this influential conceptual model of the ecosystem. It was used in the first volume of the BIOMASS research series. *Source:* Katherine A. Green, "Simulation of the Pelagic Ecosystem of the Ross Sea, Antarctica: A Time Varying Compartmental Model" (PhD diss., Texas A&M University, 1975), 48.

Research Program project in the field and was later the first woman to be chief scientist at an Antarctic research station. As a preeminent krill authority and an influential voice through unofficial social channels within the NSF, she frequently offered her opinions on the situation. In a similar vein to El-Sayed and Green, McWhinnie stated: "The antarctic marine ecosystem represents the most simple and therefore, most fragile of known ecosystems. (It lacks redundancy and cross-over in food items, restricting consumers. . . and obligating many of those consumers, to krill as food (on the by-and-large) with no significant alternate food possible)."[60] Her advice to the NSF's Division of Polar Programs was that the US position on marine living resources "be strongly based on ecosystem principles. It must represent understanding of the relative simplicity and 'direct-line' character of the food-chain sequence, recognizing that massive harvesting of krill represents the first time in human history that primary consumers (zooplankton; krill) are the target of commercial harvesting."[61]

These scientists and their research through the NSF were bolstered by the structure of environmental protection and regulation emerging during the 1970s in the United States, particularly the Council on Environmental Quality (CEQ) and the MMC. Established by the National Environmental Policy Act (NEPA) of 1969, the CEQ became the leading policy advice body to the US president on environmental issues, both domestic and international, and was especially important in developing the environmental impact assessment processes NEPA had instigated.[62] Its leading scientific officer was Lee Talbot, an ecologist with a doctorate from Berkeley and a prominent conservationist, who had held several positions with the International Union for the Conservation of Nature (IUCN) before taking up his position as senior scientist and director of international affairs with the CEQ in 1970. From the beginning of their work on Antarctica, Talbot and his staff emphasized that the environmental impacts of any exploitation in the Antarctic, be it minerals or fisheries, would occur to the ecosystem as a whole. A CEQ paper of January 1975, after noting the historic and potential exploitation of the Southern Ocean, stated: "The food chain in the Antarctic is known to be extremely simple consisting basically of phytoplankton to krill to fish to ocean mammals. . . in a simple ecosystem such as the one in the Antarctic potential effects of destruction of one member of a food chain are the destruction of all higher members of such a chain."[63] In mid-1976 Talbot again justified substantial CEQ investigation of krill on the basis of the impact on the Antarctic ecosystem and also framed the Antarctic oceans as central to the "biological productivity of much of the world's oceans, because of the ocean currents and circulation."[64] In his substantial policy offerings on this issue, Talbot always referred to the protection of the whole Antarctic ocean system, from the animals in the food chain to their physical environment.[65] Talbot's importance in disseminating and entrenching this ecosystem approach was recognized; in an oral history interview in 2000, the British ecologist Martin Holdgate stated his belief that Talbot could claim some credit for CCAMLR's ecosystem approach.[66]

The other major agency that had arrived in American Antarctic matters by the 1970s was the MMC. Created by the Marine Mammal Protection Act of 1972—which had been enacted following substantial changes to public and scientific ideas about the nature of marine mammals and the necessity of protecting them—the commission was required to bring a science-based ecosystem approach to conservation and management.[67] One of the act's central aims was to ensure that "species and population stocks should not be permitted to diminish beyond the point at which they cease to be a significant functioning element in the ecosystem of which they are part."[68] Because of its statutory obligations it was natural, even required, that the MMC would strongly support an ecosystem approach in Antarctica. Moreover, personnel within the young commission had strong Antarctic connections: John Twiss, the first executive director, had experience in Antarctic research and management within the NSF, and Robert Hofman, the scientific program director, who would represent the MMC on US delegations to the CCAMLR negotiating conferences, had worked on Antarctic seals under Don Siniff at the University of Minnesota between 1968 and 1975.[69] From its first advocacy of ecosystem conservation, the MMC did not, unsurprisingly, deviate from its position. It further reinforced that position by commissioning scientific research, including ecosystem modeling work by Katherine Green.[70]

These government agencies and the scientists in them were building on significant contemporaneous developments in the practice of wild resource management. From a fisheries perspective, the concept of maximum sustainable yield, which had governed fisheries management for several decades, was clearly under strain. The idea that a portion of any fish stock could be harvested without diminishing that stock was challenged by manifest experience; fish stocks were under pressure in many regions, and fisheries science was also becoming more sophisticated.[71] Scientists and resource managers were searching for solutions. In light of the uniform experience of resource depletion and following significant developments in ecosystem ecology as part of the American effort in the International Biological Program, a group of thirty-four scientists, conservationists, and resource managers met in 1974 and 1975 to examine critically the conceptual basis for resource management.[72] The scientists—all Americans save for Sidney Holt and John Gulland, both British and from the Food and Agriculture Organization (FAO)—argued that achieving "the maintenance of resource systems in desirable states" required "a sophisticated approach to conservation that takes into account the ecosystem as well as the selected species or stocks considered to have special value at some particular time. Ecologically simplistic concepts such as maximum sustainable yield are not adequate for that purpose."[73] They outlined four principles of resources use: first, "the ecosystem should be maintained in a desirable state such that a. consumptive and nonconsumptive values could be maximized on a continuing basis, b. present and future options are ensured, and c. risk of irreversible change or long-term adverse effects as a result of use is minimized"; second, all management should include a safety factor, an early articulation of a principle later labeled the "precautionary principle"; third, wise management should avoid wasteful use of other resources; and finally, survey, analysis, and assessment should precede planned use and accompany actual use.[74] Though the papers were not published until 1978, the ideas circulated among scientists and resource managers in positions of official influence; at least seven of the participants had some official or scientific Antarctic connection. Donald Logan, the British diplomat at the CCAMLR negotiations, quoted from the report at the first session of negotiations.[75]

By late 1976 the idea that the whole Southern Ocean ecosystem should be protected and managed was well entrenched in the responsible US agencies.[76] By August 1977 that position was carried over into official policy, dominating the approach to the marine living resource issue in the Antarctic Policy Group's report to the National Security Council; all policy options grew from this foundation.[77] The Antarctic Policy Group's August 1977 report was an important articulation of the complex tangle of reasons for America's pursuit of a conservation and management regime for marine living resources. First in that account, and notably so, was the rationale of US international food policy, which argued "for development, consistent with sound environmental practices, of the significant new sources of protein the Antarctic waters may offer." Second was America's commitment to "the preservation and protection of the Antarctic environment," especially recognizing "the importance of the

Antarctic environment to the global environment." In addition to this, US policy stated that preserving Antarctica "as a 'laboratory' for investigating global processes and obtaining base line data, serves the scientific interests of the U.S. as a leading nation in Antarctic research." Third was that the United States was committed to preventing Antarctica becoming a source of international conflict, as specifically enumerated in the treaty. And finally, the United States had "taken the lead, as a matter of both domestic and international policy, in efforts to protect marine mammals."[78] The strong, almost trenchant positions of well-respected and highly placed scientists—El-Sayed, Talbot, and Twiss, among others—were central to these developments and resonated with the sensibilities of the time.

SCAR Encompasses the Ecosystem

In the now familiar pattern of Antarctic affairs, SCAR played a central part in framing the treaty parties' engagement with the Antarctic environment. In this case, SCAR gave the imprimatur of international science to the ideas of ecosystem conservation that had been developing among certain of its members, particularly the American and British marine biologists and oceanographers. With the growing interest in Southern Ocean fisheries, along with other political and economic developments, other international nongovernmental and intergovernmental bodies began to show interest in Antarctic matters. SCAR, though certainly active all the time, faced concerted interest from the Intergovernmental Oceanographic Commission (IOC) and the FAO. In the delicately poised world of Antarctic diplomacy there might only be room for one major scientific institution in the political ecosystem. SCAR's ability to keep its dominant position in shaping the research agenda for the Antarctic and Southern Ocean was consequential for the development of an ecosystem focus for the Southern Ocean.

The initial impetus for SCAR's actions was the work in the late 1960s of the IOC (a body within UNESCO), which had established, following a Soviet initiative, the Southern Ocean Co-ordination Group.[79] The SCAR Working Group on Oceanography discussed the IOC's initiatives in September 1970 and generally agreed with moves to do a comprehensive study of the Southern Ocean. It insisted, however, that the scientific problems to be studied had to be more precisely identified.[80] Eventually, in January 1972, SCAR's Executive Committee agreed with the IOC recommendations, but requested that the Working Group on Biology also offer its opinion on the research program, specifically on krill research.[81]

That SCAR scientists refused to let the IOC keep a major stake in the developments probably reflected the apparently low opinion those oceanographers had of the IOC, especially as an organization that emphasized data collection—as preferred, it seems, by the Soviets and their "domineering. . . presence," as Jacob Hamblin has argued—rather than problem-oriented research.[82]

In August 1972 the Working Group on Biology established the Subcommittee on Marine Resources, chaired by the leading American marine biologist and oceanographer, El-Sayed.[83] The working group had the most prominent scientists of the Southern Ocean on it and was dominated by British and American scientists, including El-Sayed, Laws, Inigo Everson, George Llano, Bruce Parker, and Siniff; other important participants were the New Zealander George Knox, the Frenchmen Jean Prévost and Jean Claude Hureau, and the Australian Donald Tranter, with a Japanese representative notably absent and only one Soviet member. Their agreed collective position was quite clear: "Any future development in the exploitation of these resources [krill, inter alia] should be viewed in the context of the total ecosystem in which krill plays a key role."[84]

SCAR's position developed slowly. In May 1974 the Subcommittee on Marine Living Resources met to make recommendations about scientific work, and these were eventually endorsed in modified form by the Working Group on Biology. These recommendations built on the ecosystem as the intellectual foundation of scientific and fisheries approaches to the Southern Ocean. The working group insisted that more data had to be collected in anticipation of further fisheries exploitation and that the "gaps in our knowledge" had to be filled before "wise management" could occur. This recommendation also progressed ideas about a concerted and planned international scientific investigation of the Southern Ocean.[85] Having asserted its intellectual dominance in this area—especially by insisting on the biology of the Southern Ocean rather than only physical oceanography—the working group was tasked by the IOC with preparing practical proposals.[86] The working group's aim was to insist on resource management based on comprehensive data.

Following the eighth consultative meeting in Oslo in 1975, the SCAR Executive Committee upgraded the status of the subcommittee and renamed it the SCAR Group of Specialists on Marine Living Resources of the Southern Ocean. El-Sayed continued as convener. The terms of reference for this group included its existing intellectual foundations of assessing and developing the state of knowledge of the ecosystem and added a liaison role with the Scientific Committee on Oceanographic Research (SCOR), the IOC, and the FAO, as well as a requirement to respond to the recommendations of the treaty consultative meetings.[87] The change of name had an element of politics about it, as George Hemmen, executive secretary of SCAR, had mooted such a change of designation and place within the SCAR hierarchy to Laws as a move to trumpet SCAR's greater interest in the topic and to improve the group's impact and influence among the various other interested bodies: the IOC, the FAO, the United Nations Environment Programme, and others.[88]

Building on plans developed by the SCAR Group of Specialists in October 1975, fifty-nine scientists attended a conference at Woods Hole, Massachusetts, in August 1976 to review the present knowledge of Southern Ocean living resources and to propose a coordinated international scientific program to extend that knowledge. No Soviet scientists attended this meeting. The meeting agreed to a proposal for a scientific study titled Biological Investigations of Marine Antarctic Systems and Stocks (with the context-appropriate acronym BIOMASS).[89] The BIOMASS proposal was accepted by SCAR in October 1976,[90] which allowed firm plans by each of the participating countries to take shape, and the content of the BIOMASS proposal was finalized by the SCAR Group of Specialists in June 1977.[91]

The vision and hope for BIOMASS were substantial.[92] It was arguably SCAR's first major attempt at a large-scale multinational research program. The Woods Hole meeting agreed that "the principal objective of the BIOMASS program is to gain a deeper understanding of the structure and dynamic functioning of the Antarctic marine ecosystem as a basis for the future management of potential living resources."[93] Understanding the ecosystem was intimately linked, therefore, with future potential exploitation. Krill research was certainly a substantial element of the program, but other proposals, including ecosystem modeling and research on all members of the ecosystem, were advanced. Detailed plans were also drafted, and the planned duration of the research was a decade.[94]

The Woods Hole meeting was not a simple triumph of an ecosystem-focused conservation ethic. In the political and economic flux of the 1970s, control of the research agenda for the Southern Ocean was more fraught than the outward agreement suggests; influence even in the ostensibly objective processes of science was important. El-Sayed, firmly wedded to SCAR and conservation oriented, had prepared the bulk of the draft proposal presented at the Woods Hole meeting, with major assistance from

Knox, a New Zealand marine biologist who was prominent in the workings of SCAR, succeeding Tore Gjelsvik as president in 1978.[95] El-Sayed and Knox were two among the many conservation-minded biologists and ecologists present at Woods Hole; the other broad group present included the exploitation-oriented fisheries scientists and officials. Llano, leader of the biological program at the US Division of Polar Programs, noted that the exploitation-oriented fisheries were interested in the "technico-economic problems of Southern Ocean fisheries." "Basically," Llano continued, "the latter's principal interest was where krill swarming occurs; how large are the stocks and how much can be taken."[96] That the BIOMASS program should tend to favor the conservation and ecosystems approach, but still include aspects of the fisheries interests, shows that the resolution of these ideas was of some consequence and suggests that even in the international scientific community, an ecosystem-dominated research program was not preordained, however objective it was as a scientific category.

Owing to the changing legal status of the world's oceans, the FAO fisheries department took an active interest in underdeveloped fisheries throughout the world. While it was not quite a vacuum, the lack of an organizing regime for the Southern Ocean gave the FAO fisheries technocrats an opportunity to add another region to their bailiwick. Shaping the BIOMASS program in favor of research relating directly to exploitation rather than a fundamental understanding of the stocks and systems was one way of achieving their ends. Llano, for example, observed that John Gulland, a longtime member of the FAO staff and a very well-respected scientist, "deflected the discussion from scientific questioning."[97] Gulland and others in the FAO would continue to have quite different scientific and research needs and outlooks than SCAR; in August 1978 Louis DeGoes of the US National Research Council referred to Gulland and Sidney Holt as the "FAO 'Mafia,'" whose intentions were to control BIOMASS planning.[98]

There was, of course, nothing inherently wrong in this approach. Gulland and his FAO colleagues were clear in their research direction as fisheries scientists working within a resource development and management organization. Writing to El-Sayed in September 1977, Gulland wrote of BIOMASS: "Our interest in FAO is more in developing the basis for future management than in contributing to the general understanding of the world ocean," and went on to note that "these of course are not independent and certainly not in conflict." He stated, "I think it is important to realise that extremely detailed knowledge of a resource is neither a necessary nor a sufficient condition for good management," for "participants in exploitation must have a willingness to take appropriate action," and with that willingness good management might be successful. Gulland wanted to know more about krill stocks and thought that krill biology and ecosystems modeling, while interesting, did not contribute to management.[99] To complicate this matter, however, it is important to note that Gulland and Holt might be usefully separated from other FAO actors as being quite ardent conservationists themselves; recall Holt's participation in and editing of the "New Principles for the Conservation of Wild Living Resources" monograph of 1978, building on work in 1974–1975.

There was substantial disagreement with the FAO approach. Hemmen's and DeGoes's positions have already been suggested; they perhaps tended toward a kind of bureaucratic hegemony, building SCAR's stocks at the expense of other organizations. There were, in addition, strong scientific disagreements. McWhinnie had an interesting view of the Woods Hole meeting and plans emerging from it. Her stance articulated the strength of an anti-exploitation, preservationist approach of US scientists in positions of influence within the US government, especially the NSF. An impassioned letter from her to DeGoes in November 1976 emphasized the substantial cleavage between exploiters and conservationists: "Lou, I'm a suspicious character from way back; whatever Gjelsvik, Hemmen, you, Sayed, Llano, I, anyone thinks, hopes or plans, (or writes), USSR, Poland, West Germany, Japan, others? U.K.? are going to fish krill, (and other species) no matter the beautiful verbiage of the final BIOMASS document (no matter how 'pure and holy' IOC and others bring it to read)."[100] By McWhinnie's account, it took everything in her and El-Sayed's power (and presumably that of other conservation-inclined scientists) to steer the articulation of research priorities away from the development of better ways to exploit the marine resources to more fundamental science.[101] Llano noted that "there was [a] tendency to drift off into discussions on tonnage and catches."[102] The conviction, passion, and emotion of McWhinnie's position may not have been shared by all, but it is certainly suggestive of a divide that is not apparent in the final BIOMASS documents.

The BIOMASS initiative, supported by the foremost scientists in their fields (many, of course, working within publicly funded organizations) and combined with internal developments in the treaty parties, particularly the United States, provided a tight intellectual environment for the treaty consultative parties to work within. It also continued the trend of embedding SCAR as the premier international scientific organization that spoke for the Antarctic environment and projected its expertise and shaping of knowledge well into the future.

Negotiating the Ecosystem

Though there had been a sense among some treaty party diplomats and officials as early as 1968 that the exploitation of Antarctic marine living resources would be a topic for discussion at a future consultative meeting, it was not until the 1975 consultative meeting in Oslo that the matter appeared on the agenda. Greatly overshadowed by negotiations on the minerals question, the marine living resources item received less time for discussion even though it was beginning to dawn on some parties that, in the words of the British delegation report, it "may turn out to be much more important than Antarctic minerals."[103] The ecosystem was also not present in this discussion, with the emphasis being rather on the issues as a more traditional fisheries and resource problem.[104] The meeting's eventual recommendation (VIII-10) did not mention the ecosystem, calling only for the parties to "initiate or expand" their scientific programs, especially so as to contribute "to the development of effective measures for. . . conservation."

The discussions in Oslo were brief and not especially specific. Yet if the outward agreement seemed less than substantial, contemporaneous world events provided the Oslo consultative meeting with relevance and significance. The meeting occurred only weeks after the news broke that the Soviet whaling fleet had been operating in the North Pacific outside of quotas set by the International Whaling Commission (IWC). This revelation had been delivered to the world by the actions of the relatively new Greenpeace activists, who also demonstrated that the Soviet activities were going on close to the American coast.[105] The fate of whales, therefore, became one of the themes of the meeting. Charles Craw, the New Zealand representative, implored his colleagues to "bear in mind what has happened to the whale"—which was reported favorably by the New Zealand press as "our men in Oslo fighting to save the krill."[106] Resources and individual species were at the heart of the meeting. The ecosystem had not quite become the topic of conversation.

The mid-1970s were also the early years of negotiations toward the new and comprehensive law of the sea convention, and fisheries were an important part of that effort. In these wider fisheries negotiations the same two pressures of conservation and development were present. A March 1975 US memorandum updating President Gerald Ford on the negotiations noted that there was "a clear trend in the Conference for broad coastal state control over fisheries," but that this was "subject to duty to conserve and ensure full utilization of such resources"; these were equal duties, therefore, in tension.[107] The tensions between exploitation and conservation and between resources and the ecosystem were manifest and difficult to escape. The way the parties approached drafting measures suggests just how significant the intellectual, political, and legal jump to an ecosystem approach was.

The parties at Oslo had not had the benefit of major SCAR interventions in the subject. By 1977, though, SCAR's moves in instituting BIOMASS, as well as the longer scientific and intellectual developments, were a forceful context for the discussions of the treaty parties at the ninth consultative meeting in London. In a substantial resolution, the treaty parties agreed to three major points. First, they should cooperate as much as possible in scientific research, particularly through the BIOMASS program. Second, the parties agreed to observe basic interim guidelines for living resources conservation, particularly to take care in harvesting species without "jeopardizing the Antarctic marine ecosystem as a whole." Finally, and most consequentially, the delegates agreed that the Antarctic Treaty parties should conclude a "definitive regime" for the conservation of marine living resources by the end of 1978, specifically including in such a regime, among other political considerations, provision "for the effective conservation of the marine living resources of the Antarctic ecosystem as a whole," extending north of 60° south latitude "where that is necessary for the effective conservation of species of the Antarctic ecosystem."[108] The London meeting's resolution was ostensibly emphatic and contained a basic settlement of ideas that was to guide further negotiations.

The recommendation of the 1977 consultative meeting bound the parties to further action. Yet given the differing opinions about and hopes for a marine living resources convention, it was perhaps not the agreement it outwardly seemed. John Heap for one was unsure about the appreciation the parties had for their actions in London. He wrote in January 1978:

> For a number of reasons, differing from country to country and largely unacknowledged, the Consultative Parties agreed at London that what they would try to do was to conserve the Antarctic marine

> ecosystem. This is the sort of "imaginative response" called for by Ted Rowlands in his speech opening the London Meeting *but very few recognise it as such* or have any ideas on how to embody the principle in a convention (the Australian and South African draft conventions, as well as the Argentine draft, hardly begin to provide mechanisms that would be appropriate for the conservation of such a gigantic ecosystem).[109]

Heap's note here should not be interpreted as praise per se or as censure that the parties should have done more. It is not clear that before the consultative meeting he had given any particular thought to centering a marine living resources regime on the ecosystem; conceptual complexity and disagreement would disrupt the rather more technocratic approach Heap envisioned, concentrating on statistics and management, looking back to the convention on seals rather than forward as other states did.[110]

As agreed at London, the consultative parties convened for a special meeting to negotiate a convention in Canberra between February 27 and March 16, 1978. Despite the outward agreement at London, though, there were still divisions between those parties who demanded a conservation agreement for the whole ecosystem and those who wanted an agreement that regulated the exploitation of marine living resources. The Soviet delegation in particular, though joined by the Japanese delegation, was the most outspoken on the need for the convention under negotiation to adequately cover and regulate exploitative activities.[111] The Soviets were particularly incensed that these living resources might be left unutilized. In one intervention, the delegate stated that if the resources were not utilized, "then it is a great loss for mankind," implying that it would be more immoral to let a krill die a natural death than to take it for human use.[112]

Yet there were many delegations willing to speak up against the Soviets. The British and American delegations were—expectedly, given their histories—the loudest against them. Sir Donald Logan, head of the British delegation, was even concerned that the title of the convention was misleading, suggesting that "ecosystem" should be in the title. When speaking about the first chairman's draft, he also protested that it was "very strange that the article which sets out the conservation standards should be number 17, in this order at least, at first sight it looks like relegating it well past the middle, whereas one would have thought that the standards. . . ought to be given a good deal more prominence."[113] The conservation standard would gain a more important place at the top of the second chairman's draft. Similarly, in one of their earlier interventions the American delegation pressed hard for the ecosystem. "Everything that we have learned about the living organisms found in the Antarctic marine environment," Robert Brewster, the delegation head, said, "convinces us that effective conservation requires an approach which is not limited to individual species, but which treats the ecosystem as a whole."[114] The "we" at the beginning of that sentence is worth pausing over. Did Brewster mean the collective "we" of the consultative parties, or was he perhaps being more limited in meaning the United States? Whichever "we" was meant, the statement alluded to the long history of ecosystem engagement that the United States could perhaps hold over every other party (including its friends) and was suggestive of the methods by which it might cajole or exclude the Soviets and Japanese on the outside of such a position.

Scientific ideas about the Southern Ocean ecosystem were actively sought and central to the conduct of the meeting. Yet there were only a few scientists there. The American delegation contained the most, including Joseph Bennett, head of the NSF's Division of Polar Programs; Katherine Green, who had trained with El-Sayed and modeled the Southern Ocean ecosystem; and Robert Hofman of the MMC; to these one would certainly add John Gottschalk as a delegate with extensive experience in wildlife management. Laws of the BAS was among the most eminent scientists attending the meeting (demonstrated also in his prominent lecture to the delegates), but the Soviet oceanographer Petr Moiseev, then deputy head of the All Union Research Institute of Marine Fisheries and Oceanography and a well-known fisheries and oceans scientist, was also present. Other scientists attending included Stanislaw Rakusa-Suszczewski of Poland and those on the Australian delegation: Darry Powell (an assistant secretary at the Department of Science), Ray Garrod (the director of the Australian Antarctic Division), and Knowles Kerry (the leader of biological sciences at the Australian Antarctic Division). Other delegations also contained fisheries managers and experts.

In addition to America and Britain, many of the other parties were also enthusiastic about a strong conservation approach, Australia, New Zealand, Norway, Argentina, and Chile among them. Chile in particular—while it had not maintained an Antarctic scientific program equivalent in size and prestige to the superpowers, Britain, or Australia—nevertheless had a longer history of engagement with the seas as ecosystems, as unified entities. In the period immediately following the Second World War, as US fishing fleets boomed and entered waters near the western shores of

South America, Chile, Ecuador, and Peru responded by insisting that these seas were theirs, proclaiming two-hundred-nautical-mile zones of marine protection, control, and exploitation. These declarations came three decades before the concept of the two-hundred-mile exclusive economic zone became embedded in customary international law, and later in the law of the sea. Allied with these declarations was growing South American resistance to US fishing activities, which was capped in 1952 in Santiago at the South Pacific Fishery Conference.[115] At this meeting the Peruvian delegate, Julio Ruiz, articulated a vision of South American well-being "based on an expanded harvest from the sea, 'which contain a single biological environment of minerals, flora, and fauna'"; this prefigured the development of a "'biomass' theory that united all life on the coastal zone with the living communities of the sea."[116] One should also recall Chile's insistence on a "living resources" clause in the treaty negotiations in 1959 (as discussed in chapter 2). This intellectual heritage—at once geopolitical, scientific, and environmental—even in the absence of substantial scientific work, made Chile, through its lead delegate Fernando Zegers, an important voice in these discussions.

The ecosystem had an uneasy and mixed placed in the 1978 Canberra draft convention. The compromise between those parties who wanted the convention to acknowledge marine living resources and those who wanted an ecosystem standard meant that the draft text did not fulfill the hopes of conservation-minded scientists. At the second session of the special consultative meeting in Buenos Aires in July 1978, Laws and others kept pushing for a specific amendment to the ecosystem clause. Laws was chairman—"deft but firm" in the New Zealand delegation's estimation—of the Scientific Working Group.[117] His preferred articulation of the conservation clause read as follows:

> (a) Prevention of the depletion of harvested population:
>
> (i) for harvested populations that are not themselves subject to significant predation, depletion is defined as the reduction of a population to a state producing less than the greatest net annual increment;
>
> (ii) for any other harvested populations depletion is defined either as the reduction of a population to the state described in (i) above or to a level at which the abundance of any species dependent upon it [falls below the level described in (i)] [is substantially reduced] whichever is higher.[118]

This text attempted to specify the conservation requirements of the different trophic levels. Krill, as the principal food of the entire system, had to receive greater protection than the higher levels, that is, whales, which might be exploited along the older lines of the maximum sustainable yield. Merwyn Norrish, leading the New Zealand delegation, reported that the Soviet Union continued to find problematic the term "ecosystem," "which they said was open to too many interpretations. It looked as though they were attacking the whole concept of conservation based on the effect of harvesting not just on the resources fished but also on dependent species." In the end the Soviets' attack, Norrish reported, "turned out to be more apparent than real," with some "re-ordering of paragraphs and sub-paragraphs" mollifying them.[119] Laws's position must therefore have been too specific for the Soviets, even if it was attempting to limit the potential interpretations of this crucial article.

The text that was agreed to at Buenos Aires was a compromise between the conservationist and fishing points of view. While the substance of article II was in large part maintained, there was nevertheless a change in articulation that suggested a turn back to a more traditional fisheries agreement. After the Buenos Aires meeting, the difficulties of negotiating other aspects of the draft convention—especially those touching upon sovereignty and the position of the European Economic Community—came to the fore. Article II remained the same until CCAMLR was agreed to in May 1980.

Even in article II's final form, many scientists, including Laws, and environmentalists and conservationists such as James Barnes and the Antarctic and Southern Ocean Coalition found it wanting.[120] Nevertheless, the ecosystem was central to it. The article articulated certain "principles of conservation" to govern "harvesting and associated activities": that harvested populations should not be overharvested; that "ecological relationships between harvested, dependent and related populations" should be maintained, and "depleted populations" restored; and "prevention of changes or minimisation of the risk of changes in the marine ecosystem which are not potentially reversible over two or three decades, taking into account the state of available knowledge of the direct and indirect impact of harvesting, the effect of the introduction of alien species, the effects of associated activities on the marine ecosystem and of the effects of environmental changes." If the marine scientists and environmentalists were disappointed with the article, it was nevertheless a significant environmental achievement, for no other treaty or fisheries agreement had so extensively incorporated ecological thinking and ecosystem-level protections as did CCAMLR. Scientists and environmentalists (more the latter) would have been unreasonable to expect that all fishing could be banned in the Southern Ocean, and CCAMLR by necessity had to accommodate the demands of the fishing states and the related desire for continued stability, exclusivity, and order that all the Antarctic Treaty consultative parties valued.

Foreshadowed and Foreclosed Powers

With the agreement that a regime relating to marine living resources should be based on an ecosystem-level conservation standard, the Antarctic Treaty parties furthered their incremental and undirected transformation of the continent of ice from a seemingly inert geophysical stage for their geopolitical contestation into a significant biogeographical entity encompassing living animals, ocean, land, and ice—and of course, humans assembled in their various intellectual, disciplinary, cultural, and political communities. The convention insisted on the Antarctic as a living region, composed not simply of animals lolling about on the continent's fringes, but of a teeming and massive presence beneath the surface of the ocean. If it was an ocean that, by experience, seemed wild and untamable, it became, through science and politics, manageable and controllable. In foregrounding ecosystem relationships, the convention laid a strong foundation for future developments in environmental management and thinking in Antarctica, which continues into the present.

In seeing the Southern Ocean ecosystem and articulating and codifying that vision in international legal text, the Antarctic Treaty parties were also underpinning their power. Recall James Scott's argument that the primary moment or movement in modern statecraft, in exerting power over peoples and environments, is legibility. Through "state simplifications"—that is, rational and standardized visions of populations and individuals—or other means, "seeing" provides a capacity to use and maintain power.[121] In successfully embedding their vision of the Southern Ocean ecosystem into the treaty regime, the conservation-minded states—America, Britain, Australia, Chile, and others—could continue their historic domination of the region in political, scientific, and cultural terms. Furthermore, across the conservation-fishing divide, the Antarctic Treaty regime, as a corporate whole as it were, continued to search for legible environments (and to a small extent peoples) to bolster the collective position. In part, this suggests a need to further consider the perhaps little recognized place of "legibility" in the international and diplomatic realms.

Raising the issue of legibility in relation to the treaty regime is also a little ominous. For Scott, it was on "legible" peoples and environments that authoritarian states, imbued with "high-modernist ideology," wrought their havoc. Legibility foreshadows rather than forecloses exploitation. In the case of the Southern Ocean, it implies that the ecosystem approach, which dislodged a traditional fisheries maximum sustainable yield approach, may partake as much in the "high-modernist" enterprise as the destructive approach it ostensibly replaced.

In seeing the whole Southern Ocean ecosystem, the treaty parties continued on the path begun in the 1950s. The tensions between geographies of a whole Antarctic (whether continent or region) and more particular geographies of parts of the Antarctic (whether through territorial claims or through biogeographic specificity) had played out from the IGY through the Agreed Measures for the Conservation of Antarctic Fauna and Flora negotiations, the negotiations on seals, and the questions of the environmental impact of mining activities that immediately preceded and were coincident with the marine living resources negotiations. Despite continuing internal disagreements, the parties, with SCAR, were increasingly binding themselves together as a cohesive unit that proclaimed, owing to precedent and effort, essentially exclusive control of the region.

CCAMLR's pursuit of an ecosystem conservation standard was pathbreaking, yet it has been followed by few other treaties. Similarly, the idea that regulation should precede substantial exploitation and thoroughly regulate it broke with older ideas of fisheries management and science and was also one part of the slow development of the "precautionary principle," which was eventually codified in the Rio Declaration of 1992. Although CCAMLR has not been followed more generally in international environmental law, it was followed in the Antarctic context by the Madrid Protocol, which codified the idea of limiting impacts on "dependent and associated ecosystems" in the Antarctic regime. Yet scientists' and diplomats' involvement in codifying the ecosystem had ramifications for the Antarctic political settlement and the vexed question of territorial sovereignty. The negotiation and settlement of the renewed territorial ferment caused by expanding environmental concerns is the subject of the next chapter.

5

The Plenitude of Nature and Sovereignty

BOUNDARIES OF INSIDERS AND OUTSIDERS

THE SOUTHERN OCEAN, from the ocean floor to the crest of its waves and from the coastline to that transition zone of the Antarctic Convergence, was a challenge to the Antarctic Treaty consultative parties. They had agreed in October 1977 in London that they would negotiate a regime for the conservation of Antarctica's marine living resources. As part of that future regime, they agreed that the ecosystem as a whole should be conserved and that the principles embodied in article IV of the treaty regarding sovereignty and territory should be extended to activities in marine areas. The complexities of effecting that agreement were apparent to the parties in London but became quite stark when they convened in Canberra in February 1978. The opening days of their meeting were filled with talk of the many challenges before them. What had begun as a commercial challenge with the exploitation of krill had developed into a scientific and environmental challenge emanating from the activities of scientists and the Scientific Committee on Antarctic Research (SCAR). There was simultaneously a legal challenge from the new law of the sea under negotiation, especially pressure emerging from the Third World for economic justice and development. Buffeted by these external forces, torn between eight draft texts and a selective amnesia about what had been discussed only five months before, the opening days of the three-week session lacked direction or agreement. The treaty parties felt they had to draw boundaries to control and order the contest over resources and standing in relation to Antarctic nature.

Environments and polities have boundaries. The confident assertion by scientists in the 1970s of an ecosystem vision for the Antarctic both challenged and provided opportunities for the treaty parties to draw new boundaries to articulate their geopolitical claims, both individually and collectively. Just as the activities of the International Geophysical Year (IGY) had created a sense of a geophysically whole continent and challenged Antarctic politics to respond to that vision, the articulation (by Anglo-American biologists and SCAR through BIOMASS and other venues) of a biogeographically whole Antarctic region whose web of life was simple and fragile presented a similar challenge. Furthermore, the Third United Nations Conference on the Law of the Sea (UNCLOS) was a new and inescapable context for considering how to impose political boundaries on the oceans. Just as the geophysical wholeness of the 1950s had been exploited by some parties and resisted and rejected by others, this moment of a new environmental spatialization of the region in the 1970s would be taken advantage of or rejected anew.

A boundary is not simply about a line on a map, but fundamentally about human engagements: with each other, with environments, and with the past, present, and future. The lines of boundaries, what they include and exclude, have been fundamentally important to the dynamics of human history, especially since the development of the modern state system in the early modern and modern periods.[1] Just as Thomas Gieryn has written of the "boundary work" at the heart of the scientific endeavor—demarcating what is science and what is not science—so too there has been Antarctic boundary work.[2] The definition of what Antarctica is and what Antarctica is not is affected by the boundaries put around it. The bounding of the Antarctic in the late 1970s was a forceful attempt to make it only for certain states.

There were two contentious aspects of Antarctica's boundaries in the second half of the 1970s. The first was the boundary between the Antarctic and the world, a boundary in geographic and physical terms between the cold waters of the Southern Ocean and its ecosystem and the warmer waters of oceans to the north, and in political terms between the Antarctic Treaty parties and other states, international organizations, and nongovernmental organizations (NGOs). If the rest of the world had prevailed, the Antarctic Convergence would not have become a political boundary. Instead, the Antarctic's boundaries would have fully conformed to the spirit of the UN Law of the Sea negotiations then underway, especially as a part of the "common heritage of mankind." Because of this, each of the treaty parties wanted a boundary between Antarctica and the world to protect its interests and its history. The second boundary was between the treaty parties themselves, especially the troublesome issue of the Antarctic seas for the balance of claims to territorial sovereignty and the rejection and nonrecognition of those claims. These boundaries between parties were more difficult to negotiate, for at the center of these negotiations was the territorial settlement of the Antarctic Treaty. Both the claimant and the nonclaimant states wanted to enjoy the plenitude of power suggested by the (potential) plenitude of nature that was now so apparent to them.

In this period sovereignty was a resurgent issue at the center of Antarctic affairs. The first decade of treaty diplomacy had seen a relatively subdued presence of sovereignty issues—perhaps a sign of article IV's success. Some of the treaty parties were concerned to use the system within the capacity of the treaty document rather than redefine or battle over its foundational content. By the 1970s the delicate article IV compromise became increasingly contested and buffeted by changes in state practice and discourse. The more forthright and belligerent claimants found new opportunities to pronounce their sovereign identities and rights, and the nonclaimants continued to deny and ignore them. Antarctica's changing boundaries presented a challenge in these years to the existing norms of sovereignty and territoriality. Just as scientific practice during the IGY had confronted tenuous claims to sovereignty, so did reimaginings of the scope and contents of the Antarctic region in the 1970s offer an opportunity for changing the terms of interstate relations. We can ascribe this change, in great part, to the developments in the law of the sea, which had brought the words and ideas of sovereignty and its attendant rights to the forefront of international affairs.[3] At a more tectonic level, decolonization and its consequent shifts in the global political economy, sometimes subtle and sometimes all too evident, suggested new contours for and limits to sovereignty, Western dominance, and traditional hegemonies.[4]

As the times changed so too did the potential subjects of sovereignty. Given the relatively circumscribed conceptions of what Antarctica was in the 1950s, claims to sovereignty seemed correspondingly hollow. In highly abstract and therefore unconvincing terms, those claims were directed to the defense of territorial wholeness and impenetrability. It was a hollow sovereignty, as nothing, or very little, could be done to bolster it—there were no navies or armies, and only a few token inspectors of wildlife, coroners, and magistrates—and it was abstract because it was asserted over resources or subjects minimally or implausibly conceived. Ironically, the changing Antarctic visions in the years of treaty diplomacy gave the signatories, specifically the claimants, more subjects for sovereignty, more things, living and nonliving, to draw boundaries around. The accretion of new agreements and conceptions concerning fauna and flora, seals, the environment, minerals, marine living resources, and ecosystems destabilized the very Antarctica that the claimants had claimed in the interwar years and defended in the 1950s and that the nonclaimants had not recognized in those years. The corollary to this was that the treaty regime itself had more to its name than any of the negotiators in 1958 and 1959 might have imagined.

Boundaries were at the heart of changes in the Antarctic's political and legal character in the second half of the 1970s. This is a significant issue, as it helps us understand two important things: first, how the original 1959 settlement fared under the intense scrutiny of a changed Antarctic and world situation, and second, the shape of politics and law under which the treaty parties worked in the 1980s, during the negotiations for Convention on the Regulation of Antarctic Mineral Resource Activities (CRAMRA). By the time they signed the Convention on the Conservation of Antarctic Marine Living Resources (CCAMLR) in May 1980, the treaty parties had recommitted to an exclusive and strictly bounded Antarctica. That conception would provide a central dynamic of Antarctic politics that has persisted into the present.

"For the Benefit of Mankind": The Boundaries of North and South

The idea of Antarctica emerging by the mid-1970s was by turns one of environmental abundance, in the form of mineral and marine living resources, and environmental fragility, with the specter of pollution and over-exploitation. The image of abundance attracted the eye of the Third World and non-treaty parties, and the specter of fragility attracted the concerns of the emerging global environmental movement. The years 1974 to 1980 were a fitful prelude to the more forceful external assaults on the treaty parties and their regime in the 1980s. Though these years of skirmishing among treaty parties and outsiders came to little in the short term, they were the first major outsider disruption to the Antarctic Treaty in its lifetime. Through the United Nations Law of the Sea Conference, the Non-Aligned Movement, and the Food and Agriculture Organization

(FAO), various voices from the Third World made their presence and potential danger felt by speaking of the "common heritage of mankind" and the "New International Economic Order."

Gathering in London in September 1977, the treaty consultative parties were acutely aware of the forces amassing to challenge the regime they had been building since 1959. Most of the parties were deeply protective of their positions. There was a sense, in the words of a New Zealand High Commission telegram reporting the meeting's opening, "that all delegations regard the Ninth ATCM as the most important yet held." The questions of mineral and marine living resources were on the agenda, and each of the parties believed, the telegram continued, "that if the Treaty powers do not act quickly the international community will step in and the Antarctic will be internationalised as the 'common heritage of mankind.' " That would have been an unthinkable scenario for the nonclaimants as much as the claimants. The parties were even being hectored by "widespread press, radio and television interest" and a public mood that was "critical of a carve up of resources between the Treaty powers." One delegate even had to endure the attacks of a London cab driver, who "accused him of representing a closed exclusive club."[5] The sensitivities to that external assault were articulated in the interventions of several, though not all, parties, when they began negotiating the marine living resources convention in Canberra in February 1978. The Norwegian delegate did not want the treaty parties to be seen as "ravenous vultures . . . about to now join forces to find the formal basis for sharing the spoils of the resources in Antarctica."[6]

The parties' response to these incursions on their sphere of interest was to baldly proclaim their centrality to Antarctic affairs and to insist on their exclusive competence for the region. Their position was codified in article V, paragraph 1 of CCAMLR: "The Contracting Parties which are not Parties to the Antarctic Treaty acknowledge the special obligations and responsibilities of the Antarctic Treaty Consultative Parties for the protection and preservation of the environment of the Antarctic Treaty area." The idea of "special obligations and responsibilities" had been emerging slowly since about 1975. At the 1972 and 1975 consultative meetings, the recommendations relating to mineral resources had stated "that the Antarctic Treaty places a special responsibility upon the Contracting Parties" (VII-6 and VIII-14). In London in 1977, these sentiments were expressed differently, speaking only of "the special responsibilities of Consultative Parties" (recommendation IX-1). The shift in these sentiments is subtle and typical of the nuances of formal Antarctic language. In the earlier articulations, the "special responsibilities" emanated from the treaty. In the later articulations, the "special obligations and responsibilities," though certainly associated with the treaty, simply existed, without need for further elaboration or justification.

These years constituted one of Antarctica's explicit postcolonial moments. Yet they have not been discussed by historians in anywhere near the detail of the Indian challenge in the United Nations in 1956 and 1958 or the Malaysian challenge in the United Nations beginning in 1982.[7] The 1970s, then, was the period of the second of three major challenges by the Third World to the parties' insularity and efforts at Antarctic hegemony. Furthermore, another challenge to the treaty regime arose, though in a very different register, in the form of international environmental NGOs.

AT THE FIRST substantive session of the Third UNCLOS, beginning in June 1974, the Antarctic Treaty parties saw a potential challenge to their grip on the continent. The purpose of the negotiations was to agree on a regime covering such subjects as the idea of the territorial sea, economic zones, economic rights to the continental shelf, freedom of navigation, rights relating to scientific research, and obligations regarding the protection of the marine environment.[8] The conference was convened following two major initiatives, one coming from the superpowers and the other from smaller states and the Third World.

In mid-1967 the Soviet Union approached the United States and other major powers on the subject of the limits of the territorial sea. An exact limit in nautical miles had not been resolved in the 1958 Convention on the Territorial Sea and the Contiguous Zone, and the Soviet Union was pushing for twelve miles. In the spirit of the emerging détente, the United States and others responded to these overtures and began negotiations, though these faced many interruptions.[9] Theirs was a minimally conceived vision for an agreed law of the sea, concentrating on codifying the limits of the territorial sea: both superpowers especially wanted to ensure the right of passage for their enormous navies and merchant fleets.

The second pressure behind UNCLOS came from a lengthy and detailed speech by the Maltese diplomat Arvid Pardo at the United Nations General Assembly. On November 1, 1967, Pardo delivered a speech on "the question of the reservation exclusively for peaceful purposes of the sea-bed and the ocean floor." Pardo saw that "rapidly developing technology makes possible the exploitation of the world's sea-beds and much of its ocean floor." Seeing that this was leading to national exploitation and benefits, he wondered if some debate should occur about whether, in fact, the seabed should have some form of international control and internationalized benefit. He considered that "a properly established international regime" should be acceptable to all, "rich and poor countries, strong and weak, coastal and landlocked States." Central to his speech was the concept of the "common heritage of mankind": "The sea-bed and the ocean floor are a common heritage of mankind and should be used and exploited for peaceful purposes and for the exclusive benefit of mankind as a whole. The needs of poor countries, representing that part of mankind which is most in need of assistance, should receive preferential consideration in the event of financial benefits being derived from the exploitation of the sea-bed and ocean floor for commercial purposes."[10] This provocative statement found much favor among small and developing states, even if exploitation of the seabed—just like mining in Antarctica—seemed distant and almost unfathomable. It also went much further than either the Soviet Union or United States was hoping. Debate over the international rules and norms for the exploitation of the seabed were incredibly divisive and were among the very last to be resolved before the UN Law of the Sea convention could be agreed to in 1982—and even then, US displeasure with the measures has meant that it has still not ratified the agreement.[11]

The Antarctic Treaty parties, especially the claimants, feared the "common heritage of mankind," considering it a dangerous concept that could undermine their rights.[12] In a world where basically no other state recognized Antarctic territorial claims, the Antarctic, its seas, and its continental shelf could be seen as part of the common heritage of humanity. The simultaneous interest in the mineral and marine living resources of Antarctica and the UN Law of the Sea negotiations made world attention all the more engaged. The treaty claimants would not stand for it, however. In August 1974 they met secretly at the second session of UNCLOS in Caracas. Convened by the Australian delegate Ralph Harry—an experienced Antarctic hand with a long diplomatic career—the outcome of the meeting was general agreement among the claimants "that the Antarctic was not part of the 'common heritage of mankind,' [and] that a boundary had to be drawn between the International Authority's area and the Antarctic and that no reference whatsoever should be made to the Antarctic in any meeting of the present Conference."[13]

Most of the treaty parties went to great lengths to keep Antarctica off the UN Law of the Sea agenda. This was a continuing and trying task, given the fact that the negotiations continued over so many years. At one point this stretched as far as erasing Antarctica and the Southern Ocean from the map. Defining the range of the continental shelf—the area of the ocean floor beyond the exclusive economic zone over which states could claim economic rights—was a central but difficult task for UNCLOS. Those states with significant continental shelf areas stood to gain great swaths of actual and potential mineral resources. In June 1977 the UNCLOS Second Committee requested that a study, in both maps and figures, be undertaken to ascertain the extent of the continental shelf using various formulas. The map that emerged by April 1978—produced by the Lamont-Doherty Geological Observatory of Columbia University—was poorly received by the Antarctic Treaty parties (see figure 5.1).

The Australian diplomat Keith Brennan, as the lead negotiator of CCAMLR, convened a meeting of the consultative parties in Geneva on April 17, 1978. Their first task was to discuss the map. Brennan criticized its "lack of perspective and the distortion of the Antarctic, vis-à-vis the Arctic Circle." Fernando Zegers of Chile complained "that the marine spaces of Antarctica in the map were, due to Mercator's projection, shown as disproportionately large in size," a sentiment the French representative shared.[14] The Soviet representative asked if the secretariat even had "a mandate to draw lines around Antarctica." Jan Witek of Poland—which had in 1977 been the first country admitted to consultative status under the treaty, in addition to the original twelve—thought the parties should attempt "to deprive the map of any 'legal validity', that is, to reduce its status as much as possible." Concerned with the distortions of the map and prejudicial lines, the parties agreed that if "suppression" was out of the question, then all the shortcomings of the map and its lines should be made clear.[15] Because of the weight and complexity of other issues under consideration at UNCLOS, the map seems not, in the end, to have precipitated any major attack on the treaty parties' positions; the Antarctic's boundaries seemed secure against the challenge of the map and the proliferation of lines in so many other places in the world oceanic realm.

THE LAW OF the Sea Conference was not the only forum in which Antarctic affairs faced scrutiny. Whispers and rumors of non-treaty incursions into the Antarctic haunted the treaty parties. Word came through in July 1975 that Sri Lanka was considering placing the Antarctic on the agenda of the United Nations General Assembly. The Sri Lankan legal adviser on the Law of the Sea, Christopher Pinto, revealed his intentions in a conversation

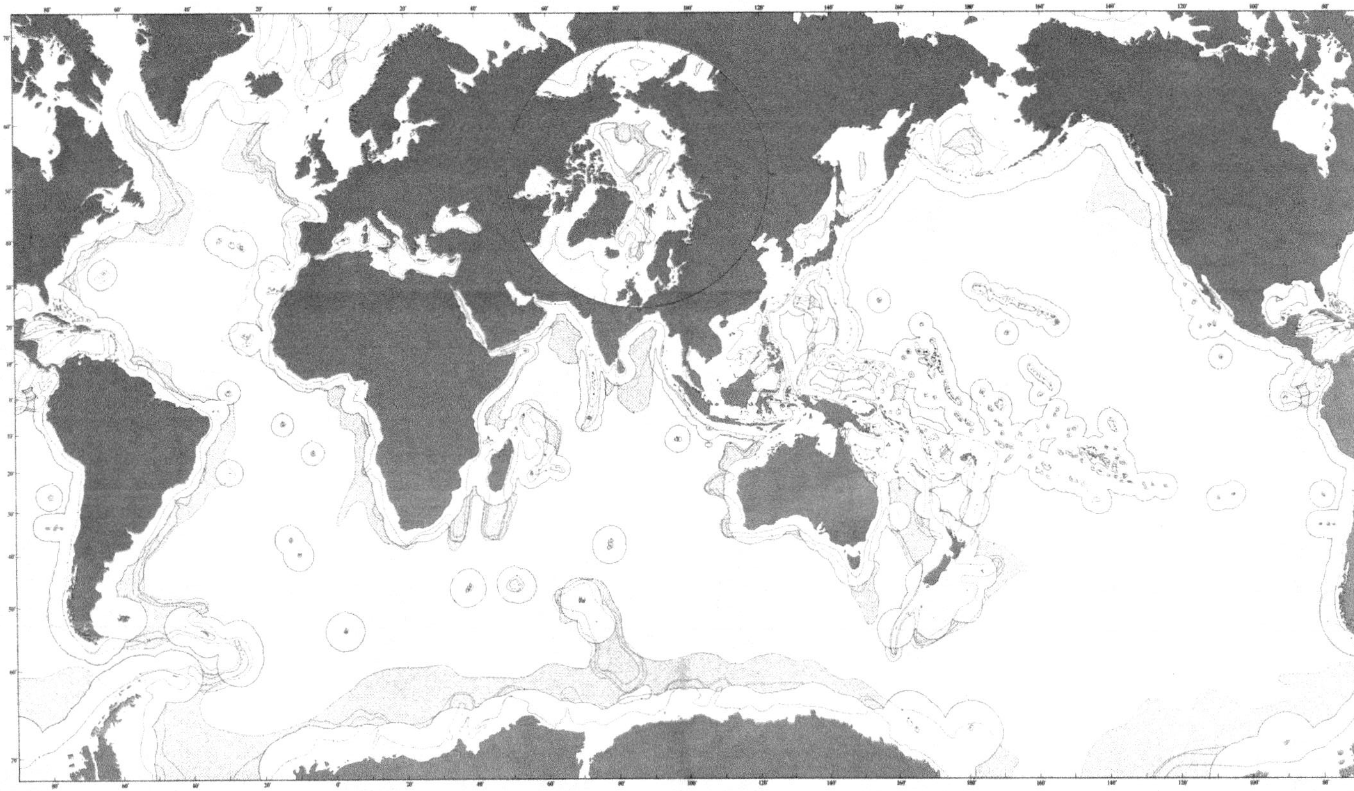

FIGURE 5.1 This world map was commissioned by the Secretariat of the Third United Nations Law of the Sea Conference to illustrate the various proposed formulas for delimiting the extended continental shelf (A/CONF.62/C.2/L.98). The treaty parties were privately disquieted by the enormous presence Antarctica had on the map and the implications that its continental shelf was hiding significant riches. *Source:* United Nations, Division for Ocean Affairs and the Law of the Sea.

with the Chilean representative Zegers, who immediately tried to dissuade Pinto from the action. Zegers was quickly joined in his efforts to suppress those intentions by the delegates from Australia, New Zealand, and the United Kingdom.[16] Investigations and discussions in the first few weeks of August 1975 revealed that the supposed "Sri Lanka proposal" was nothing more than Pinto's personal initiative, and the proposal was unlikely to go further, especially as another Sri Lankan, Hamilton Shirley Amerasinghe, was the president of the Law of the Sea Conference and conscious of the need to keep certain actors on the side and certain issues off the table.[17]

Despite the reprieve, this passing shadow precipitated much discomfort. The New Zealand Ministry of Foreign Affairs wrote: "Looking forward a little . . . it is clear that international interest in Antarctica is growing. Some states (eg Brazil) might be willing to pursue their interest within the framework of the Treaty but it is also probably that pressure for a greater UN involvement in Antarctica will increase."[18] With a full sense of self-entitlement, Hugh Gilchrist, a senior Australian diplomat, confidently stated that "everyone would be the poorer" with UN administrative interest, especially as "The Treaty powers' record to this date is one of benign control and advances in a host of areas." He added, with an imperialistic sensibility, that UN involvement would "import extraneous and essentially political problems and the Third World people associated with them. PLO, Namibia, 'the new economic order boys' and what else might get in the way of rational development of the Antarctic regime."[19] But what to do about it? Full obstruction and opposition would only go so far. New Zealand's hope was for "a strategy aimed at directing UN interest along reasonably benevolent channels."[20] Such a channel would direct discussions away from resources, where the treaty parties would seem grasping and rapacious, toward environmental and conservation questions, on which they might just come across as wise and benevolent.[21]

The Sri Lankan scare was repeated in August 1976. As host of the Fifth Conference of Heads of State or Government of Non-Aligned Countries, Sri Lanka (again, Pinto) thought it could profitably include Antarctic matters on the agenda. There were even rumors that "a senior Yugoslav official" was now interested in the Antarctic; even more distressing to the treaty parties was the second part of that rumor, that the United States "was quietly and actively encouraging non-aligned countries to raise the question of Antarctica at their forthcoming meeting and thereafter at the General Assembly"—though the Australians doubted this was true.[22] Again worrying in this circumstance was that Antarctica would probably feature in the economic section of the Non-Aligned meeting, concentrating on the equitable distribution of and access to the world's natural resources.[23] Luckily, with Argentina in the Non-Aligned Movement, the treaty parties had a claimant insider that was ready to obstruct such moves.[24] In the end, the 1976 Non-Aligned meeting did not speak of Antarctica.

THE NEXT ASSAILANT on Antarctica's boundaries was the FAO. As part of its general mission to assist with the development of fisheries industries, the members of the fisheries department of the FAO began to take an interest in Antarctic waters from about 1972. Beginning with an "informal consultation" on krill in October 1974, the FAO joined up with the United Nations Development Programme (UNDP) in late 1975 to begin an initial survey of krill stocks, current scientific knowledge, and potential industry methods.[25] At the same time, members of the FAO fisheries department had been taking part in the SCAR development of BIOMASS (discussed in chapter 4). Not only FAO officers, but also non-treaty states, used the forum of the FAO Committee on Fisheries to undermine the "special relationship" claims that underpinned the Antarctic Treaty parties' boundary making.

Though easily framed as a technical program, the FAO's efforts and the forum it provided manifested the North-South politics of the 1970s. It was clear to the New Zealand representative in May 1976 "that the Group of 77, led in Rome by Guinea, are likely to perceive the [Southern Ocean] project in a political context."[26] The language of the FAO's intervention in Antarctica had deep affinities with the New International Economic Order and law of the sea discussions about the "common heritage of mankind." The New Zealand Department of Foreign Affairs in November 1975 wrote of an early FAO paper: "While seeming innocuous, [it] makes certain assumptions about a regime for exploration and exploitation of Antarctic marine resources which are at present under consideration by the Treaty powers. The words 'for the benefit of all mankind' clearly imply that Antarctic fisheries should be subject to the international regime foreseen in law of sea discussion."[27] Such analyses persisted for several years. Taking a similar tone in April 1977, the New Zealand department wrote: "We believe that the FAO proposals are in fact the thin edge of a wedge which is being driven into the Antarctic Treaty framework by various countries and in various fora. . . . Clearly one of the long term objectives is to internationalise Antarctica using 'common heritage of mankind' type agreements. Naturally this line of argument is particularly attractive to the developing countries. It is however essentially destructive of the Treaty itself."[28] If the treaty parties saw the FAO's technical disposition as cover for more expansive political moves, they did not turn that criticism inward to see themselves as wishing to retain power under the cover of environmental discourse. The greening of Antarctica was as much a tool of diplomatic exclusion as it was a development arising from scientists, scientific disciplines, and environmental aspirations.

The FAO was not only a forum for state discussion on development and fisheries. As an international organization, its structure and staff expertise gave it the character of a bureaucracy seeking work and influence. The greatest problem for the fisheries department of the FAO was that the newly forming, exclusive economic zones off coastal states were removing areas of international ocean capable of international development under FAO auspices.[29] A New Zealand Ministry of Foreign Affairs telegram of April 1977 expressed the sentiments of several treaty parties when it opined that the Southern Ocean program "offers the Fisheries Division the prospect of a new empire at a time in which the proliferation of 200 mile zones is rapidly doing them out of a job."[30]

The treaty parties' responses to the FAO were complicated by the recognition that, depending on its attitude, the FAO might be a constructive actor in the Antarctic. The British certainly thought that the FAO had a legitimate interest in Antarctic marine matters, unless its plans were "scientifically or technically ill conceived." The Antarctic Treaty had foreseen and allowed for "cooperative working relations" with the UN's specialized agencies (article III, 2).[31] The Australians even somewhat welcomed the FAO, as any of its studies would offer "the best access available to Australia to consolidated information on the Southern Oceans."[32] Given the parameters though, and as plans started to develop, Colin Keating of the New Zealand Department of Foreign Affairs noted: "We have to decide whether to beat them or join them."[33]

Once more the treaty parties banded together against outsiders. For this FAO intrusion, they put their trust in one of their number to lead negotiations and keep a watching brief in Rome: first the British diplomat John Heap in 1977 and then the Australian Brennan in 1978. While FAO work on the Southern Ocean remained in its investigative stage and in draft form, the treaty parties could work behind the scenes to shape the tone and scope of the outcomes. Eventually, though, those programs would have to be endorsed in an open international forum, in which case the treaty parties would have to counter the FAO's work in public. This occurred in April 1977 and June 1978.

The treaty parties' diplomacy was evidently already working. The Southern Ocean paper for the April 1977 meeting was, in Heap's estimation, "completely different in structure from the earlier drafts and marked a further move by FAO away from active participation in Southern Ocean development towards an information and coordination paper."[34] The New Zealand delegate to the Fisheries Committee in Rome reported that the 1977 meeting "was not lively or aggressive"; importantly, the secretariat "gave a very fair account of the Antarctic Treaty."[35] The non-Antarctic Treaty countries whose representatives spoke—Guinea, Senegal, Sri Lanka, Cuba, Brazil, and Portugal, among others—"argued that all the world should benefit." The general treaty party line was that, while FAO had a role to play, there were other priorities, and the UNDP/FAO project should be allowed to complete its work. Argentina and Chile took a hard line on sovereignty.[36]

For much of this period, it seemed to treaty party diplomats that FAO interest in Antarctica was being motivated by only a few individuals, as had been the case with Pinto and his proposed General Assembly debate. Heap and others felt that it was Mario Ruivo—a Portuguese marine biologist, chair of the FAO Fisheries Committee, and a senior negotiator of the UN Law of the Sea—who was out to advance his own position in diplomatic circles. Ruivo did explicitly note his interest in Antarctic fisheries conservation matters to several treaty party diplomats, as well as his willingness to intervene in the matters.[37] Brennan thought that should he not get his way, Ruivo might be "a dangerous opponent."[38] The treaty parties, however, refused to allow Antarctica and the Southern Ocean to be appropriated by FAO officers for an expanded mission in the wake of the law of the sea.

Despite assurances from Ruivo and other leading FAO officials that their interests were in helping developing states to develop "unconventional fisheries resources" and "management of their EEZs," the specter of FAO interference haunted the treaty parties.[39] That specter even encouraged a sense of urgency—more than, perhaps, even the prospect of one of the treaty parties engaging in large-scale exploitation in the Southern Ocean. At the first session of the special consultative meeting in March 1978, the New Zealand delegate reported the "widespread feeling" that the parties had only a short time to negotiate a convention in the face of a reported FAO push to seek "a watching brief on behalf of the 'Third World' over the Antarctic's marine resources," a possibility that apparently "horrified the Russians and the Poles."[40]

The final discussion on the Southern Ocean in the FAO Fisheries Committee occurred in June 1978. Coming between the first two sessions of the marine living resources special consultative meeting, it was a sensitive time, especially as the Canberra meeting in February–March had not, apparently, progressed negotiations far enough to be confident of making the end of 1978 deadline for a decisive conference. As with the 1977 meeting, foregoing discussions shaped the outcomes; other agenda items dominated the meeting and "shortened the debate" on the Southern Ocean question.[41] The New Zealand representative reported that Brennan, Heap, and Zegers "were the professional Antarctic 'heavies'. . . . They had the experience—and the time—and did the lobbying. . . . They also negotiated the re-nomination of Ruivo as Chairman of COFI[,] a move which, it seems, earned Ruivo's gratitude and provided a chairman that treated the item in a very cool, businesslike way."[42] The representatives of the developing countries and the FAO officers were backed into a corner in which the proposed program became a minimally conceived exercise in scientific and technical aspects of the fisheries. For the moment, the FAO would be kept north of the Antarctic Convergence.

IT WAS NOT only developing states and international organizations that mustered around the treaty parties. NGOs and global civil society, which had firmly established themselves in many spheres by this time, especially in relation to areas of concern to postwar environmentalism, now started to eye the Antarctic. NGOs began to appear in Antarctic affairs from the early 1970s, especially in the context of the negotiation of the Convention for the Conservation of Antarctic Seals (discussed in chapter 3). These organizations and individual actors walked the line between antidevelopment, preservationist rhetoric and positions promoting equitable access to, and distribution of, Antarctic resources by all nations.

The treaty parties were greeted at the beginning of 1977 with a provocative cover on an issue of *New Scientist* and a challenging article inside (see figure 5.2). The January 13 issue was released with a hyperbolic, garish blue and white cover with the question "Whose Antarctica?" It stoked intense public interest and a strong refusal on the part of some environmental activists to accommodate the traditional positions of the treaty parties. Drawn by the British political cartoonist and environmentalist Richard Willson,[43] the magazine's cover portrayed nine of the twelve

FIGURE 5.2 The provocative image from the January 13, 1977, cover of *New Scientist* that stoked public disquiet about resource exploitation in Antarctica and defensiveness on the part of the Antarctic Treaty parties.

treaty parties (Belgium, France, and Japan were excluded) in high stereotype. The bloated, cigar-smoking American oil baron rests atop an offshore oil platform; the hardened and blokey Australian maneuvers an enormous and menacing tractor claw with rapacious intent; the hawk-eyed New Zealander aims an explosive harpoon into the whale's home; the swarthy and shady South Americans, Argentina and Chile, bare their teeth greedily; and the Soviet ship's captain drags a trawling net while staring into the heart of the ice. The Norwegian and British characters seem benign in their tiny boats, but perhaps something sinister lurks behind their quiet faces. The international pariah South Africa sits glumly on his coastline. And all the while, a solitary and slightly bemused-looking penguin awaits the onslaught.[44]

The article inside was a little more equivocal in tone and argument than the cover suggested. Written by Barbara Mitchell, a research associate at the International Institute for Environment and Development (IIED) an international NGO founded by Barbara Ward in 1971, this article was one of Mitchell's earliest public works, following the IIED's adoption of the mineral and living resources issues in 1975–1976.[45] From the very first paragraphs she foregrounded what she saw as deeply troubling: the fact that "only 12 countries"—a "privileged few," a "club"—participated in meetings dealing with the fundamentally important issues of Antarctic resources and environmental protection. She did concede that the historic and intense links "the 12" had with the Antarctic were not to be lightly ignored, and that the Antarctic Treaty had established "unparalleled cooperation" and "the world's first non-militarised, nuclear-free zone." Nevertheless, she argued that the "very nature" of mineral and living resources "demand a cooperative development by nations rather than an expansionary approach."[46]

The cover and the article did not go unnoticed. The New Zealand High Commission in London took particular umbrage, with the high commissioner himself writing to *New Scientist*'s editor to insist that New Zealand was absolutely not a whaling country and that it was, in fact, in the process of protecting all sea mammals in its waters.[47] Tom Caughley, also of the New Zealand High Commission, reported that Mitchell had approached and interviewed Heap and had given him the opportunity to comment on her draft, but most of his suggested changes were rejected. Heap objected to the article, "particularly because of its 'frequent use of innuendo employed in a heavy-handed press-type way.' "[48]

It was mainly in the United States that environmentalist groups achieved a place in Antarctic affairs. Only the US government had a policy of including, where possible, representatives of these organizations on delegations to international diplomatic conferences.[49] Patricia Scharlin of the Sierra Club joined several US delegations to consultative meetings from 1977, and James Barnes of the Antarctic and Southern Ocean Coalition (ASOC) was invited to join the marine living resources delegations. Other governments also responded to NGO activism, but with varying degrees of engagement, including providing briefings on the development of negotiations.[50]

At the first session of the special consultative meeting in Canberra in February 1978, the local branch of the Friends of the Earth engaged with Antarctic diplomacy by publishing a newsletter titled *Ice*. The first issue complained, "There is obviously a lack of knowledge of Antarctica within Australia. The public does not know or is not told and many members of parliament and government do not know or do not bother to find out."[51] A later issue stated that *Ice* was being published "in an attempt to relate to as wide an audience as possible the danger which threatens Antarctica."[52] The Friends of the Earth were fundamentally opposed to "any exploitation of Antarctic 'resources' at this stage and in the foreseeable future," doubtful of the ability of exploiters to interfere in the Antarctic ecosystem without causing harm and doubtful even of the need for exploitation.[53] Friends of the Earth activists stalked the Academy of Science building where the meeting was taking place, sending forth one of their members in a penguin suit, naming her Ché d'squark. They attacked the closed nature of the meeting and the exclusivity of the treaty parties. The issues of *Ice* (which would become *Eco* at later meetings) were filled with calls for restraint, information, cartoons, and images. *Ice* tried to puncture the inflated and disingenuous rhetoric of diplomatic compromise and continually connected the marine living resources issue with future mineral exploitation.[54]

Perhaps the most notable development in the late 1970s in this area was the founding of ASOC. It was composed of a diverse and international group of environmentalist organizations and included many national branches of Friends of the Earth and Greenpeace; several branches of the World Wildlife Fund; and other organizations, especially based in Australia, the United States, and some other Western and Northern European countries. ASOC drew much of its intellectual and organizational force from Barnes, an American lawyer whose advocacy had begun in Washington, DC, as lobbyist for the Center for Law and Social Policy (CLSP).[55] ASOC lobbied for tighter environmental protections during the CCAMLR negotiations, both through the position of Barnes on the American delegation to the special consultative meetings and through correspondence with each of the treaty party governments.[56] ASOC was the only specifically Antarctic environmental NGO, so throughout the 1980s it became the leading voice expressing global environmentalist concerns to the treaty parties. As a result, it became the only body of its kind to be admitted as an observer to Antarctic Treaty consultative meetings in 1991.

Environmentalist groups, appearing late on the stage and limited to the American delegations, were not especially influential in the negotiations for CCAMLR or the mineral discussions of the 1970s. ASOC and others, including Greenpeace, would take on a much more dramatic and public place in Antarctic affairs after the mid-1980s. What they insisted on was respect for the plenitude of nature *as* nature, as something separate from the needs or demands of sovereign states seeking to bolster or aggrandize themselves by projecting into the far South.

THESE CHALLENGES BETWEEN 1974 and 1980—the law of the sea, the Non-Aligned Movement, the FAO, and the new constellation of global civil society and environmentalists—did not succeed in fundamentally altering the situation. The consultative parties maintained their positions as the states with the most direct interests in the Antarctic. Yet challenges they were, and the parties managed to temporarily stifle, deflect, or accommodate each of them. At the heart of their response was the environment. Because they had raised elements of Antarctic nature to the status of geopolitical concern and had assembled it as an international environment, the treaty parties felt they could proclaim, as they did in CCAMLR's article V, their "special obligations and responsibilities . . . for the protection and preservation of the environment of the Antarctic Treaty area."

The "Plenitude of Sovereignty": Unsettling the Relationship of Claimants and Nonclaimants

For all the challenges from outsiders to the Antarctic Treaty's boundaries and assumptions, there was also internal dissent and tension among the treaty parties. As much as it seemed an external threat, the new law of the sea under negotiation was also used by the claimant states to advance their positions in the treaty regime. The prospect of restated territorial seas, newly appurtenant fishing zones and exclusive economic zones, and protruding continental shelves was a boon to the more forthright claimants and a sticking point with the rest who had never recognized claims. The problem was one of the relationship of land and sea, how the region hung together as a whole. The seas and oceans surrounding the Antarctic continent had been a major part of the region's history. Yet Antarctica's seas disappeared, in effect, with the negotiation and ratification of the treaty. Bringing the seas back into the agreement required intellectual and textual efforts. Through CCAMLR, the potential expansion of treaty party competence to the Antarctic Convergence challenged the original treaty settlement, for Antarctic lands and ocean had different meanings and characters, which until the 1970s had not been brought into a single political and legal settlement.

The central problem was that any marine living resource convention boundary that would include the whole Antarctic marine ecosystem would problematically cover two sovereignty dispositions. Antarctic lands south of 60°S were covered by article IV of the treaty. This placed territorial and sovereignty issues related to those lands in abeyance for the life of the treaty. Subantarctic islands north of 60°S would also be covered by the proposed convention, and on this issue hinged a complex point of international law and potentially the scope and effectiveness of a convention. These islands included the Australian Heard Island; the French island groups of Kerguelen and Crozet; the South African Prince Edward Islands; the Norwegian Bouvet Island; and the British South Georgia, South Sandwich, and South Orkney island groups. With the exception of Argentina's dispute with Britain over South Georgia, sovereignty was not contested over these islands.

At the head of the charge to test sovereignty's purchase and muscle—of naturalizing sovereignty, as it were—was Australia and its leading Antarctic diplomat, Brennan. Appointed Australia's ambassador to Switzerland in 1974, Brennan was also Australia's principal negotiator for Antarctic matters (from the 1975 consultative meeting in Oslo to the 1980 decisive conference on marine living resources) and from 1977 the head of Australia's delegation to UNCLOS. A devout Catholic, Brennan began his career in the Australian Department of External Affairs in 1947. Before his Antarctic and law of the sea work in the 1970s, he was noted in Canberra for his "patience, kindliness and sense of humour" when leading the administration and personnel division of the department during the greater part of the 1960s. In addition to his patience, his Antarctic and law of the sea diplomacy also demonstrated a persistence of energy and intellectual force that made him well-regarded by his diplomatic colleagues. Not only was he an effective negotiator, demonstrating on several occasions his ability to build compromise in often hopelessly fractured situations (as was the case in the last sessions of UNCLOS between 1980 and 1982), but he was also a forceful, perhaps even at times too forceful, advocate for the Australian position.[57]

It was at the 1976 Special Preparatory Meeting on minerals in Paris that Brennan emerged as one of the vociferous proponents of sovereignty. The New Zealand delegation reported that Brennan demanded that "the political fact of sovereignty must be recognized," perhaps out of his own force of thinking, perhaps out of a "tactical brief" to stand out as a "most extreme proponent of sovereignty."[58] That "fact" was that the Antarctic territorial claims generated territorial seas, exclusive economic zones or exclusive fishing zones, and continental shelves over which it could assert rights. Exclusive economic zones were not simply abstract spaces of sovereignty, but spaces in which states could benefit from the plenitude of nature, which had so recently been revealed through scientific and environmental work. John McArthur, New Zealand's ambassador in Paris, on several occasions shared with Brennan his opinion that the Australian brief was a "tactical one," but Brennan responded with "an irate lecture on sovereignty and the limits of Australian freedom to manoeuvre on each occasion."[59] At that same meeting, the New Zealand delegation was disquieted when Brennan "reacted with some hostility" to their paper on minerals and described it as "essentially destructive of the Australian position"—a phrase to which Brennan, McArthur noted, was "somewhat addicted."[60]

McArthur's future encounters with Brennan at the London consultative meeting in 1977 were equally frustrating, if combined with a growing sense that Brennan had the diplomatic wherewithal to bring the nonclaimants along with his sometimes belligerent tone. In his report to Wellington, McArthur noted that during discussion of the sovereignty question and living resources, "constant and harassing interventions by Keith Brennan were one of the dominant features of the meeting," going on to place Brennan's actions in the same class as those of the "paranoid" Chilean and Argentinean delegations.[61] If Brennan was harassing, though, his clarity of expression and incisive understanding of the problems were important in advancing debate. In July 1977, at the London extended preparatory meeting, the New Zealand delegation reported that Brennan's ability to articulate "the dilemma" of marine sovereignty attached to Antarctic territory "without drawing down the fire of the non-claimants" was an achievement.[62]

What was seen as a clear exposition of issues might also be seen as a subtle but meaningful evasion and parsing of the Antarctic Treaty on Brennan and Australia's part. In one sense, an important tactic was to sidestep the treaty per se by insisting that there were seven claimants, and that was a political fact—the claimants were, in a sense, a natural part of

Antarctica along with its other natural environmental attributes. At a June 1977 meeting of Brennan, the Australian legal adviser Eli Lauterpacht, and the Soviet delegate to UNCLOS Valentin Romanov, Brennan reported that he and Lauterpacht "asked that the Soviet Union should give sympathetic consideration to our view that the existence of claims was a political reality which could not simply be ignored in the search for a solution to the resource problems which were under discussed." Romanov did not see the claims as a "political reality," responding that he thought "that any attempt to 'reactivate' claims would destroy the Antarctic Treaty."[63]

In addition to evading the treaty by naturalizing the claimants, Brennan and other claimants began to subtly parse and restrict the commonly accepted meanings of the treaty. At the 1977 London consultative meeting, Brennan insisted that a "freedom of exploitation" clause in any future marine living resources or minerals agreement was not equivalent to the "freedom of scientific research" clause in the Antarctic Treaty. Article IV of the treaty, his argument went, put sovereignty questions into abeyance for very specific purposes, one of which was freedom of scientific research. Brennan pressed that it should not be assumed that freedom of exploitation would immediately and without negotiation receive the same reprieve.[64] It is unclear the extent to which the other parties accepted Brennan's new interpretation of the treaty. The recommendation of the London meeting, though an important outcome for the claimants, did not so specify the limits of article IV, saying only that its provisions should not be affected by the marine living resources regime to be negotiated and should be safeguarded in the marine areas south of 60° south latitude (recommendation IX-2).

The struggle, however, was hardly won, and some parties helpfully forgot the tenor and substance of discussion at London when they came to Canberra in February 1978 (see figure 5.3). On his home turf, Brennan continued his defense of Australian sovereignty, using the newly codified concept of the exclusive economic zone to further naturalize Australia's and other claimants' positions within Antarctica, making them as central to the Antarctic environment as krill, seals, and ice. Both the Soviet Union and Japan as the principal fishing states took most issue with this new balance for the seas. Concerned most with the attitudes of the Soviet Union, Brennan made great efforts to convince its delegation head, Oleg Khlestov, of the Australian position. Brennan reported that Khlestov stated "that for Australia to declare an EEZ off its Antarctic Territory would 'destroy' the Treaty."[65]

FIGURE 5.3 Three of the influential delegates to the first session of the special consultative meeting on Antarctic marine living resources, Canberra, February 1978. Donald Logan (left) and John Heap (right), leaders of the British delegation, have their picture taken with the Australian diplomat Keith Brennan (center). *Source:* NAA: A6180, 28/2/78/11.

In Canberra Brennan emphasized Australia's need for a "retention of the balance of claim and non-recognition."[66] What Australia saw as necessary was an adaptation of article IV of the treaty for CCAMLR's new circumstances. In a spectacular intervention, emphatic, insistent, and forceful, Brennan delivered a demanding lecture couched in terms of self-proclaimed reasonableness:

> But all that Australia is asking, this is all we're asking, is not to be prevented by entering into this convention from asserting that we have territorial seas and that we have got economic zones south of 60 degrees, now that's all we're asking. . . . And we feel that it

> would be highly prejudicial to us, highly prejudicial if this convention should prevent us from saying that. Nothing in the Antarctic Treaty prevents us from saying that we've got territorial sovereignty down there—in fact we say it every day of the week! And nothing in the Antarctic Treaty prevents others from saying "No you haven't!" And they say it at least as frequently as we assert that we've got it. Now we feel that in the new convention it is necessary to transplant that same principle so that we are not estopped or debarred from saying that we have got territorial seas and that we have got exclusive economic zones south of 60 degrees as well as north and that those colleagues that agreed with us, and there are such, will say yes you have, and those colleagues disagree with us will say no you haven't. Now there's no way of resolving that basic difference of national policy between us, and all I am asking and all our article sought to do was to retain that situation intact.[67]

This was a restatement of Brennan's "political reality" argument.

Despite New Zealand's position between the late 1950s and early 1970s not to be among the forthright claimants, in Canberra it joined Australia in parsing the treaty for the new situation in which it found itself.[68] Gerald Hensley, the New Zealand delegate, posed the questions: "What is the subject matter of the Antarctic Treaty? What are the substantive obligations which the claimant countries have accepted and which they then say shall not be considered as prejudicing their positions?" Hensley conveyed the New Zealand position that there were "perhaps three incidences of sovereignty" covered by the treaty. First, treaty parties could enter the claimants' territories for the purposes of scientific research without the claimants exercising "immigration controls." Second, the treaty parties had "agreed not to use or implement military force in Antarctica." And third, the parties had agreed to "establish rules regarding the denuclearization of Antarctica" and had agreed "not to dump nuclear material." Each of these was a specific "derogation" of sovereignty that the claimants had accepted and that were covered by the "balance" of article IV as negotiated in 1959.[69]

The resolution to this problem of sovereignty was an approach labeled "bifocalism" by the negotiators. The label—apparently coined by Donald Logan[70]—referred to the two ways in which signatories to the eventual convention could view the settlement of the issue of sovereignty and coastal state jurisdiction. For claimants, bifocalism meant that the convention would protect their territorial claims over both the continent and the subantarctic islands. For nonclaimants, bifocalism would allow them to see the convention as applying to subantarctic islands over which there was no sovereignty dispute and as not applying to the continental territorial claims that they had never recognized.[71]

Between Canberra and the second round of the special consultative meeting in Buenos Aires, Brennan flew to Moscow to continue Australia's overtures at the Soviet Foreign Ministry. Brennan and his colleague Michael McKeown spoke with Khlestov and three of his colleagues, several of whom had been at Canberra. Brennan's telegram back to Canberra on the evening of the meeting is my only source for this meeting, but it is nevertheless pregnant with the issues at stake and the manner in which they were handled. While all present had a chance to speak, the report conveys a competition of two individual voices, Brennan and Khlestov. Brennan cabled: "Most of the morning was taken up with a discussion about the degree to which claimant states have forgone their standing to assert sovereignty against another Antarctic Treaty partner."[72] Brennan's language includes and excludes; it looks to history, yet it looks for a fresh beginning. The Soviet Union, in spite of its historic unwillingness to recognize Australian sovereignty, was a treaty "partner," not simply another party to the treaty; both parties had endured the same trials of the FAO and Non-Aligned Movement's challenges. Australia remained a sovereign, and Brennan an agent of that sovereignty. The Soviet Union could insouciantly ignore Australia's "sovereignty," but Khlestov could not ignore Brennan.

The telegram continued with the back and forth of argument, point and counterpoint. The crux of the argument was the interpretation of article IV of the treaty and its reality in 1978. Brennan noted that "Khlestov developed the line that claimant states under the Treaty had recognised the right of non-claimant states not to recognise claims and it would therefore be contrary to the Treaty for a claimant state to attempt to enforce jurisdiction under any circumstances against another party." Brennan could not accept this interpretation, so he "asserted that the claimant states retained the plenitude of sovereignty and their standing to assert it against another party except in those respects, principally scientific research, in which an abatement was specifically written into the Antarctic Treaty." Khlestov and his colleagues did not accept Brennan's interpretation. Words would articulate the settlement, so they mattered and were worth the effort to parse and win. The phrases "coastal state jurisdiction" and "jurisdiction in marine areas" were unacceptable to the Soviets within the Antarctic

Treaty area; the conversation seemed to glide over the subantarctic islands, though Khlestov expressed "serious reservations about 'bifocalism.'"[73]

When the parties reconvened in Buenos Aires in July 1978, sickness, new leadership, and intransigence kept the parties from making better advances on their negotiations. Brennan's efforts had taken a physical toll, and he suffered a heart attack in Buenos Aires just before the opening of the meeting. The British delegation report noted, though, that "he kept in touch from his bed in the British hospital."[74] The Soviet delegation head, new to Antarctic affairs, was also apparently ill, but the British report was not so sympathetic about his ailments.[75] Perhaps, feeling that they had conceded too much at Canberra, the Soviet, Japanese, and Polish delegations stood firm on their opinions that a marine living resources convention could not extend the treaty's article IV compromise to include areas of the Southern Ocean.

Sovereignty—naturalizing its own presence—was not only an Australian obsession. Argentina and Chile were notably vociferous on the issue, and the three countries were often lumped together in British and New Zealand reports as the strong claimants—noteworthy in that both Britain and New Zealand were themselves claimants, and New Zealand had been taking such a specific line on sovereignty. Argentina and Chile were, at the time, in conflict over their boundaries in the Beagle Channel, so they could not appear to soften in their attitudes on questions of sovereignty in any place. The claimants, particularly in the articulations of Brennan and, more subtly, Hensley, were trying to naturalize the highly political question of territorial and ocean sovereignty, just as the natural and environmental had been enrolled and apprehended into the geopolitical. The material life of the Antarctic—both the humans and nature—had to be carefully woven together through the subtle dance of diplomacy and the precision of international legal language.

It was the French who became, rather unexpectedly, a major impediment to agreement. After the early rounds of the special consultative meeting, the French declared that they could not accept a convention that included the Kerguelen and Crozet Islands, or their exclusive economic zones, within its boundaries without specific safeguards for French actions. The situation, which was labeled the "French islands issue," was an uncomfortable repeat of the 1959 position of the French that had almost foreclosed the treaty's being concluded.

Why did France obstruct the negotiations? The answer remains unclear and will remain so without research in the French archives. Several explicit and implicit reasons were recognized by others at the time. An explicit concern was that the French wished to control their own fisheries; the plenitude of sovereignty was tightly linked to the productivity of nature for them. The development of exclusive economic zones in the late 1970s was a particular gain for the French, who, owing to their remaining empire consisting mainly of isolated islands, gained vast tracts of ocean to exploit.[76] A conservation regime that put quotas in the hands of a commission was not, perhaps, an ideal outcome in a situation with majority voting, but with the Antarctic tradition of unanimous voting, the French had some protections.

Another more implicit problem, and only alluded to in bilateral discussions, was the Soviet presence in the Southern Ocean. On the one hand, as the lead French negotiator Patrick Henault put it, the Soviets "were trying to introduce north of 60 degrees the ambiguities over sovereignty applying in the Antarctic Treaty area."[77] On the other hand was a sense of a general Soviet expansion into the area of the French subantarctic islands.[78] Henault wanted to be "firm with the Russians."[79] The final suggested reason for French difficulty was that the area might be of some potential military use for them. This was definitely speculative, but the Australian ambassador in Paris, John Rowland, reported his feeling based on several factors, including "hints . . . about the possibility of French military activities which might 'deplete fish' in the waters surrounding the islands." Rowland specifically thought that the French wanted "to leave open the possibility of conducting nuclear tests in these waters."[80]

Though these speculations about French motives provided understandable reasons for French obstruction, several other parties found the position untenable and at times basically truculent. Well into the issue in September 1979, Heap felt that the French "at times behaved badly by making concessions and then withdrawing them."[81] What was most enraging to parties was that the other claimants with subantarctic islands were not similarly obfuscating; Australian and British records, for example, suggest that they were not even secretly happy that the French were pursuing this issue, as the matter had been resolved to their satisfaction.

Perhaps the French position on France's subantarctic islands is a symptom of adjustments to new territorialities and thinking about sovereignty at a time of great change. France stood to gain immensely from the law of the sea under negotiation, including substantial exclusive economic zones around the Kerguelen and Crozet islands. Collectively managing the Antarctic marine ecosystem was therefore a challenge to the French.

Taking control of natural resources out of the global commons and into national jurisdiction and control was one of the two great movements of the new law of the sea, the other movement being the codification of the global commons itself. As a New Zealand report of July 1979 put it, "The issue is rapidly crystallising into a major dispute on the nature of coastal state jurisdiction in the 200 mile zone."[82]

The parties resolved the "French islands issue" at side meetings at the tenth consultative meeting in Washington, DC, in October 1979. They agreed that the chairman of the decisive conference on marine living resources would make a statement to be included in the final act of that conference and to be accepted by all parties. An exercise in mollifying the French, the statement was a kind of exegesis of elements of the convention with the French islands of Kerguelen and Crozet in mind. It affirmed that France could continue to promulgate its own conservation measures but would be still be bound by those passed by the commission—which it could veto in any case. The statement continued that the CCAMLR conservation measures would only be enforced over the French islands by France, and that inspections foreseen by the convention would only be carried out by France or in an agreed manner. The statement's final element was that as far as it applied to the French islands, it would also apply to other subantarctic islands within the convention area.[83]

With the signing of CCAMLR, the relationship of claimants and nonclaimants was reforged with new environmental parameters in the form of the ecosystem and in new global circumstances. If in some ways it seemed to maintain the status quo—that is, maintaining article IV, keeping concord—the sovereignty talk within the CCAMLR negotiations was a rehabilitation, an effort in sustaining notions meant to be quieted by the treaty. Rather than some absolutely quality, "sovereignty" involved, as historian James Sheehan has suggested, "not only asserting power but also constantly testing, extending, and sometimes accepting power's limitation."[84] If scholars interrogating Antarctic politics and history have perhaps tended to see sovereignty in rather more theoretical and pure terms, the diplomats of the claimants states, whether Keith Brennan or any other, have known sovereignty, and claims and proclamations of it, as enacted and realized in the real world and with limits. In the Antarctic, this meant that any enhancement or enlargement of what elements of the Antarctic environment were considerable, or textually and discursively real within the regime, must occur simultaneously with, using Sheehan's words, "a collection of claims and counterclaims" regarding sovereignty there.[85]

Strong Boundaries, Strong Claims

With CCAMLR the treaty parties expanded the boundaries of their activities and embedded their centrality to Antarctic life. They erected and renewed these boundaries in response to several challenges, especially that of the wandering and dynamic lines and volumes of the ocean environment and its denizens. It was a sense of nature's abundance that attracted the eye of the Third World, and it was a sense of ecological fragility that attracted the agitations of global civil society. It was the issue of demarcating zones of sovereignty, territory, and internationality of that environment that promised to unhinge the relationships of the treaty parties among themselves. The Antarctic Treaty only settled a limited range of issues. Each of the treaty parties, whether claimant or nonclaimant, had some claim to a specifically assembled place, which had to be accommodated. The greening of Antarctica through the treaty regime had, however, shifted the ground beneath the parties' feet and unsettled those claims. Though the original negotiators were not blind to the future, they could not have anticipated the major changes of the 1970s. And so the boundaries needed resettlement.

Along with the renewed attempt to increase standing within the regime, this resettlement brought the claimants and nonclaimants closer to one another. Given the changing circumstances of international law and territoriality, the 1970s saw the claimants restate their claims with renewed vigor. Though some of the nonclaimants, especially the Soviet Union, tried to oppose such a restatement of claims, they did not succeed. Rather ironically, they tied themselves to the "political fact," as Brennan would have put it, that it was the claimants' positions that allowed the nonclaimants to join in on the enclosure of the Antarctic with such a strong boundary. Brennan was quite sensitive to the situation, musing in a telegram of April 1979:

> It occurs to me that the only ground that can be advanced for treating living and non-living resources in Antarctica otherwise than as resources falling outside national jurisdiction is the existence of national claims. Therefore the USA, the USSR, Japan, etc. are pursuing conflicting policies in the Law of the Sea Conference and in the Antarctic consultative meetings. In the latter they should, if they are to be consistent, be urging parallel access for an enterprise and for national operators on the continental shelf or the Antarctic mainland. But the thought of equipping an enterprise to

prospect for oil on the Antarctic continental shelf or to prospect for minerals on the Antarctic mainland is a quelling one.[86]

The nonclaimants, especially the Soviet Union and the United States, who had in some ways cowed the claimants in 1959, were now dependent on the claimants for their own positions, which insisted on the centrality of treaty diplomacy for environmental protection. The ties of nature and sovereignty were strengthened, not weakened.

In their simultaneous assertions of the plenitudes of sovereignty and nature, the treaty parties were acting in a drama of high territoriality, against outsiders and against one another. The historian Charles Maier has argued that the 1970s and 1980s were the twilight of a regime or "epoch" of the territoriality of nation-states that had emerged from around 1860.[87] In that century, nation-states were consolidated and "decision" and "identity" spaces overlapped in single territorial units. This began to dissipate after 1970 or so, and territory, physical space, "fade[d] in importance as a political or economic resource."[88] While the Antarctic experience of the late 1970s might seem merely a delayed instance of Maier's thesis, a remnant site of territoriality experiencing a delayed modernity, it does, in fact, highlight an absence in his account: the environment. Just as he argues that technological changes "have tended to make physical space a less relevant resource,"[89] so too I suggest that changing conceptualizations of the earth emerging in the "age of ecology" and shifts in thinking about the environment subtly changed what it was that both states and individuals felt needed their attention and their agreement. "Territory" and "environment" are certainly not fully overlapping terms, but they share a materiality. If territoriality is, in part, a contest for political control of some ground, the discursive formation of that material ground constantly renews or destabilizes territorial projects; even as this book has suggested the "greening of Antarctica" as an intellectual as much as a material development, the contest for status and claim in Antarctica is inescapably one about a physical, material environment, with real living and mineral things, as it is for other global and international environments.

By the time the treaty parties signed CCAMLR, they had demonstrated in the strongest possible terms their belief in an exclusive and bounded Antarctic region, expansively conceived to include the entire Southern Ocean. The rationale for that exclusivity and boundedness, the individual and collective territoriality, was by 1980 deeply rooted in an ethic of environmental authority and protection. The signing of CCAMLR also demonstrated that, within the regime, the forthright claimants would not allow the internationalized experience of Antarctic governance to derogate from their histories and beliefs of sovereignty. If CCAMLR was only one-half of a comprehensive resources settlement—the other half being a settlement on minerals, which would begin in 1981—it articulated a range of interstate, state-environment, and territorial-environmental relationships and concepts that have been foundational to Antarctic Treaty diplomacy and a motor of Antarctic geopolitics in the decades since. The geographic and geopolitical boundaries raised in the late 1970s, while not impenetrable, have been durable and robust.

Epilogue

THE FATE OF THE GREEN ANTARCTIC

THE FIRST TWO decades of the Antarctic Treaty produced not simply a collection of international agreements, but a profound body of diplomatic and scientific thought about the Antarctic environment itself, new relationships among peoples and physical nature, and the authority to interpret and manage that environment. It was, in short, an international environment. While seeking the advancement of their own positions, the treaty parties and the internationally organized scientists also genuinely sought peace and stability and endeavored to fix the contested visions of the Antarctic into legal documents upon which they could rely; they also enrolled Antarctica's living and nonliving nature in their search for stability and power. In 1959 the Antarctic powers saw the continent as a stage on which to enact their geopolitical, imperial, and colonial dramas; there was little sense of environmental fragility or dynamism. In 1980 the Antarctic powers saw a region filled not only with a fragile and very extensive ecosystem but also with themselves and their scientists as a fundamental part of it. Could the treaty parties have foreseen in 1959 what would become of the treaty? Of course not. Rather, the important issue is how they reacted, individually and collectively, to the challenges they faced in the years following.

The emergence of this international Antarctic environment was a slow process that took decades. The developments were sometimes deliberate and at other times incidental, sometimes consciously pursued and at other times unintentional. The protection of the Antarctic environment and the management of resource exploitation were not the only concerns of the states and scientists; they also wanted to give meaning and shape to the relationships among themselves. Diplomats and scientists continually sought geopolitical or epistemic authority for Antarctica. Furthermore, ideas about nature and the environment in the Antarctic mutually developed with ideas about the wider diplomatic and political order. Defining an environment's natural elements was inseparable from defining *who* was connected to it and might benefit from it. The foundations of the contemporary Antarctic Treaty System in the 1960s and 1970s have not yet become a matter of concerted research among historians and other scholars of Antarctic affairs. This book has offered, for the first time, critical histories of the negotiations of three central Antarctic documents—the Agreed Measures for the Conservation of Antarctic Fauna and Flora (AMCAFF), the Convention for the Conservation of Antarctic Seals (CCAS), and the Convention on the Conservation of Antarctic Marine Living Resources (CCAMLR)—and of the first phase of the minerals debate, as well as how the agreements articulated the linked contest for power and the formation of environmental sensibilities. Authoring and negotiating ideas and sensibilities and fixing them into international legal texts was a delicate and long process.

The Antarctic was not, and is not, a timeless and unchanging region, either in environmental or human terms. It was invested with new meanings over the 1960s and 1970s, and it was seen and made legible in different and new ways; it was thus a very different assemblage of concepts, ideas, histories, sciences, and material things in 1980 than in 1959. There were two movements in this regard: one, geographical, of expansion from the continent to the region; and the other, environmental, about the progressive and iterative inclusion within the management vision of fauna and flora, seals, minerals, continental shelves, marine living resources, exclusive economic zones, and an "ecosystem." What these developments meant, therefore, was that the Antarctic was not simply, as Stephen Pyne put it, "a white spot on the globe" after its exploration, but rather a complex region of life with an equally complex human regime engaging with and managing it.[1] That continuing and renewing complexity, an environment evading simplification, ensured that Antarctica remained a problem for diplomacy. The problem of sovereignty re-emerged as awareness and knowledge of the complex, fragile, and extensive Antarctic environment grew. As the Australian historian Tom Griffiths has written, "Antarctic voyagers of the nineteenth century had originally wanted rock. They wanted rock, and soil they could plant a flag in and claim for their country."[2] If continental ice could not substitute for soil, a region of living and extensive nature—realized through science and developing environmental sensibilities—might accommodate the flag and the sovereignty it represented. Diplomats and scientists imagined new ground for their contest.

The Greening of Antarctica has explored the slow emergence of an international environment out of competing and conflicting visions of Antarctic nature, both scientific and political, in the 1960s and 1970s. At the same time, it has been as much about the maintenance of the Antarctic Treaty as it has been about the creation of new instruments. The agreements of the 1960s and 1970s—AMCAFF, CCAS, and CCAMLR—remain in force, and therefore their ideas persist into the present. The developments in these two decades were the foundation on which the minerals debate of 1982 to 1988, and then the environmental protection negotiations of 1988 to 1991, were built. Both the Convention on the Regulation of Antarctic Mineral Resource Activities (CRAMRA) and the Madrid Protocol repeated and included essential elements of AMCAFF and perpetuated the ecosystem vision first enunciated in CCAMLR, as well as other earlier provisions; international law scholar Davor Vidas has gone so far as to note that the Madrid Protocol and its annexes "evolved from a 'cut and paste' operation."[3] The creation of this environmental regime was not an easy or simple manifestation of the latent potentials of the Antarctic Treaty, but rather a process of contested and concerted intellectual effort. It continually, if subtly, wrestled with the implications and ideas of the treaty and the materiality of the Antarctic and kept the treaty under permanent negotiation. It was also a process that brought to bear on Antarctica long genealogies of concern for the protection of nature and resource conservation of the temperate world, as well as younger traditions of environmentalism and the regulatory approaches of the age of ecology.

ANTARCTIC POLITICS CERTAINLY did not stop in 1980—just as it did not end in 1959—and the contest for authority and power over the region and its environment continues into the present. All the elements of the Antarctic order established and constituted in the two decades following the treaty channeled the energies of treaty party diplomats and scientists in the subsequent decades. The challenges and developments since 1980 have all drawn to a significant extent on the foundational moments and hewed to the contours established in the early decades, though of course they had particular, immediate dynamics and contexts too and were not simply blind repetitions. Though I want to avoid any crude suggestion of path dependency after the early 1980s, the diplomats and scientists of the

Antarctic Treaty System were heirs to an already complex, sophisticated, and compelling body of thought, policy, and action.

The 1980s were a busy time in Antarctic history but can be seen in many ways as an extension of the ideas and negotiating positions of the 1970s. The Malaysian-led challenge to the Antarctic Treaty in the United Nations beginning in 1982 was met using the same language of exclusivity and environmental concern that the treaty parties had generated in responding to the Food and Agriculture Organization and law of the sea challenges in the 1970s. Expansion of the number of consultative parties was the new response—though conservative in effect—in that context.[4] Though eventually rejected, CRAMRA, signed in 1988, reflected the balance of conservation and exploitation, environmental management and protection, that CCAMLR had initiated and manifested. Indeed, it explicitly perpetuated a vision of the Antarctic as a fragile ecosystem.[5] The Madrid Protocol that was negotiated to fill the void left through the Franco-Australian rejection of CRAMRA was so quickly achieved because it drew extensively on the environmental protection frameworks and ideas first instituted by AMCAFF in 1964 and all the environmental impact talk of the 1970s. Even the recent and highly contentious negotiations over the institution of marine protected areas in the Southern Ocean through CCAMLR reflect the foundational cleavages between conservation and exploitation clearly articulated during its negotiations. All the environment talk and environment making that had gone on by 1980 fairly constrained the range of options that the treaty parties thought they still enjoyed.

One element of the Antarctic that has been absent from this book's account, but is worth reflecting on, is ice. Ice dominates and defines Antarctica. It might seem like a supreme oversight of this book to have ignored ice, but it has not been a central concern of the Antarctic Treaty System. Though albedo (reflectiveness of solar radiation) was discussed at the margins of the minerals debate in the 1970s, and iceberg harvesting was intermittently mentioned in the 1970s and 1980s, ice has not been a diplomatically considerable element; it has not been extensively enrolled in the international environment I have described. This is surely deeply problematic given the realities of climate change that we are faced with. Glaciologists have established clearly that there has been significant ice mass loss from the Antarctic Peninsula and the West Antarctic Ice Sheet; the East Antarctic Ice Sheet presents a more complex picture of change. The data and knowledge gained from Antarctic ice have certainly become germane to the Intergovernmental Panel on Climate Change and the global climate regime. Yet ice still has not become a central diplomatic concern of the Antarctic Treaty parties. The Antarctic and Southern Ocean Coalition (ASOC) has attempted to politicize the ice through interventions in recent Antarctic Treaty consultative meetings. With the anthropologist Jessica O'Reilly as lead author, ASOC has tabled information papers to urge the consultative parties to see—simply to see—the West Antarctic Ice Sheet and its current and future diminished body. ASOC's political project since the late 1970s has been to recast Antarctic politics toward a more fundamentally preservationist and globalist mindset, with mixed results. Enrolling the West Antarctic Ice Sheet in the project has yet to bear much fruit; the ice, which was so minimized and tangential to treaty business, may yet become central to it.[6] What is the fate of the green Antarctic as ice slides off its bedrock and onto the international diplomatic agenda?

THOSE DIPLOMATIC, SCIENTIFIC, and nongovernmental actors who participate in the Antarctic Treaty system today treasure its distinctiveness. States and scientists generally, and to an extent rightly, congratulate themselves on the maintenance of peace in the region and the protection of its environment. Even as environmental troubles clearly loom, the Antarctic Treaty System is often held up as a regime to be copied for other international environmental problems. Yet histories often puncture valorized portrayals of the past. Though worthy in many ways, the Antarctic environment as it has been constituted is still a highly political assemblage of actors, both human and nonhuman, relationships, and ideas. Each of the Antarctic agreements I have explored in *The Greening of Antarctica* has its historical tensions and cleavages, as well as the benefits that saw it signed in the first place.

If we neglect to explore critically the manner in which the parties came to their agreement in 1959—and their further agreements in 1964, 1972, 1980, and so on—it weakens our capacity to think incisively about the contemporary regime and its future. Critical histories that explore the paths almost taken, and that recognize the past's present and futures, can usefully lengthen foreshortened visions. As Tom Griffiths has urged, "History down south, as in any society, is a practical and spiritual necessity, but especially so in a place where human generations are renewed every summer and the coordinates of space and time are warped by extremes."[7]

The Antarctic is a central element in our understanding of the current global environmental crisis. Because of this, the heroic and continent-bound endeavors of the early explorers, as famous and remembered as they are in the public imagination, can no longer dominate Antarctic history's field of vision. For all its contemporary frustrations, anxieties, and faults, the Antarctic Treaty System and those who work within it have produced ideas, geographies, and obligations that balance many competing interests and pressures. This balance is a result of the vigorous and consequential intellectual labors of diplomats, scientists, and other officials working productively to create an orderly international environment. Their thoughts and actions have profoundly shaped our continuing engagement with the Antarctic.

Notes

INTRODUCTION

1. This English-language version of the original Russian-language comment is taken from the transcript of the simultaneous translation heard by the English-speaking delegates at the Conference on Antarctica, Committee I, Verbatim Record, October 26, 1959 (NACP: RG 43, Antarctic Conference, US Delegation Program Records, 1959).
2. Richard Casey, the Australian minister for external affairs, recorded in his diary that Tunkin, though "amiable and accommodating," had "the reputation of being able to prove that black is white" (October 16, 1959, NLA: MS 6150, Series 4, Volume 24).
3. Conference on Antarctica, Committee I, Verbatim Record, October 26, 1959 (NACP: RG 43, Antarctic Conference, US Delegation Program Records, 1959).
4. Conference on Antarctica, Committee I, Verbatim Record, October 29, 1959 (NACP: RG 43, Antarctic Conference, US Delegation Program Records, 1959).
5. Conference on Antarctica, Committee I, Verbatim Record, October 30, 1959 (NACP: RG 43, Antarctic Conference, US Delegation Program Records, 1959); Casey had also expressed these ideas to his delegation two days before, see Diary, October 28, 1959 (NLA: MS 6150, Series 4, Volume 24).
6. US Department of State, *The Conference on Antarctica, Washington, October 15–December 1, 1959: Conference Documents, the Antarctic Treaty and Related Papers* (Washington, DC: US Department of State, 1959). The delegates were: from Belgium, Baron Gaston de Gerlache de Gomery; from Chile, Oscar Pinochet de la Barra; from the Soviet Union, Mikhail Mikhailovich Somov and Alexander Mikhailovich Gusev; and from the United Kingdom, Brian Roberts. A few other delegates had direct Arctic experience.
7. Richard Casey, Diary, November 5, 1959 (NLA: MS 6150, Series 4, Volume 24).
8. As of 2018, there were twenty-nine consultative parties to the Antarctic Treaty, with a further twenty-four nonconsultative signatories. Fourteen of the seventeen non-original consultative parties were admitted to consultative status between 1977 and 1990.

9. The system of Antarctic international governance initiated with the Antarctic Treaty is now generally called the Antarctic Treaty System (ATS), because of both the passage of "recommendations" and agreements within the Antarctic Treaty structure and the creation of new treaties and structures. This is, of course, the major subject of this book, but to avoid using an anachronism, I generally do not refer to the ATS, as that designation arose and stabilized from the late 1980s through the 1990s.
10. I have chosen "international," rather than "transnational" or "global," specifically to center nation-states in this history. Here I also note Joseph Taylor's call for historians to be "deliberate" in their deployment of "boundary terminology." Joseph E. Taylor III, "Boundary Terminology," *Environmental History* 13, no. 3 (2008): 454–81.
11. Many acronyms in the Antarctic Treaty System, as in other international regimes, are pronounced as if they were words. Therefore, AMCAFF is pronounced with two syllables: "am-caff." CCAS is also pronounced in this way: "sea-cass." CCAMLR has two distinct pronunciations as far as I have heard from English-speakers: "camel-r/are" or, with two longish syllables, "cam-lar."
12. Erik Mueggler, *The Paper Road: Archive and Experience in the Botanical Exploration of West China and Tibet* (Berkeley: University of California Press, 2011), 16.
13. For recent scholarship that focuses on the imagined Antarctic, see the contributions in Peder Roberts, Lize-Marié van der Watt, and Adrian Howkins, eds., *Antarctica and the Humanities* (London: Palgrave Macmillan, 2016).
14. There are many popular accounts of the expeditions and many biographies of the explorers of the "heroic era." The term was coined in 1933 by J. Gordon Hayes in *The Conquest of the South Pole: Antarctic Exploration 1906–1931* (New York: Macmillan, 1933). The following works provide strong narratives on the scientific, geographical, and political aspects of these early twentieth-century expeditions: Edward R. Larson, *An Empire of Ice: Scott, Shackleton, and the Heroic Age of Antarctic Science* (New Haven, CT: Yale University Press, 2011); Chris Turney, *1912: The Year the World Discovered Antarctica* (Melbourne, Australia: Text, 2012); and David Day, *Antarctica: A Biography* (North Sydney, Australia: Knopf, 2012). Max Jones's work is a sophisticated and fine exploration of the meanings of Robert Scott's *Terra Nova* expedition and the reception of his death in Edwardian Britain: Max Jones, *The Last Great Quest: Captain Scott's Antarctic Sacrifice* (Oxford: Oxford University Press, 2003). The heroic era also receives critical attention in Stephen J. Pyne, *The Ice: A Journey to Antarctica* (Seattle: University of Washington Press, [1986] 1998); and Tom Griffiths, *Slicing the Silence: Voyaging to Antarctica* (Sydney, Australia: University of New South Wales Press, 2007).
15. This is a feature of work on international environmental regimes, led especially by the political scientist Oran Young and associated scholars. See Oran R. Young, "The Politics of International Regime Formation: Managing Natural Resources

and the Environment," *International Organization* 43, no. 3 (1989): 349–75; Oran R. Young and Gail Osherenko, eds., *Polar Politics: Creating International Environmental Regimes* (Ithaca, NY, and London: Cornell University Press, 1993); Peter M. Haas, Robert O. Keohane, and Marc A. Levy, eds., *Institutions for the Earth: Sources of Effective International Environmental Protection* (Cambridge, MA: The MIT Press, 1993); and Oran R. Young, ed., *The Effectiveness of International Environmental Regimes: Causal Connections and Behavioral Mechanisms* (Cambridge, MA: The MIT Press, 1999). Antarctic politics scholarship has often focused on questions of regime formation, legitimacy, and effectiveness; see particularly Olav Schram Stokke and Davor Vidas, eds., *Governing the Antarctic: The Effectiveness and Legitimacy of the Antarctic Treaty System* (Cambridge, UK: Cambridge University Press, 1996). Some works within international environmental history have also, at least partly, addressed concerns about regime effectiveness. See contributions in Erika Marie Bsumek, David Kinkela, and Mark Atwood Lawrence, eds., *Nation-States and the Global Environment: New Approaches to International Environmental History* (New York: Oxford University Press, 2013); Kurkpatrick Dorsey, *The Dawn of Conservation Diplomacy: U.S.-Canadian Wildlife Protection Treaties in the Progressive Era* (Seattle: University of Washington Press, 1998); and Kurkpatrick Dorsey, *Whales and Nations: Environmental Diplomacy on the High Seas* (Seattle: University of Washington Press, 2013).

16. On the minerals negotiations of the 1980s, see Francisco Orrego Vicuña, *Antarctic Mineral Exploitation: The Emerging Legal Framework* (Cambridge, UK: Cambridge University Press, 1988); Rüdiger Wolfrum, *The Convention on the Regulation of Antarctic Mineral Resource Activities: An Attempt to Break New Ground* (Berlin: Springer-Verlag, 1991); and Andrew Jackson and Peter Boyce, "Mining and 'World Park Antarctica', 1982–1991," in *Australia and the Antarctic Treaty System: 50 Years of Influence*, ed. Marcus Haward and Tom Griffiths (Sydney, Australia: University of New South Wales Press, 2011), 243–73.

17. The 1960s and 1970s have received some increased attention in the last few years. Peter Beck's classic book *The International Politics of Antarctica* (London: Croom Helm, 1986) does chronicle these decades, but relies on open-source documents and is more concerned with high-level policy questions. From historians, see Marcus Haward and Tom Griffiths, eds., *Australia and the Antarctic Treaty System: 50 Years of Influence* (Sydney, Australia: University of New South Wales Press, 2011); Adrian Howkins, "Melting Empires? Climate Change and Politics in Antarctica since the International Geophysical Year," *Osiris* 26 (2011): 180–97; Lize-Marié van der Watt, "Return to Gondwanaland: South Africa, Antarctica, Minerals and Apartheid," *The Polar Journal* 3, no. 1 (2013): 72–93; and Simone Turchetti et al., "On Thick Ice: Scientific Internationalism and Antarctic Affairs, 1957–1980," *History and Technology* 24, no. 4 (2008): 351–76.

18. As such, this book also adds historical depth to a range of Antarctic scholarship focused on contemporary Antarctic political and environmental issues.

For example, see Alan D. Hemmings, Donald R. Rothwell, and Karen N. Scott, eds., *Antarctic Security in the Twenty-First Century: Legal and Policy Perspectives* (London and New York: Routledge, 2012); Anne-Marie Brady, ed., *The Emerging Politics of Antarctica* (Abingdon, UK: Routledge, 2013); and Jessica O'Reilly, *The Technocratic Antarctic: An Ethnography of Scientific Expertise and Environmental Governance* (Ithaca, NY: Cornell University Press, 2017).

19. My use of the assembly metaphor draws upon and takes conceptual and analytical insights from two now significant bodies of literature. First, it draws from actor-network theory: Bruno Latour, *Reassembling the Social: An Introduction to Actor-Network-Theory* (Oxford: Oxford University Press, 2005). Second, it draws from the "assemblage theory" associated with the work of Gilles Deleuze and Felix Guattari, especially in Gilles Deleuze and Félix Guattari, *A Thousand Plateaus: Capitalism and Schizophrenia*, trans. Brian Massumi (Minneapolis: University of Minnesota Press, 1987). For a short explication see J. Macgregor Wise, "Assemblage," in *Gilles Deleuze: Key Concepts*, ed. Charles J. Stivale (Montreal and Kingston, ON: McGill-Queen's University Press, 2005), 77–87. I have drawn especially from the use of this work within the critical human geography literature—see Ben Anderson and Colin McFarlane, "Assemblage and Geography," *Area* 43, no. 2 (2011): 124–27 and the associated special issue; and Jane Bennett, "The Agency of Assemblages and the North American Blackout," *Public Culture* 17, no. 3 (2005): 445–65.
20. Pyne, *The Ice*, 68.
21. This position draws on critical geopolitics scholarship, which speaks to the ways in which practitioners of geopolitics depict the world in certain ways, "geographing," to justify and perpetuate certain geopolitical projects. See Gearóid Ó Tuathail and John Agnew, "Geopolitics and Discourse: Practical Geopolitical Reasoning in American Foreign Policy," *Political Geography* 11, no. 2 (1992): 190–204; Gearóid Ó Tuathail, *Critical Geopolitics: The Politics of Writing Global Space* (Minneapolis: University of Minnesota Press, 1996); and Martin Müller, "Text, Discourse, Affect and Things," in *The Ashgate Companion to Critical Geopolitics*, ed. Klaus Dodds, M. Kuus, and J. Sharp (Farnham, UK: Ashgate, 2012), 49–68.
22. The treaty was created in four languages: English, French, Spanish, and Russian. Two contemporaneous articles still provide important legal and historical insights into the treaty: John Hanessian, "The Antarctic Treaty 1959," *International and Comparative Law Quarterly* 9, no. 3 (1960): 436–80; Robert D. Hayton, "The Antarctic Settlement of 1959," *American Journal of International Law* 54, no. 2 (1960): 349–71.
23. These formal dates should not obscure the fact that explorers often claimed territories during their expeditions and that some countries, Argentina in particular, often referred generally to claims and interests without making formal and strictly defined claims. For details of the dates and relevant legal instruments, see Robert Keith Headland, *A Chronology of Antarctic Exploration: A Synopsis*

of Events and Activities from the Earliest Times until the International Polar Years, 2007–09 (London: Quaritch, 2009), 24–26.

24. Adrian Howkins, *Frozen Empires: An Environmental History of the Antarctic Peninsula* (New York: Oxford University Press, 2017).
25. James Spiller, *Frontiers for the American Century: Outer Space, Antarctica, and Cold War Nationalism* (Houndmills, UK: Palgrave Macmillan, 2015).
26. "Embassy of the Soviet Union to the Department of State, Memorandum," June 8, 1950 in US Department of State, *Foreign Relations of the United States, 1950*, Vol. 1, National Security Affairs; Foreign Economic Policy (Washington, DC: US Government Printing Office, 1977), 911–13; Irina Gan, "Red Antarctica: Soviet Interests in the South Polar Region Prior to the Antarctic Treaty, 1946–1958" (PhD thesis, University of Tasmania, 2009).
27. Ronald E. Doel, "Constituting the Postwar Earth Sciences: The Military's Influence on the Environmental Sciences in the USA after 1945," *Social Studies of Science* 33, no. 5 (2003): 635–66. See also Jacob Darwin Hamblin, *Oceanographers and the Cold War: Disciples of Marine Science* (Seattle: University of Washington Press, 2005); Jacob Darwin Hamblin, *Arming Mother Nature: The Birth of Catastrophic Environmentalism* (Oxford: Oxford University Press, 2013); Jon Agar, *Science in the Twentieth Century and Beyond* (Cambridge, UK: Polity, 2012); and Allan A. Needell, *Science, Cold War and the American State: Lloyd V. Berkner and the Balance of Professional Ideals* (Amsterdam: Harwood Academic Publishers in association with the National Air and Space Museum Smithsonian Institution, 2000).
28. On the IGY generally, see Walter Sullivan, *Assault on the Unknown: The International Geophysical Year* (New York: McGraw-Hill, 1961); Dian Olson Belanger, *Deep Freeze: The United States, the International Geophysical Year, and the Origins of Antarctica's Age of Science* (Boulder: University Press of Colorado, 2006); Klaus Dodds, "Assault on the Unknown: Geopolitics, Antarctic Science, and the International Geophysical Year (1957–8)," in *New Spaces of Exploration: Geographies of Discovery in the Twentieth Century*, ed. Simon Naylor and James R. Ryan (London: I. B. Tauris, 2010), 148–72; Christy Collis and Klaus Dodds, "Assault on the Unknown: The Historical and Political Geographies of the International Geophysical Year (1957–8)," *Journal of Historical Geography* 34, no. 4 (2008): 555–73; Adrian Howkins, "Reluctant Collaborators: Argentina and Chile in Antarctica During the International Geophysical Year, 1957–58," *Journal of Historical Geography* 34, no. 4 (2008): 596–617; Adrian Howkins, "Science, Environment, and Sovereignty: The International Geophysical Year in the Antarctic Peninsula Region," in *Globalizing Polar Science: Reconsidering the International Polar and Geophysical Years*, ed. Roger D. Launius, James Rodger Fleming, and David H. DeVorkin (Houndmills: Palgrave Macmillan, 2010), 245–64; Alessandro Antonello, "Australia, the International Geophysical Year and the 1959 Antarctic Treaty," *Australian Journal of Politics and History* 59, no.

4 (2013): 532–46; and Colin P. Summerhayes, "International Collaboration in Antarctica: The International Polar Years, the International Geophysical Year, and the Scientific Committee on Antarctic Research," *Polar Record* 44, no. 231 (2008): 321–34. On SCAR's history, see David W. H. Walton, Peter D. Clarkson, and Colin P. Summerhayes, *Science in the Snow: Fifty Years of International Collaboration through the Scientific Committee on Antarctic Research* (Cambridge, UK: Scientific Committee on Antarctic Research, 2011).

29. H. Robert Hall, "International Regime Formation and Leadership: The Origins of the Antarctic Treaty" (PhD thesis, University of Tasmania, 1994), 128–43.

30. The following works by international law scholars provide legally focused interpretations of Antarctic Treaty structures and law: F. M. Auburn, *Antarctic Law and Politics* (London: C. Hurst & Co., 1982); Donald R. Rothwell, *The Polar Regions and the Development of International Law* (Cambridge, UK: Cambridge University Press, 1996), 51–154; Christopher C. Joyner, *Antarctica and the Law of the Sea* (Dordrecht, Netherlands: Martinus Nijhoff Publishers, 1992); Christopher C. Joyner, *Governing the Frozen Commons: The Antarctic Regime and Environmental Protection* (Columbia: University of South Carolina Press, 1998); and Arthur Watts, *International Law and the Antarctic Treaty System* (Cambridge, UK: Grotius Publications, 1992). Another classic and sound account of Antarctic diplomatic and scientific structures is Beck, *International Politics of Antarctica.*

31. Two prominent examples of this are Paul Arthur Berkman, *Science into Policy: Global Lessons from Antarctica* (San Diego, CA: Academic Press, 2002) and Paul Arthur Berkman et al., eds., *Science Diplomacy: Antarctica, Science, and the Governance of International Spaces* (Washington, DC: Smithsonian Institution Scholarly Press, 2011). For more sophisticated approaches, see Aant Elzinga, "Antarctica: The Construction of a Continent by and for Science," in *Denationalizing Science: The Contexts of International Scientific Practice*, ed. Elisabeth Crawford, Terry Shinn, and Sverker Sörlin (Dordrecht, Netherlands: Kluwer Academic Publishers, 1993), 73–106; Klaus Dodds, "The Great Game in Antarctica: Britain and the 1959 Antarctic Treaty," *Contemporary British History* 22, no. 1 (2008): 43–66; Klaus Dodds, "Guest Editorial—the 1959 Antarctic Treaty: Reflecting on the 50th Anniversary of a Landmark Agreement," *Polar Research* 29 (2010): 145–49; and Howkins, *Frozen Empires.*

32. Klaus Dodds and Alan D. Hemmings, "Britain and the British Antarctic Territory in the Wider Geopolitics of the Antarctic and the Southern Ocean," *International Affairs* 89, no. 6 (2013): 1429–44.

33. This conception of the society of states draws on Hedley Bull, *The Anarchical Society* (New York: Columbia University Press, 1977). See also Barry Buzan, *An Introduction to the English School of International Relations: The Societal Approach* (London: Polity, 2014).

34. The distinction between "regime" and "order" is important here. There is a well-developed literature on regimes, especially in the disciplines of political

science, international relations, and international law, with Stephen Krasner's work being an important foundation: Stephen D. Krasner, "Structural Causes and Regime Consequences: Regimes as Intervening Variables," *International Organization* 36, no. 2 (1982): 185–205. Oran Young and associated figures have led in the study of environment and international natural resource questions in regimes (see note 15).

35. In this sense, this book moves beyond the rather more institutionally focused histories of environmental diplomacy and international environmental politics that earlier, foundational, works have taken. Examples are Robert Boardman, *International Organization and the Conservation of Nature* (London: Macmillan, 1981); and John McCormick, *Reclaiming Paradise: The Global Environmental Movement* (Bloomington: Indiana University Press, 1989). Carmel Finley's work in marine environmental history effectively takes this larger approach: on the concept of maximum sustainable yield, see Carmel Finley, *All the Fish in the Sea: Maximum Sustainable Yield and the Failure of Fisheries Management* (Chicago: University of Chicago Press, 2011); and in relation to tuna and the idea of "highly migratory stocks," see Carmel Finley, "Global Borders and the Fish That Ignore Them: The Cold War Roots of Overfishing," in *Nation-States and the Global Environment: New Approaches to International Environmental History*, ed. Erika Marie Bsumek, David Kinkela, and Mark Atwood Lawrence (New York: Oxford University Press, 2013), 62–75. Mark Lawrence et al. also make clear that, although they are central, it is not just states that constitute "the international"; see Mark Atwood Lawrence, David Kinkela, and Erika Marie Bsumek, introduction to *Nation-States and the Global Environment: New Approaches to International Environmental History*, ed. Erika Marie Bsumek, David Kinkela, and Mark Atwood Lawrence (New York: Oxford University Press, 2013), 1–21.

36. On sealing, see Rhys Richards, *Sealing in the Southern Oceans 1788–1833* (Wellington, New Zealand: Paremata Press, 2010). On whaling, see J. N. Tønnessen and A. O. Johnsen, *The History of Modern Whaling* (London and Canberra, Australia: C. Hurst & Co. and ANU Press, 1982); D. Graham Burnett, *The Sounding of the Whale: Science and Cetaceans in the Twentieth Century* (Chicago: University of Chicago Press, 2012); and Dorsey, *Whales and Nations*.

37. There is now a large literature on the authority of science and scientists in relation to environments and nature. Particularly relevant vis-à-vis this study, see Samuel P. Hays, *Beauty, Health, and Permanence: Environmental Politics in the United States, 1955–1985* (Cambridge, UK: Cambridge University Press, 1987); Stephen Bocking, *Nature's Experts: Science, Politics, and the Environment* (New Brunswick, NJ, and London: Rutgers University Press, 2004); Stephen Bocking, "Science and Spaces in the Northern Environment," *Environmental History* 12, no. 4 (2007): 867–94; Burnett, *Sounding of the Whale*; Libby Robin, *How a Continent Created a Nation* (Sydney, Australia: University of New South Wales Press, 2007);

Mark Carey, *In the Shadow of Melting Glaciers: Climate Change and Andean Society* (New York: Oxford University Press, 2010); and Mark Carey, "Science, Models, and Historians: Toward a Critical Climate History," *Environmental History* 19, no. 2 (2014): 354–64.

38. There is now a wide range of literature that investigates international environmental history. Two important recent collections are Bsumek, Kinkela, and Lawrence, *Nation-States and the Global Environment*; and Wolfram Kaiser and Jan-Henrik Meyer, eds., *International Organizations and Environmental Protection: Conservation and Globalization in the Twentieth Century* (New York and Oxford: Berghahn, 2016). Two early works with wide coverage are McCormick, *Reclaiming Paradise*; and Boardman, *International Organization and the Conservation of Nature*. Environmental diplomacy in the first half of the twentieth century is analyzed by Dorsey, *Dawn of Conservation Diplomacy*; and Mark Cioc, *The Game of Conservation: International Treaties to Protect the World's Migratory Animals* (Athens: Ohio University Press, 2009). On global environmentalism, see Thomas Robertson, *The Malthusian Moment: Global Population Growth and the Birth of American Environmentalism* (New Brunswick, NJ, and London: Rutgers University Press, 2012); and Frank Zelko, *Make It a Green Peace! The Rise of Countercultural Environmentalism* (New York: Oxford University Press, 2013). On the global environment and the Cold War, see J. R. McNeill and Corinna R. Unger, eds., *Environmental Histories of the Cold War* (Washington, DC, and New York: German Historical Institute and Cambridge University Press, 2010). On the climate system and climate change, see Clark A. Miller and Paul N. Edwards, eds., *Changing the Atmosphere: Expert Knowledge and Environmental Governance* (Cambridge, MA: The MIT Press, 2001); and Joshua P. Howe, *Behind the Curve: Science and the Politics of Global Warming* (Seattle: University of Washington Press, 2014). On marine pollution and nuclear dumping, see Jacob Darwin Hamblin, *Poison in the Well: Radioactive Waste in the Oceans at the Dawn of the Nuclear Age* (New Brunswick, NJ, and London: Rutgers University Press, 2008). On an "international river," see Mark Cioc, *The Rhine: An Eco-Biography, 1815–2000* (Seattle: University of Washington Press, 2002). On global population (enfolding many other issues), see Alison Bashford, *Global Population: History, Geopolitics, and Life on Earth* (New York: Columbia University Press, 2014). On "sustainable development," see Stephen J. Macekura, *Of Limits and Growth: The Rise of Global Sustainable Development in the Twentieth Century* (New York: Cambridge University Press, 2015). On biodiversity, see Rafi Youatt, *Counting Species: Biodiversity in Global Environmental Politics* (Minneapolis: University of Minnesota Press, 2015).

CHAPTER 1

1. International Union of Geodesy and Geophysics, *Antarctic Symposium, Buenos Aires 17–25 Novembre 1959*, Monograph No. 5 (Paris: Institut Géographique

National, 1960), 19–20. Carrick's original paper as written and presented in Buenos Aires does not seem to have survived in the pertinent Australian archives; his 1960 published article in the *SCAR Bulletin* is the earliest extant version.

2. The historical literature on conservation is significant, a reflection of the multifaceted nature and complexity of the subject. Some of this literature is referenced here, especially as it relates to conservation and environmental protection as a subject of international relations. General and important works include Samuel P. Hays, *Conservation and the Gospel of Efficiency: The Progressive Conservation Movement, 1890–1920* (Cambridge, MA: Harvard University Press, 1959); Samuel P. Hays, *Beauty, Health, and Permanence: Environmental Politics in the United States, 1955–1985* (Cambridge, UK: Cambridge University Press, 1987); Thomas Dunlap, *Nature and the English Diaspora: Environment and History in the United States, Canada, Australia, and New Zealand* (Cambridge, UK: Cambridge University Press, 1999); Tina Loo, *States of Nature: Conserving Canada's Wildlife in the Twentieth Century* (Vancouver: University of British Columbia Press, 2006); Libby Robin, *Defending the Little Desert: The Rise of Ecological Consciousness* (Melbourne, Australia: Melbourne University Press, 1998); John Sheail, *Nature in Trust: The History of Nature Conservation in Britain* (Glasgow, UK: Blackie, 1976); Roderick P. Neumann, *Imposing Wilderness: Struggles over Livelihood and Nature Preservation in Africa* (Berkeley: University of California Press, 1998); Ian Tyrrell, *Crisis of the Wasteful Nation: Empire and Conservation in Theodore Roosevelt's America* (Chicago: University of Chicago Press, 2015); and Emily Wakild, *Revolutionary Parks: Conservation, Social Justice, and Mexico's National Parks, 1910–1940* (Tucson: University of Arizona Press, 2011).
3. On extinction in this period, see Mark V. Barrow Jr., *Nature's Ghosts: Confronting Extinction from the Age of Jefferson to the Age of Ecology* (Chicago: University of Chicago Press, 2009). A useful entry point for the large literature on wilderness is Roderick Frazier Nash, *Wilderness and the American Mind*, 5th ed. (New Haven, CT: Yale University Press, 2014).
4. Stephen Bocking, *Ecologists and Environmental Politics: A History of Contemporary Ecology* (New Haven, CT: Yale University Press, 1997).
5. Ronald E. Doel, "Constituting the Postwar Earth Sciences: The Military's Influence on the Environmental Sciences in the USA after 1945," *Social Studies of Science* 33, no. 5 (2003): 635–66.
6. Carl R. Eklund and Joan Beckman, *Antarctica: Polar Research and Discovery During the International Geophysical Year* (New York: Holt, Rinehart and Winston, 1963), 9–10.
7. Ibid., 11.
8. Ibid., 14.
9. Philip Ayres, *Mawson: A Life* (Melbourne, Australia: Miegunyah Press, 1999), 205–6.
10. Examples of these regulations can be found in W. M. Bush, ed., *Antarctica and International Law: A Collection of Inter-State and National Documents* (London: Oceana, 1982).

11. N. A. Mackintosh, "The Work of the Discovery Committee," *Proceedings of the Royal Society B* 137, no. 887 (1950): 137–38; Peder Roberts, *The European Antarctic: Science and Strategy in Scandinavia and the British Empire* (New York: Palgrave Macmillan, 2011), 32–34; and D. Graham Burnett, *The Sounding of the Whale: Science and Cetaceans in the Twentieth Century* (Chicago: University of Chicago Press, 2012), 103–15.
12. As Australia's Antarctic policy and engagement developed and intensified in the early 1950s, effective administration became a central concern for perfecting the claim to the Australian Antarctic Territory. The appointment of magistrates, coroners, and other officers, including inspectors of wildlife, was part of this general policy. Instruments of appointment of coroners and inspectors can be found in the files of the Australian Department of External Affairs (NAA: A1838, 1495/3/2/2, Parts 1–2).
13. Tyrrell, *Crisis of the Wasteful Nation*; Wakild, *Revolutionary Parks*; and Bernhard Gissibl, Sabine Höhler, and Patrick Kupper, eds., *Civilizing Nature: National Parks in Global Historical Perspective* (New York: Berghahn, 2012).
14. Bernhard Gissibl, "German Colonialism and the Beginnings of International Wildlife Preservation in Africa," *German Historical Institute Bulletin Supplement*, no. 3 (2006): 126–29; Bernhard Gissibl, *The Nature of German Imperialism: Conservation and the Politics of Wildlife in Colonial East Africa* (New York and Oxford: Berghahn, 2016), chs. 6–7; and John M. MacKenzie, *The Empire of Nature: Hunting, Conservation and British Imperialism* (Manchester, UK: Manchester University Press, 1988), 205.
15. Mark Cioc notes that the convention did not cover all of Africa, despite its title; Mark Cioc, *The Game of Conservation: International Treaties to Protect the World's Migratory Animals* (Athens: Ohio University Press, 2009), 34–40.
16. Kurkpatrick Dorsey, *The Dawn of Conservation Diplomacy: U.S.-Canadian Wildlife Protection Treaties in the Progressive Era* (Seattle: University of Washington Press, 1998); Cioc, *The Game of Conservation*; Tyrrell, *Crisis of the Wasteful Nation*; and Sherman Strong Hayden, *The International Protection of Wild Life: An Examination of Treaties and Other Agreements for the Preservation of Birds and Mammals*, Studies in History, Economics and Public Law (New York: Columbia University Press, 1942).
17. MacKenzie, *The Empire of Nature*, chs. 8 and 10. Americans also had some involvement with this late imperial agreement; see Barrow, *Nature's Ghosts*, 150–52. See also Gissibl, Höhler, and Kupper, *Civilizing Nature*; and Patrick Kupper, "Science and the National Parks: A Transatlantic Perspective on the Interwar Years," *Environmental History* 14, no. 1 (2009): 58–81.
18. Barrow, *Nature's Ghosts*, ch. 6. See also Cioc, *The Game of Conservation*, 88–94 for a discussion of the 1936 convention and 94–97 for the 1940 convention.
19. J. N. Tønnessen and A. O. Johnsen, *The History of Modern Whaling* (London and Canberra: C. Hurst & Co. and Australian National University Press, 1982), chs. 20–25.

20. On initiatives following the Second World War, especially the establishment of the United Nations Educational, Scientific and Cultural Organization (UNESCO) and the International Union for Conservation of Nature (IUCN), see Robert Boardman, *International Organization and the Conservation of Nature* (London: Macmillan, 1981), 35–46; John McCormick, *Reclaiming Paradise: The Global Environmental Movement* (Bloomington: Indiana University Press, 1989), ch. 2; and Anna-Katharina Wöbse, "'The World after All Was One': The International Environmental Network of UNESCO and IUPN, 1945–1950," *Contemporary European History* 20, no. 3 (2011): 331–48. On the developments in fisheries, some details can be found in Carmel Finley, *All the Fish in the Sea: Maximum Sustainable Yield and the Failure of Fisheries Management* (Chicago: University of Chicago Press, 2011), chs. 7 and 8. On the Convention on Fishing and Conservation of the Living Resources of the High Seas, signed at the Geneva Conference on the Law of the Sea in April 1958, see Arthur H. Dean, "The Geneva Conference on the Law of the Sea: What Was Accomplished," *American Journal of International Law* 52, no. 4 (1958): 625–27.
21. Kurkpatrick Dorsey, *Whales and Nations: Environmental Diplomacy on the High Seas* (Seattle: University of Washington Press, 2013), chs. 4 and 5.
22. Ron Doel suggests that there was also a broader shift at this time away from "environment" defined through geophysics to "environment" defined through biology and ecology. See Doel, "Constituting the Postwar Earth Sciences."
23. International Union of Geodesy and Geophysics, *Antarctic Symposium*, 19.
24. Carrick's position as the initiator of SCAR's conservation efforts has been identified and briefly discussed in Martin J. Riddle and Paul M. Goldsworthy, "Environmental Science and the Environmental Ethos of ANARE," in *Australian Antarctic Science: The First 50 Years of ANARE*, ed. Harvey J. Marchant, Desmond J. Lugg, and Patrick G. Quilty (Kingston, Tasmania: Australian Antarctic Division, 2002), 565–66. See also Alan D. Hemmings and Julia Jabour, "Already a Special Case? Australian Antarctic Policy in the First Decade of the Antarctic Treaty," in *Australia and the Antarctic Treaty System: 50 Years of Influence*, ed. Marcus Haward and Tom Griffiths (Sydney, Australia: University of New South Wales Press, 2011), 127.
25. He had already dealt with the topic in a broad way at the March 1959 SCAR meeting in Canberra: "Third meeting of S.C.A.R. held in Canberra, 2 to 6 March 1959," *SCAR Bulletin*, no. 3 (September 1959): 594.
26. Gordon Robin, Letters to Robert Carrick, April 8, 1960, and May 17, 1960 (NAA: A9697, C5/65).
27. J. S. Cumpston, *Macquarie Island*, ANARE Scientific Reports, Series A(1) (Melbourne, Australia: Antarctic Division, Department of External Affairs, 1968).
28. G. M. Dunnet, "Robert Carrick 1911–88," *Scottish Birds* 15, no. 2 (1988): 93. J. J. Jenkins, "Obituary Dr. Robert Carrick," *Aurora: ANARE Club Journal* 8, no. 3 (1989): 13–14; Libby Robin, "Nature Conservation as a National Concern: The Role of the Australian Academy of Science," *Historical Records of Australian*

Science 10, no. 1 (1994): 1–24; Libby Robin, *The Flight of the Emu: A Hundred Years of Australian Ornithology 1901–2001* (Melbourne, Australia: Melbourne University Press, 2001), 153–54, 161–63, 203, 432n46; George Main, ed. *Of Beauty Rich and Rare: Fifty Years of CSIRO Wildlife and Ecology* (Canberra, Australia: CSIRO Division of Wildlife and Ecology 1999); and Cameron Muir, *The Broken Promise of Agricultural Progress: An Environmental History* (Abingdon, UK, and New York: Routledge, 2014), 153.

29. Robert Carrick, "Conservation of Nature in the Antarctic," *SCAR Bulletin*, no. 6 (September 1960): 299.
30. Ibid., 300.
31. Ibid., 301.
32. Ibid., 302.
33. Ibid., 299.
34. Ibid., 299–300.
35. Stephen Bocking, "Nature on the Home Front: British Ecologists' Advocacy for Science and Conservation," *Environment and History* 18, no. 2 (2012): 261–81.
36. Carrick, "Conservation of Nature in the Antarctic," 303.
37. Robert Cushman Murphy, *Logbook for Grace: Whaling Brig Daisy, 1912–1913* (New York: Macmillan, 1947), 239.
38. Robert Cushman Murphy, "Antarctic Conservation," *Science* 135, no. 3499 (1962): 195. On Murphy, see Dean Amadon, "In Memoriam: Robert Cushman Murphy, April 29, 1887–March 20, 1973," *The Auk: A Quarterly Journal of Ornithology* 91, no. 1 (1974): 1–9; Gregory T. Cushman, "'The Most Valuable Birds in the World': International Conservation Science and the Revival of Peru's Guano Industry, 1909–1965," *Environmental History* 10, no. 3 (2005): 477–509; and Gary Kroll, *America's Ocean Wilderness: A Cultural History of Twentieth-Century Exploration* (Lawrence: University Press of Kansas, 2008), ch. 2. It is worth noting that Murphy, as the main American scientist in this situation, did not deploy the language of wilderness that was so significant a part of American environmental politics at the time, given the lobbying for and passage of the Wilderness Act in 1964.
39. British Section, International Council for Bird Preservation, Letter to British Foreign Secretary, July 18, 1960 (TNA: FO 371/147718).
40. Carrick shared his conservation paper in advance with Robert Falla and W. J. L. Sladen; Carrick, Letter to Gordon Robin, May 4, 1960 (NAA: A9697, C5/46). Carrick was also a frequent correspondent of Gordon Robin. It is difficult to know if this was simply because Robin was the secretary of SCAR and in frequent contact with all working group chairs (which is likely), or also because Carrick and Robin had perhaps known each other in Canberra, where Carrick was based and where Robin had been for a short time as a fellow of the Australian National University in 1957.
41. Mark V. Barrow Jr., *A Passion for Birds: American Ornithology after Audubon* (Princeton, NJ: Princeton University Press, 1998).

42. Gordon Robin, Letter to Robert Carrick, April 5, 1960 (NAA: A9697, C5/65).
43. Robert Carrick, Letter to Gordon Robin, May 4, 1960 (SCAR Secretariat).
44. Simone Turchetti et al., "Accidents and Opportunities: A History of the Radio Echo-Sounding of Antarctica, 1958–79," *British Journal of the History of Science* 41, no. 3 (2008): 427.
45. Alessandro Antonello, "The Greening of Antarctica: Environment, Science and Diplomacy, 1959–1980" (PhD thesis, Australian National University, 2014), 47–53.
46. Gordon Robin, Letter and attachment to Robert Carrick, April 5, 1960 (NAA: A9697, C5/65).
47. Brian Roberts, "Conservation of Living Resources in the Antarctic," September 15, 1960 (TNA: FO 371/147720).
48. "Conservation of Nature in Antarctica," *SCAR Bulletin*, no. 8 (May 1961): 532.
49. "Conservation of Nature in Antarctica," *SCAR Bulletin*, no. 8 (May 1961): 532–40.
50. Adrian Howkins, "Science, Environment, and Sovereignty: The International Geophysical Year in the Antarctic Peninsula Region," in *Globalizing Polar Science: Reconsidering the International Polar and Geophysical Years*, ed. Roger D. Launius, James Rodger Fleming, and David H. DeVorkin (Houndmills, UK: Palgrave Macmillan, 2010), 257.
51. Paul A. Siple, "Geographic Basis for Antarctic Scientific Observations," *Proceedings of the National Academy of Sciences* 40, no. 10 (1954): 979.
52. "First meeting of S.C.A.R. held at The Hague, 3 to 5 February 1958," *SCAR Bulletin*, no. 1 (January 1959): 364.
53. US Department of State, "Tentative Proposals of the State Department (not U.S. Government)," c. January 1958 (TNA: FO 371/131905).
54. British Embassy, Washington, Telegram 580 to London, March 12, 1958 (TNA: FO 371/131906).
55. D. F. Muirhead (British Embassy, Washington), Letter to H. A. A. Hankey, June 20, 1958 (TNA: FO 371/131910).
56. "Aide-Memoire from the Department of State to Certain Embassies," March 24, 1958, in US Department of State, *Foreign Relations of the United States, 1958–1960*, Vol. 2, United Nations and General International Matters (Washington, DC: US Government Printing Office, 1991), 497; and H. A. A. Hankey (FO), letter to Oslo, April 22, 1958 (TNA: FO 371/131907).
57. A copy of this treaty draft can be found in TNA: FO 371/131916.
58. D. F. Muirhead (British Embassy, Washington), Letter to H. A. A. Hankey, June 26, 1959 (TNA: FO 371/138966).
59. See, for example, Francis Wilcox, Memorandum to Paul Daniels, December 16, 1958 (NACP: RG 59, Subject Files of Francis O Wilcox, Assistant Secretary of State for International Organization Affairs, 1958–1959).
60. Conference on Antarctica, verbatim record, Committee II, October 22, 1959, and Working Paper COMII/SR/4, "Summary Record—Fourth Meeting of Committee II," October 22, 1959 (NACP: RG 43, Antarctic Conference, US Delegation Program Records, 1959).

61. Conference on Antarctica, Working Paper COMII/SR/5, "Summary Record—Fifth Meeting of Committee II," October 23, 1959 (NACP: RG 43, Antarctic Conference, US Delegation Program Records, 1959).
62. Conference on Antarctica, Working Paper COMII/P11, "Provision for Administrative Measures: Proposal by the Delegation of Chile with Regard to Article VIII," October 24, 1959 (NACP: RG 43, Antarctic Conference, US Delegation Program Records, 1959).
63. Finley, *All the Fish in the Sea*, chs. 7 and 8
64. New Zealand, Department of External Affairs, "Antarctic Conference, 1959: Report of the New Zealand Delegation," December 10, 1959 (ANZ: ACIE, 8798, 208/5/4/5 Part 1).
65. Conference on Antarctica, Working Paper COMII/SR/6, "Summary Record—Sixth Meeting of Committee II," October 26, 1959 (NACP: RG 43, Antarctic Conference, US Delegation Program Records, 1959).
66. Conference on Antarctica, verbatim record, Committee II, October 27, 1959 (NACP: RG 43, Antarctic Conference, US Delegation Program Records, 1959).
67. Conference on Antarctica, Working Paper COMII/SR/7, "Summary Record—Seventh Meeting of Committee II," October 27, 1959 (NACP: RG 43, Antarctic Conference, US Delegation Program Records, 1959).
68. C. W. Harders (Australia, Attorney-General's Department), "Conference on the Antarctic—Appraisal Prepared for the Solicitor-General," November 26, 1959 (NAA: A1838, 1495/3/2/1 Part 21).
69. Malcolm Templeton writes that article IX 1(f) "got into the Treaty . . . almost by accident," though he does not really investigate why this was so, and neither does he see it as part of a broader debate about what the treaty would do. Malcolm Templeton, *A Wise Adventure: New Zealand in Antarctica 1920–1960* (Wellington: Victoria University Press in association with the New Zealand Institute of International Affairs, 2000), 266.
70. D. L. Benest (British Embassy, Washington), Letter to H. A. A. Hankey, January 27, 1960 (TNA: FO 371/147715).
71. Klaus Dodds, *Pink Ice: Britain and the South Atlantic Empire* (London: I. B. Tauris, 2002).
72. Brian Roberts, "Conservation of Living Resources in the Antarctic," September 15, 1960 (TNA: FO 371/147720).
73. K. G. McInnes, Minute, A15214/80, September 20, 1960 (TNA: FO 371/147720).
74. "Recommendations" were the negotiated agreements of the consultative meetings; they were framed as recommendations rather than agreements or rules, because the government of each party still had to approve the measures, and the measures only came into effect once all governments had ratified them.
75. Recommendation I-VIII, in "Report of First Consultative Meeting, Canberra," 1961.

76. Robert Carrick, Letter to Gordon Robin, July 17, 1961 (NAA: A9697, C5/65).
77. Brian Roberts, Personal Journal, First Antarctic Treaty Consultative Meeting, Canberra, 1961, July–August 1961, July 11, 1961 (SPRI: MS1308/11).
78. The treaty states that the first meeting of parties would take place in Canberra within two months of the treaty's coming into force. Australia, Argentina, and Chile were the last ratifications; Australia so it could control the date of the meeting, while Argentina and Chile got bogged down in their domestic politics.
79. Brian Roberts, Personal Journal, First Antarctic Treaty Consultative Meeting, Canberra, 1961, July–August 1961, July 25, 1962 (SPRI: MS1308/12).
80. Brian Roberts, Letter to Gordon Robin, July 28, 1962 (TNA: FO 371/162064).
81. Second Antarctic Treaty Consultative Meeting, Working Paper P3, "Draft Convention on the Conservation of Wild Life in the Antarctic," July 17, 1962.
82. W. H. Mills (US State Department), Memorandum to Philip Smith (NSF), April 22, 1963, and W. H. Mills (State), Memorandum to Philip Smith (NSF), April 30, 1963 (NACP: RG 307, OAP, Central Subject Files 1961–1969).
83. USSR, "Notes on the Draft Convention for the Conservation of Wild Life of the Antarctic" (UK translations, July 17, 1963), June 4, 1963 (TNA: FO 371/167776).
84. K. W. Piddington (New Zealand Mission, Brussels), Memorandum to Wellington, June 10, 1963 (ANZ: ABHS, 7148, LONB 68/2 Part 1).
85. Australian Embassy, Brussels, Memorandum to Canberra, June 10, 1963 (NAA: A1838, 1495/3/2/14 Part 1).
86. Though apparently not enough of a bombshell for the New Zealand delegate to report; K. L. Press (New Zealand Mission, Brussels), Memorandum to Wellington, September 11, 1963 (ANZ: ABHS, 7148, LONB 68/2 Part 1).
87. Brian Roberts, Minute, November 8, 1963 (TNA: FO 371/167776); and Henry Carr (British Embassy, Brussels), Letter to Anthony Parsons (FO), November 26, 1963 (TNA: FO 371/167776).
88. K. L. Press (New Zealand Mission, Brussels), Memorandum to Wellington, November 15, 1963 (ANZ: ABHS, 7148, LONB 68/2 Part 1).
89. US Embassy, Wellington, Note Verbale, January 7, 1964 (ANZ: ABHS, 950, 208/1/10 Part 1).
90. US Department of State, Airgram A60 to Brussels, October 28, 1963 (NACP: RG 59, Central Foreign Policy Files, 1963).
91. J. W. C. Cumes (Australian Embassy, Brussels), Memorandum to Canberra, April 9, 1964 (NAA: B1387, 1996/839); Brian Roberts, Letter to Phillip Law, May 14, 1964 (NAA: B1387, 1996/840).
92. USSR, "Notes on the Draft Convention for the Conservation of Wild Life of the Antarctic" (UK translations, July 17, 1963), June 4, 1963 (TNA: FO 371/167776).
93. J. W. C. Cumes (Australian Embassy, Brussels), Memorandum to Canberra, February 12, 1964 (NAA: B1387, 1996/839); US Embassy, Brussels, Airgram A794 to Washington, February 18, 1964 (NACP: RG59, Central Foreign Policy Files, 1964–1966).

94. Brian Roberts, Letter to Phillip Law, May 14, 1964 (NAA: B1387, 1996/840).
95. Foreign Office, Working Paper, "Proposed Agreement on the Conservation of Wild Life in the Antarctic," February 28, 1964 (ANZ: ABHS, 950, 208/1/10 Part 2).
96. US Department of State, Airgram A60 to Brussels, October 28, 1963 (NACP: RG 59, Central Foreign Policy Files, 1963).
97. J. W. C. Cumes (Australian Embassy, Brussels), Memorandum to Canberra, April 9, 1964 (NAA: B1387, 1996/839).
98. Another helpful account of AMCAFF's details can be found in David Anderson, "The Conservation of Wildlife under the Antarctic Treaty," *Polar Record* 14, no. 88 (1968): 26–30.
99. Etienne Benson charts similar developments in the United States after the passing of the Marine Mammal Protection Act of 1972 and the Endangered Species Act of 1973. Etienne Benson, "Endangered Science: The Regulation of Research by the U.S. Marine Mammal Protection and Endangered Species Acts," *Historical Studies in the Natural Sciences* 42, no. 1 (2012): 30–61.
100. Robert Carrick, Letter to J. L. Lavett, August 4, 1966 (NAA: B1387, 1996/841).

CHAPTER 2

1. Brian Roberts, Personal Journal, Fourth Antarctic Treaty Consultative Meeting, Santiago, Chile, 1966, November 16, 1966 (SPRI: MS 1308/15).
2. W. Nigel Bonner and Richard M. Laws, "Seals and Sealing," in *Antarctic Research: A Review of British Scientific Achievement in Antarctica*, ed. Raymond Priestley, Raymond J. Adie, and G. de Q. Robin (London: Butterworths, 1964), 176–77.
3. Simon Lyster, *International Wildlife Law* (Cambridge, UK: Grotius Publications, 1985), 49. Lyster's text was among the very first on the subject of international wildlife law, was certainly the most substantial and wide-ranging available at the time, and was therefore influential for some years.
4. Sealers were excellent explorers but often kept discoveries to themselves for commercial purposes or simply had little interest in publishing exploration accounts. G. E. Fogg, *A History of Antarctic Science* (Cambridge, UK: Cambridge University Press, 1992), 38–41.
5. Richard M. Laws, "The Seals of the Falkland Islands and Dependencies," *Oryx* 2, no. 2 (1953): 88; R. J. Campbell, ed., *The Discovery of the South Shetland Islands: The Voyages of the Brig* Williams *1819–1820 as Recorded in Contemporary Documents and the Journal of Midshipman C. W. Poynter* (London: Hakluyt Society, 2000); A. G. E. Jones, "British Sealing on New South Shetland, 1819–1826, Part I," *The Great Circle* 7, no. 1 (1985): 9–20; A. G. E. Jones, "British Sealing on New South Shetland, 1819–1826, Part II," *The Great Circle* 7, no. 2 (1985): 74–85; and Rhys Richards, *Sealing in the Southern Oceans 1788–1833* (Wellington, New Zealand: Paremata Press, 2010).

6. Richards, *Sealing in the Southern Oceans*, 23–58; Briton Cooper Busch, *The War against the Seals: A History of the North American Seal Fishery* (Kingston, ON: McGill-Queen's University Press, 1985), 175; and Kenneth J. Bertrand, *Americans in Antarctica 1775–1948*, Special Publication No. 39 (New York: American Geographical Society, 1971).
7. Busch, *The War against the Seals*, 36; and Richards, *Sealing in the Southern Oceans*, 12.
8. A. B. Dickinson, *Seal Fisheries of the Falkland Islands and Dependencies: An Historical Review* (St. John's, NL: International Maritime Economic History Association, 2007), 152.
9. Busch, *The War against the Seals*, 184; Richard M. Laws, *The Elephant Seal (*Mirounga Leonina *Linn.): II, General, Social and Reproductive Behaviour*, Falkland Islands Dependencies Survey, Scientific Reports, no. 13 (London: Her Majesty's Stationery Office, 1956): 8; and Bjørn L. Basberg and Robert K. Headland, "The Economic Significance of the 19th Century Antarctic Sealing Industry," *Polar Record* 49, no. 4 (2013): 381–91.
10. Gerald L. Kooyman, *Weddell Seal: Consummate Diver* (Cambridge, UK: Cambridge University Press, 1981), 11.
11. Laws, "The Seals of the Falkland Islands and Dependencies," 88.
12. Ibid., 96.
13. L. Harrison Matthews, "The Natural History of the Elephant Seal with Notes on Other Seals Found at South Georgia," *Discovery Reports* 1 (1929): 249.
14. Dickinson, *Seal Fisheries of the Falkland Islands and Dependencies*, 146.
15. L. Harrison Matthews, *Sea Elephant: The Life and Death of the Elephant Seal* (London: MacGibbon & Kee, 1952), 28.
16. Dickinson, *Seal Fisheries of the Falkland Islands and Dependencies*, 143.
17. Bonner and Laws, "Seals and Sealing," 187.
18. W. H. Thompson (Colonial Secretary, Falkland Islands), Letter to Vivian Fuchs (BAS), April 1, 1965; Martin Holdgate (BAS), Letter to Vivian Fuchs, May 6, 1965; and Vivian Fuchs, Letter to W. H. Thompson, May 7, 1965 (BAS: AD3/1/AS/107/8(1)).
19. Canada, Royal Commission on Seals and the Sealing Industry in Canada, *Seals and Sealing in Canada* (Ottawa: Canadian Government Publishing Centre, 1986), 3:514–15 and ch. 19.
20. T. Øritsland, "Sealing and Seal Research in the South-West Atlantic Pack Ice, Sept.–Oct. 1964," in *Antarctic Ecology*, ed. M. W. Holdgate (London and New York: Academic Press, 1970), 367–76; and Martin Holdgate, Letter to Sidney Holt (FAO), November 2, 1964 (SCAR Secretariat).
21. Martin Holdgate, Letter to Gordon Robin, November 2, 1964; Holdgate, Letter to Sidney Holt, November 2, 1964; Holdgate, Letter to Johan Ruud (University of Oslo), December 9, 1964 (SCAR Secretariat).
22. George Llano (OAP), Memorandum to Tom Jones and Henry Francis (OAP), July 15, 1964 (NACP: RG 307, OAP, Central Subject Files 1961–1969).

23. Ibid.; see also J. Clausen (Lauritzen), Letter to Phillip Law (AAD), September 2, 1964, and Phillip Law, Letter to J. Clausen, September 28, 1964 (NAA: B1387, 1996/840).
24. Tim Bowden, *The Silence Calling: Australians in Antarctica 1947–97* (St. Leonards, Australia: Allen & Unwin, 1997), 92.
25. Ibid., 192–95.
26. David M. Lavigne, Victor B. Scheffer, and Stephen R. Kellert, "The Evolution of North American Attitudes toward Marine Mammals," in *Conservation and Management of Marine Mammals*, ed. John R. Twiss Jr and Randall R. Reeves (Washington, DC: Smithsonian Institution Press, 1998), 24; Canada, Royal Commission on Seals and the Sealing Industry in Canada, *Seals and Sealing in Canada* (Ottawa: Canadian Government Publishing Centre, 1986), 2:66.
27. H. G. R. King and Ann Savours, eds., *Polar Pundit: Reminiscences about Brian Birley Roberts* (Cambridge, UK: Scott Polar Research Institute, 1995). Klaus Dodds gives considerable attention to Roberts's place in the broader sphere of governance of the Falkland Islands Dependencies in the 1950s in Klaus Dodds, *Pink Ice: Britain and the South Atlantic Empire* (London: I. B. Tauris, 2002), and also to his particular part in the British delegation to the 1959 Antarctic Conference, in "The Great Game in Antarctica: Britain and the 1959 Antarctic Treaty," *Contemporary British History* 22, no. 1 (2008): 43–66. Peder Roberts has also offered an appraisal of Brian Roberts, but concentrating on his part in a culture of polar exploration at the University of Cambridge, particularly the Scott Polar Research Institute: Peder Roberts, *The European Antarctic: Science and Strategy in Scandinavia and the British Empire* (New York: Palgrave Macmillan, 2011), ch. 4.
28. Brian Roberts, "Working Paper for an International Agreement on the Conservation of Fauna on Antarctic Floating Ice, with Special Reference to Pelagic Sealing," February 17, 1966 (TNA: FO 371/185125).
29. Ibid.
30. D. Graham Burnett, *The Sounding of the Whale: Science and Cetaceans in the Twentieth Century* (Chicago: University of Chicago Press, 2012), 29 and ch. 2 more generally.
31. Victor Scheffer (US Department of the Interior), Letter to Henry Francis (NSF), July 20, 1966 (NAS: Committee on Polar Research 1961–1966 Collection). Scheffer changed his position in later years; see Victor B. Scheffer, *Adventures of a Zoologist* (New York: Charles Scribner's Sons, 1980).
32. Carleton Ray, Letter to H. W. Wells (US National Academy of Sciences), July 15, 1966 (NAS: Committee on Polar Research 1961–1966 Collection).
33. Philip Smith (NSF), Memorandum to T. O. Jones, July 27, 1966 (NACP: RG 307, OAP, Central Subject Files 1961–1969).
34. Torger Øritsland (Fiskeridirectoratets Norway), Letter to Martin Holdgate, June 27, 1966 (SCAR Secretariat).

35. For an analysis of the long Anglo-Norwegian connections with regard to whaling, see Roberts, *The European Antarctic.*
36. Martin Holdgate (Nature Conservancy), Letter to E. W. Momber (UK Department of Education and Science), September 30, 1966 (TNA: FO 371/185160).
37. Ibid.
38. Brian Roberts, October 5, 1966 (TNA: FO 371/185160); and Foreign Office, Brief for the Delegation to the Fourth Antarctic Treaty Consultative Meeting, October 24, 1966 (TNA: FO 371/185128).
39. SCAR Working Group on Biology, "Pelagic Sealing and the Taking of Fauna in the Pack Ice," IX SCAR-39, September 23, 1966 (TNA: FO 371/185160).
40. W. J. L. Sladen (Johns Hopkins University), "Report on the Biology Working Group Meetings, IX SCAR Santiago," September 27, 1966 (NAS: Committee on Polar Research 1961–1966 Collection).
41. Foreign Office, Brief for the Delegation to the Fourth Antarctic Treaty Consultative Meeting, October 24, 1966 (TNA: FO 371/185128).
42. Brian Roberts, Personal Journal, Fourth Antarctic Treaty Consultative Meeting, Santiago, Chile, 1966, November 11, 1996 (SPRI: MS 1308/15); and US Department of State, Position Paper, "Pelagic Sealing," October 3, 1966 (NACP: RG 59, Central Foreign Policy Files, 1964–1966). The US delegation's instructions read: "The United States would prefer to have a moratorium on all sealing until adequate scientific data is available, and has been evaluated by the scientific community."
43. Brian Roberts, Personal Journal, Fourth Antarctic Treaty Consultative Meeting, Santiago, Chile, 1966, Annex LXXXIV (SPRI: MS 1308/15).
44. Brian Roberts, Personal Journal, Fourth Antarctic Treaty Consultative Meeting, Santiago, Chile, 1966, November 16, 1966 (SPRI: MS 1308/15). The poem was also read at the signing of the Final Act at the Conference on the Conservation of Antarctic Seals in London in February 1972. Ralph Harry, "Antarctic Fauna and Flora," read at midnight on February 11–12, 1972 (TNA: FCO 7/2349).
45. Foreign Office, "The Fourth Antarctic Treaty Consultative Meeting," AZ 1071/66, December 5, 1966 (TNA: FO 371/185129).
46. US Department of State, "Report on the Fourth Consultative Meeting under the Antarctic Treaty," January 25, 1967 (NACP: RG 307, OPP, Office Files of Henry S Francis).
47. Brian Roberts, Letter to D. C. Martin (Royal Society), March 3, 1967 (TNA: FCO 7/991).
48. "SCAR Working Group on Biology, Meeting Held in 1968," *SCAR Bulletin*, no. 32 (May 1969): 748–60. However, the brief for the British delegation suggested there was a larger group; see Brief No. 2, "Pelagic Sealing," Annex E, November 8, 1968 (FCO 7/1371).
49. Foreign Office, Brief No. 2, "Pelagic Sealing," Annex E, November 8, 1968 (FCO 7/1371).

50. Brian Roberts, Personal Journal, Fifth Antarctic Treaty Consultative Meeting, Paris, November 19, 1968 (SPRI: MS 1308/17).
51. "SCAR Working Group on Biology, meeting held in 1968," *SCAR Bulletin*, no. 32 (May 1969): 749.
52. Brian Roberts, Personal Journal, Fifth Antarctic Treaty Consultative Meeting, Paris, November 28, 1968 (SPRI: MS 1308/17).
53. "Soviet Sealing in the North Pacific Ocean," *Polar Record* 13, no. 84 (1966): 342; and "Soviet Exploitation of Seals in the Bering Sea," *Polar Record* 13, no. 87 (1967): 793–94.
54. Brian Roberts, Personal Journal, Fifth Antarctic Treaty Consultative Meeting, Paris, November 28, 1968 (SPRI: MS 1308/17); see also Henry Francis (NSF), Memorandum to C. Maechling, February 19, 1969 (NACP: RG 307, OAP, Central Subject Files 1961–1969), which corroborates the Simsarian-Tolstikov disagreement.
55. Foreign Office, "Fifth Antarctic Treaty Consultative Meeting," ALZ 2/13, December 10, 1968 (TNA: FCO 7/1373).
56. See the Foreign Office brief for the British delegation to the 1968 Consultative Meeting (FCO 7/1371).
57. "Antarctic Treaty: Fifth Consultative Meeting: Paris, France. November 18–29, 1968; Report of the New Zealand Delegation" [completed in April 1969] (ANZ: ABHS, 22310, PAR322/1/1 Part 6).
58. Lavigne, Scheffer, and Kellert, "The Evolution of North American Attitudes toward Marine Mammals"; and Burnett, *Sounding of the Whale*, ch. 6. For the period just after this, see Etienne Benson, "Endangered Science: The Regulation of Research by the U.S. Marine Mammal Protection and Endangered Species Acts," *Historical Studies in the Natural Sciences* 42, no. 1 (2012): 30–61.
59. US Department of State, "Statement of US Objectives Regarding Antarctica and Courses of Action during the Next Several Years," February 14, 1962 (NACP: RG 59, Central Decimal File, 1960–1963).
60. S. De Palma (Department of State), Memorandum to Acting Secretary, November 20, 1969, and Henry Kissinger (US National Security Adviser), Memorandum for Under Secretary of State, December 23, 1969 (NACP: RG 59, Central Foreign Policy Files, 1967–1969). This review was being conducted by the National Security Council because, as De Palma noted in his memorandum, it had not conducted a review since 1959.
61. US National Security Council, Under Secretaries Committee, Memorandum for the President, May 28, 1970 (DDRS-214063-i1-11). On Nixon's approach to foreign policy, see Frederik Logevall and Andrew Preston, eds., *Nixon in the World: American Foreign Relations, 1969–1977* (Oxford: Oxford University Press, 2008). On the Nixon administration's approach to international environmental issues and diplomacy, see J. Brooks Flippen, "Richard Nixon, Russell Train, and the Birth of Modern American Environmental Diplomacy," *Diplomatic History*

32, no. 4 (2008): 613–38; and Stephen Macekura, "The Limits of the Global Community: The Nixon Administration and Global Environmental Politics," *Cold War History* 11, no. 4 (2011): 489–518.

62. Brian Roberts, Letter to Henry Francis, October 6, 1970 (TNA: FCO7/1743).
63. "Report of the United States Delegation to the Sixth Consultative Meeting under the Antarctic Treaty," April 17, 1971 (NACP: RG 59, Subject Numeric Files, 1970–1973).
64. Henry Francis, "Report on Fifth Preparatory Meeting for Sixth Antarctic Treaty Consultative Meeting," c. June 1970 (NACP: RG 307, OPP, Central Subject Files, 1969–1975).
65. "Report of the Australian Delegation to the Sixth Antarctic Treaty Consultative Meeting," 1970 (NAA: A1838, 1495/3/2/18 Part 1).
66. See chapter 4.
67. Henry Francis, Letter to Brian Roberts, November 3, 1971 (TNA: FCO 7/2151).
68. The issue had been raised previously; J. L. Lavett (Australian Embassy, Washington), Memorandum to Canberra, August 14, 1970 (NAA: A1838, 1495/3/2/17 Part 3); J. N. Tønnessen and A. O. Johnsen, *The History of Modern Whaling* (London and Canberra: C. Hurst & Co. and Australia National University Press, 1982), ch. 33; and Burnett, *Sounding of the Whale*, ch. 5.
69. Brian Roberts, Letter to Henry Francis, November 19, 1971 (TNA: FCO 7/2151).
70. Henry Francis, Letter to Brian Roberts, January 5, 1972 (TNA: FCO 7/2347).
71. US Department of State, Airgram A946 to London, January 28, 1972 (TNA: FCO 7/2349).
72. Brian Roberts, Letter to Henry Francis, November 19, 1971 (TNA: FCO7/2151).
73. US Department of State, Airgram A946 to London, January 28, 1972 (TNA: FCO 7/2349).
74. Brian Roberts, Statement, February 7, 1972 (TNA: FCO 7/2350); a handwritten note by Roberts claimed: "This is what I said on this subject and was (I was told afterwards) responsible for killing the US proposals. These remarks were strongly supported by many speeches, but the subject is sure to rise again."
75. Passed on to the Foreign and Commonwealth Office: Comite nacional pro defense de la fauna y flora, Chile, Letter to P. Scott (UK WWF), January 5, 1972 (TNA: FCO 7/2348).
76. See Conference for the Conservation of Antarctic Seals working papers (ANZ: ABHS 7148 LONB 68/8 Part 1).
77. T. H. H. Richardson (FCO), Minute, February 3, 1972 (TNA: FCO 7/2349); in a letter to M. E. D. Poore of the UK Nature Conservancy, Brian Roberts gives a very detailed account of all the "conservation" and environmentalist groups he engaged with for the seals conference: April 13, 1972 (TNA: FCO 7/2351).
78. See Foreign and Commonwealth Office, "Report of the Conference on the Conservation of Antarctic Seals," Diplomatic Report No. 247/72, February 25, 1972 (TNA: FCO 7/3556).

79. The right to sign and accede to treaties is not always automatic. During the Cold War a persistent issue at treaty conferences was what form the accession article would take. If the accession article allowed all members of the United Nations to sign, it would exclude certain Communist countries (notably East Germany and the People's Republic of China), and this was unacceptable to the Soviet Union and its allies; if it took an "all states" formula, it would allow these states, and this would have been unacceptable to the United States and its allies. This began to change in 1969 with the "Vienna formula," codified in the Vienna Convention on the Law of Treaties, which broadened the potential scope of accession articles. In any case, by the end of 1972 the geopolitics of this question had changed, as the two Germanies had signed the Basic Treaty, which normalized relations between them and other states and allowed their admittance to the United Nations. The West also began to normalize its relations with the People's Republic of China, which had become a member of the United Nations in 1971.
80. Many of Roberts's colleagues and friends emphasize his contributions to CCAS. See contributions to King and Savours, *Polar Pundit.*
81. Brian Roberts, Personal Journal, Sixth Antarctic Treaty Consultative Meeting, Tokyo, October 28, 1970 (SPRI: MS 1308/18).

CHAPTER 3

1. For New Zealand: D. Gillman (London Holdings/Venture Associates, Sydney), Letter to Keith Holyoake (New Zealand Prime Minister), August 7, 1969; M. J. McNamara (New Zealand, Department of External Affairs), Note for file, August 14, 1969 (ANZ: ABHS, 950, 208/2/1 Part 1). For Australia: R. Hugh Wyndham (Department of External Affairs), Minute to F. B. Cooper, March 13, 1970 (NAA: A1838, 1495/3/2/17 Part 1). For Britain: FCO, "Mineral Prospecting in the Antarctic [Provisional United Kingdom Views]," June 16, 1970 (TNA: FCO 7/1742).
2. Neal Potter, *Natural Resource Potentials of the Antarctic* (New York: American Geographical Society, 1969); Neal Potter, "Economic Potentials of the Antarctic," *Antarctic Journal of the United States* 4, no. 3 (1969): 61–72; and Neal Potter, "The Antarctic: Any Economic Future?," *Bulletin of the Atomic Scientists* 26, no. 10 (1970): 94–99.
3. New Zealand Embassy, Tokyo, Memorandum to Wellington, May 29, 1970 (ANZ: AAEG, 6956, TKY322/1/1 Part 18).
4. Francisco Orrego Vicuña, *Antarctic Mineral Exploitation: The Emerging Legal Framework* (Cambridge, UK: Cambridge University Press, 1988); Rüdiger Wolfrum, *The Convention on the Regulation of Antarctic Mineral Resource Activities: An Attempt to Break New Ground* (Berlin: Springer-Verlag, 1991); Lorraine M. Elliot, *International Environmental Politics: Protecting the Antarctic*

(New York: St. Martin's Press, 1994), chs. 6–7; Andrew Jackson and Peter Boyce, "Mining and 'World Park Antarctica', 1982–1991," in *Australia and the Antarctic Treaty System: 50 Years of Influence*, ed. Marcus Haward and Tom Griffiths (Sydney, Australia: University of New South Wales Press, 2011), 243–73; and Emma Shortis, "'Who Can Resist This Guy?' Jacques Cousteau, Celebrity Diplomacy, and the Environmental Protection of the Antarctic," *Australian Journal of Politics and History* 61, no. 3 (2015): 366–80.

5. David J. Drewry, "Deep-sea Drilling from Glomar Challenger in the Southern Ocean: The Results and Their Geophysical and Geological Implications," *Polar Record* 18, no. 112 (1976): 47–77; and Walter Sullivan, "Russians Will Help U.S. in Drilling in Sea's Floor," *New York Times*, March 23, 1973, 1, 74.
6. "Eleventh Meeting of SCAR, Oslo: 17 to 22 August 1970," *SCAR Bulletin*, no. 37 (January 1971): 635–36.
7. Abundance being a leitmotif of polar history. See Adrian Howkins, *The Polar Regions: An Environmental History* (Cambridge, UK: Polity Press, 2016).
8. Samuel P. Hays, *Beauty, Health, and Permanence: Environmental Politics in the United States, 1955–1985* (Cambridge, UK: Cambridge University Press, 1987).
9. Matthew Connelly, "Future Shock: The End of the World as They Know It," in *The Shock of the Global: The 1970s in Perspective*, ed. Niall Ferguson et al. (Cambridge, MA: Belknap Press, 2010), 338, 344. Libby Robin et al. also emphasize how the "global" and the "future" are linked spatial and temporal concepts: Libby Robin, Sverker Sörlin, and Paul Warde, *The Future of Nature: Documents of Global Change* (New Haven, CT: Yale University Press, 2013), 6. See also Paul Warde, Libby Robin, and Sverker Sörlin, *The Environment: A History* (Baltimore, MD: Johns Hopkins University Press, 2018).
10. Timothy Mitchell, *Carbon Democracy: Political Power in the Age of Oil* (London and New York: Verso, 2011), 189, 192. Mitchell particularly emphasizes the centrality of oil and the machinery of finding, exploiting, moving, and using oil, which have constituted democracy, "the economy," "the market," and more recently, "the environment."
11. Douglas Mawson, "The Proposed Australasian Antarctic Expedition, 1911–1914," *Report of the ANZAAS Congress* 13 (1912): 398–400. See "Antarctica. Evidence of Mineral Wealth. Sir Douglas Mawson's Address," *Sydney Morning Herald*, February 1, 1935, 10; "The An[t]arctic. Mineral Wealth. Sir Douglas Mawson's Views," *Brisbane Courier*, September 26, 1928, 16. In "Antarctic Minerals. 'Rich Deposits Could be Worked Profitably.' Sir Douglas Mawson's Opinion," *Sydney Morning Herald*, July 9, 1938, 16, Mawson specifically rejected "the statement made by Mr B.R. O'Brien, a member of Admiral Byrd's second expedition to the Antarctic, that any commercial exploitation of mineral deposits in the ice area was impossible." See also Brigid Hains, *The Ice and the Inland: Mawson, Flynn, and the Myth of the Frontier* (Melbourne, Australia: Melbourne University Press, 2002).

12. "Antarctic Trip Suggested: Sir Douglas Mawson on Nation's Claims," *The Advertiser* (Adelaide), October 24, 1945, 6.
13. "Future Policy of Empire in Antarctic Regions," January 12, 1921 (NAA: A981, ANT 4 Part 1), quoted in David Day, *Antarctica: A Biography* (North Sydney, Australia: Knopf, 2012), 184.
14. "Proposed Antarctic Expedition," Record of conservation between Senator Pearce, Professor Masson, and Dr. Mawson, January 18, 1911 (NAA: A1, 1915/5159), quoted in Marie Kawaja, "The Politics and Diplomacy of the Australian Antarctic, 1901–1945" (PhD thesis, Australian National University, 2010), 64.
15. Adrian Howkins, "The Significance of the Frontier in Antarctic History: How the US West Has Shaped the Geopolitics of the Far South," *The Polar Journal* 3, no. 1 (2013): 17–18; see also Lisle A. Rose, *Explorer: The Life of Richard E. Byrd* (Columbia: University of Missouri Press, 2008), 408.
16. Rose, *Explorer*, 426. See also "Memorandum of Conversation, by the Deputy Director of the Office of European Affairs (Thompson)," May 24, 1949 in US Department of State, *Foreign Relations of the United States, 1949*, Vol. 1, National Security Affairs, Foreign Economic Policy (Washington, DC: US Government Printing Office, 1976), 799.
17. Peder Roberts, *The European Antarctic: Science and Strategy in Scandinavia and the British Empire* (New York: Palgrave Macmillan, 2011), 129.
18. See "Mineral Wealth Possibilities in Polar Region," *Sydney Morning Herald*, January 10, 1955, 1; and "We've made big find in Antarctica: There may be minerals in new range," *Argus* (Melbourne), January 10, 1955, 6. See also correspondence and documents in NAA: A1838, 1495/3/2/2 Part 2.
19. Telegrams between Phillip Law and Keith Waller, May 1954 (NAA: B1387, 1996/1089).
20. Adrian Howkins, "Science, Environment, and Sovereignty: The International Geophysical Year in the Antarctic Peninsula Region," in *Globalizing Polar Science: Reconsidering the International Polar and Geophysical Years*, ed. Roger D. Launius, James Rodger Fleming, and David H. DeVorkin (Houndmills, UK: Palgrave Macmillan, 2010), 257.
21. For example, Cabinet Decision 462, September 29, 1959 (NAA: A1838, TS1495/3/2/1/1 Part 2).
22. Rob Hall and Marie Kawaja, "Australia and the Negotiation of the Antarctic Treaty," in *Australia and the Antarctic Treaty System: 50 Years of Influence*, ed. Marcus Haward and Tom Griffiths (Sydney, Australia: University of New South Wales Press, 2011), 68–96.
23. D. F. Muirhead (British Embassy, Washington), Memorandum to H. A. A. Hankey (FO), June 26, 1959 (TNA: FO 371/138966).
24. Malcolm Templeton, *A Wise Adventure: New Zealand in Antarctica 1920–1960* (Wellington: Victoria University Press in association with the New Zealand Institute of International Affairs, 2000), 183–84.

25. New Zealand, Department of External Affairs, "Antarctic Conference—October 1959: New Zealand Brief" (ANZ: ACIE, 8798, 208/5/4/2 Part 1).
26. Duncan Stewart, "Antarctic Minerals," *Bulletin of the US Antarctic Projects Officer* 5, no. 4 (1963): 12; and Phillip Law, *Antarctica—1984: Sir John Morris Memorial Lecture* (Hobart: The Adult Education Board of Tasmania; D.E. Wilkinson, Government Printer, Tasmania, 1964).
27. "Remarks by New Zealand Representative, H.E. Mr. R. H. Wade at Informal Discussion of Antarctic Minerals Exploration and Exploitation," October 23, 1970 (ANZ: ABHS, 7148, LONB 68/8 Part 1).
28. "Report of the Australian Delegation to the Sixth Antarctic Treaty Consultative Meeting," October 19–31, 1970 (NAA: A1838, 1495/3/2/18 Part 1); and "Antarctic Treaty: Sixth Consultative Meeting Tokyo 19–31 October 1970: New Zealand Delegation Report," December 21, 1970 (ANZ: ABHS, 7148, LONB 68/8 Part 1).
29. "Report of the Australian Delegation to the Seventh Antarctic Treaty Consultative Meeting—Wellington, New Zealand—1972" (NAA: A1838, 1495/3/2/18 Part 4).
30. US Embassy, Wellington, Telegram 2227 to Washington, November 7, 1972 (NACP: RG 59, Subject Numeric Files, 1970–1973).
31. Daniel Yergin, *The Prize: The Epic Quest for Oil, Money & Power* (New York: Touchstone, 1991), 541 and ch. 27 generally.
32. David E. Nye, *Consuming Power: A Social History of American Energies* (Cambridge, MA: MIT Press, 1998), 218; Robert D. Lifset, "A New Understanding of the American Energy Crisis of the 1970s," *Historical Social Research/Historische Sozialforschung* 39, no. 4 (2014): 22–42; Elisabetta Bini, Giuliano Garavini, and Federico Romero, eds., *Oil Shock: The 1973 Crisis and Its Economic Legacy* (London and New York: I. B. Tauris, 2016); Daniel J. Sargent, *A Superpower Transformed: The Remaking of American Foreign Relations in the 1970s* (New York: Oxford University Press, 2015); and Mitchell, *Carbon Democracy*.
33. Nye, *Consuming Power*, 217.
34. Ibid., 231.
35. Ibid., 6. See also the special issue of the *Journal of American History*, "Oil in American History," 99, no. 1 (2012).
36. Robert Gramling, *Oil on the Edge: Offshore Development, Conflict, Gridlock* (Albany: State University of New York Press, 1996), ch. 5; and Tyler Priest, *The Offshore Imperative: Shell Oil's Search for Petroleum in Postwar America* (College Station: Texas A&M University Press, 2007), chs. 3 and 4.
37. Yergin, *The Prize*, 569–74; and Peter Coates, *Trans-Alaska Pipeline Controversy: Technology, Conservation, and the Frontier* (Bethlehem, PA: Lehigh University Press, 1991).
38. Gillian Staerck, ed., *The Development of North Sea Oil and Gas* (London: Institute of Contemporary British History, 2002).
39. On the reconstruction, see A. Gilbert Smith and A. Hallam, "The Fit of the Southern Continents," *Nature* 225, no. 5228 (1970): 140. The Gondwanaland

reconstruction was prominent in the USGS report: N. A. Wright and P. L. Williams, eds., *Mineral Resources of Antarctica*, Geological Survey Circular 705 (Reston, VA: US Geological Survey, 1974), 26–27. See also the front cover of the *Antarctic Journal of the United States* (May–June 1970); Lize-Marié van der Watt, "Return to Gondwanaland: South Africa, Antarctica, Minerals and Apartheid," *The Polar Journal* 3, no. 1 (2013): 75; and Tom Griffiths, *Slicing the Silence: Voyaging to Antarctica* (Sydney, Australia: University of New South Wales Press, 2007), 80–82.

40. Clyde Sanger, *Ordering the Oceans: The Making of the Law of the Sea* (Toronto: University of Toronto Press, 1987).
41. Sullivan, "Russians Will Help U.S. in Drilling in Sea's Floor." The scientific reports of this Antarctic leg of the Deep Sea Drilling Project were released in 1975: Dennis E. Hayes and Lawrence A. Frakes, "General Synthesis, Deep Sea Drilling Project Leg 28," *Initial Reports of the Deep Sea Drilling Project* 28 (1975): 919–42.
42. Brian Roberts suggested to the Argentine diplomat Roberto Guyer that Willett's report was "a reasonable reflection of what this group achieved but very far from a report of what was actually said!" July 19, 1973 (FCO 7/2548).
43. Richard Willett, "Report of the Scientific and Technical Working Group, Nansen Foundation Meeting," c. June 1973 (ANZ: ABHS, 7148, LONB 68/2 Part 7).
44. Ibid.
45. American Embassy, Brussels, Telegram 7939 to Washington, October 11, 1974 (NACP: RG 59, Central Foreign Policy Files, 1973–1979).
46. Henry Francis, Background Paper 5, "Non-scientific Uses, Economic Potentials and Commercial Development in Antarctica" (NACP: RG 307, OPP, Office Files of Henry S. Francis).
47. R. D. Yoder (Department of State), Memorandum to H. Pollack, December 13, 1972 (NACP: RG 59, Subject Numeric Files, 1970–1973).
48. Megan Black clearly demonstrates the global reach and pretentions of the Department of the Interior: Megan Black, "Interior's Exterior: The State, Mining Companies, and Resource Ideologies in the Point Four Program," *Diplomatic History* 40, no. 1 (2016): 81–110.
49. "Position paper," undated, c. January 1973 (NACP: RG 307, OPP, Central Subject Files, 1969–1975).
50. Some of the details of the review made it into the press at this time, including the *Wall Street Journal*. This caused the Department of State to send instructions to American embassies in the treaty party countries to temper any wild assumptions. See US Department of State, Telegram to Brussels, Buenos Aires, Canberra, London, Moscow, Oslo, Paris, Pretoria, Santiago, Tokyo and Wellington, April 24, 1974 (NACP: RG 59, Central Foreign Policy Files, 1973–1977).
51. "Memorandum NSC–U/DM–109B from the Chairman of the National Security Council Under Secretaries Committee (Rush) to President Nixon," May 14, 1974, in US Department of State, *Foreign Relations of the United States*,

1969–1976, Vol. E-3, Documents on Global Issues, 1973–1976 (Washington, DC: US Government Printing Office, 2009), document 12, http://history.state.gov/historicaldocuments/frus1969-76ve03/d12.

52. "Guidelines for Consultations on Antarctic Mineral Resources," October 4, 1974, in US Department of State, *Foreign Relations of the United States, 1969–1976*, Vol. E-3, Documents on Global Issues, 1973–1976 (Washington, DC: US Government Printing Office, 2009), document 56, http://history.state.gov/historicaldocuments/frus1969-76ve03/d56.
53. Wright and Williams, *Mineral Resources of Antarctica*, 1.
54. Dixy Lee Ray, Memorandum to Deputy Secretary of State, May 23, 1975 (Hoover Institution Archives: Dixy Lee Ray Papers, Box 93).
55. Brian Roberts, draft diary fragment, June 20, 1975 (SPRI: MS 1308/45).
56. Deborah Shapley, "Antarctica's Future: Will Oslo Talks on Resources Mean That Scientists Have to Move Over?," *Science* 187, no. 4179 (1975): 820.
57. New Zealand Embassy, The Hague, Telegram 62 to Wellington, February 27, 1975 (ANZ: ABHS, 950, 208/44/1 Part 1).
58. US Department of State, Telegram 40169 to Buenos Aires, London, Santiago, New York, March 4, 1975 (NACP: RG 59, Central Foreign Policy Files, 1973–1979).
59. New Zealand High Commission, London, Telegram 3882 to Wellington, June 23, 1975 (ANZ: ABHS, 7148, LONB 68/2 Part 7).
60. New Zealand High Commission, London, Telegram 3882 to Wellington, June 23, 1975 (ANZ: ABHS, 7148, LONB 68/2 Part 7). See also US Embassy, Oslo, Telegram 2597 to Washington, June 23, 1975 (NACP: RG 59, Central Foreign Policy Files, 1973–1979).
61. New Zealand High Commission, London, Telegram 3882 to Wellington, June 23, 1975 (ANZ: ABHS, 7148, LONB 68/2 Part 7).
62. Recommendation VIII-14.
63. Tore Gjelsvik, Letter to Gordon Robin, October 31, 1975 (SCAR Secretariat).
64. Tore Gjelsvik, Letter to Martin Holdgate, October 31, 1975 (SCAR Secretariat).
65. M. W. Holdgate, *Penguins and Mandarins: Memories of Natural and Unnatural History* (Whitworth Hall, Spennymoor, UK: The Memoir Club, 2003); David J. Drewry, "Gordon De Quetteville Robin," *Polar Record* 39, no. 208 (2003): 61–78; and David W. H. Walton, Peter D. Clarkson, and Colin P. Summerhayes, *Science in the Snow: Fifty Years of International Collaboration through the Scientific Committee on Antarctic Research* (Cambridge, UK: Scientific Committee on Antarctic Research, 2011).
66. "Antarctic Resources—Effects of Mineral Exploration: Initial Response by SCAR, Dated May 1976, to Antarctic Treaty Recommendation VIII-14," *SCAR Bulletin*, no. 57 (September 1977): 630.
67. Ibid., 634.
68. Ibid., 630–31.

69. Uwe Radok, Letter to George Hemmen (SCAR), October 29, 1975 (SCAR Secretariat).
70. Ibid.
71. Gordon Robin, Comments on Martin Holdgate paper (of July 25, 1975), October 3, 1975 (SCAR Secretariat).
72. James Zumberge (US Committee on Polar Research), Letter to George Hemmen (SCAR), March 30, 1976 (SCAR Secretariat).
73. Ian McLeod (SCAR Working Group on Geology), Letter to George Hemmen (SCAR), December 31, 1975 (SCAR Secretariat).
74. By "region" and "regional" here I mean "the Antarctic"—not simply the continent, but also including the seas up to the Antarctic Convergence. Alessandro Antonello, "Finding Place in Antarctica," in *Antarctica and the Humanities*, ed. Peder Roberts, Lize-Marié van der Watt, and Adrian Howkins (Houndmills, UK: Palgrave Macmillan, 2016), 185–89.
75. See "Report of the Australian Delegation to the Special Preparatory Meeting of Antarctic Treaty Consultative Parties on the Exploration and Exploitation of the Mineral Resources of Antarctica, Paris, 28 June—10 July 1976" (NAA: B1387, 1996/866 Part 3).
76. "Report of the Working Group Considering the Scientific, Ecological, Technical and Economic Aspects of Exploration and Exploitation of the Mineral Resources of Antarctic," Special Preparatory Meeting, Paris, July 1976 (NAA: B1387, 1996/866 Part 3).
77. For a short biography of Heap, see G. Hattersley-Smith, "Heap, John Arnfield (1932–2006)," in *Oxford Dictionary of National Biography* (Oxford: Oxford University Press, 2010), online edition, January 2011, http://www.oxforddnb.com/view/article/97078.
78. John Heap, Report, "Special Preparatory Meeting Held in Paris . . . ," August 13, 1976 (TNA: FCO 76/1321); and John Heap, Minute to H. M. Carless and M. F. Young, August 13, 1976 (TNA: FCO 76/1321).
79. "Fourteenth Meeting of SCAR, Mendoza: 18 to 23 October 1976," *SCAR Bulletin*, no. 56 (May 1977): 531–53.
80. Scientific Committee on Antarctic Research, Group of Specialists on the Environmental Impact Assessment of Mineral Exploration/Exploitation in Antarctica, "A Preliminary Assessment of the Environmental Impact of Mineral Exploration/Exploitation in Antarctica," August 1977, 4 (copy available at TNA: FCO 76/1682).
81. Ibid., 53.
82. Matthew J. Lindstrom and Zachary A. Smith, *The National Environmental Policy Act: Judicial Misconstruction, Legislative Indifference, and Executive Neglect* (College Station: Texas A&M University Press, 2001), 66 and ch. 5 more generally.
83. Ibid., ch. 3.
84. Hays, *Beauty, Health, and Permanence*, 279–81.

85. Stephen J. Macekura, *Of Limits and Growth: The Rise of Global Sustainable Development in the Twentieth Century* (New York: Cambridge University Press, 2015), 180–94. The history of environmental impact assessment has not been extensively investigated. Though EIAs appear as pieces of evidence or important milestones in environmental histories, they have rarely been considered as a type of action or a category demanding historical analysis. For a general consideration, see Richard N. L. Andrews, *Managing the Environment, Managing Ourselves: A History of American Environmental Policy*, 2nd ed. (New Haven, CT: Yale University Press, 2006). Stephen Bocking has published a significant case study, trying to understand how EIAs affected ecosystem science at the US Atomic Energy Agency in the early 1970s: Stephen Bocking, "Ecosystems, Ecologists, and the Atom: Environmental Research at Oak Ridge National Laboratory," *Journal of the History of Biology* 28, no. 1 (1995): 32–35. On the place of environmental review in an international development context—including both the United States Agency for International Development and the World Bank—see Macekura, *Of Limits and Growth*, ch. 5.
86. R. E. Munn and SCOPE Workshop on Impact Studies in the Environment, eds., *Environmental Impact Assessment: Principles and Procedures* (Toronto: Scientific Committee on Problems of the Environment (SCOPE), 1975), 12. By 1979 this definition had changed subtly but importantly, foregrounding effects on ecosystems equally with human impacts: "An *environmental impact assessment* is an activity designed to identify and predict the impact of an action on the biogeophysical environment and on man's health and well-being, and to interpret and communicate information about the impacts." R. E. Munn, ed., *Environmental Impact Assessment: Principles and Procedures*, 2nd ed. (Chichester, UK: Scientific Committee on Problems of the Environment (SCOPE) and John Wiley & Sons, 1979), xvi.
87. "Report of the Australian Delegation to the Special Preparatory Meeting of Antarctic Treaty Consultative Parties on the Exploration and Exploitation of the Mineral Resources of Antarctica, Paris, 28 June–10 July 1976" (NAA: B1387, 1996/866 Part 3).
88. The overlapping two were Pedro Lesta of Argentina and Dirk C. Neethling of South Africa. A full list of the members of EAMREA can be found at Scientific Committee on Antarctic Research, Group of Specialists on the Environmental Impact Assessment of Mineral Exploration/Exploitation in Antarctica, "A Preliminary Assessment of the Environmental Impact of Mineral Exploration/Exploitation in Antarctica," August 1977; a full list of members of the 1977 Consultative Meeting's group of experts can be found at "Report of the Ninth Consultative Meeting, London, 19 September–7 October 1977" (London: Foreign and Commonwealth Office, 1977), 73.
89. "Report of the Ninth Consultative Meeting, London," 56–73.
90. Tore Gjelsvik, Letter to John Heap, January 6, 1978 (SCAR Secretariat).

91. John Heap, Letter to Tore Gjelsvik, February 2, 1978 (SCAR Secretariat).
92. Ibid.

CHAPTER 4

1. Recommendation IX-2, para 3(c).
2. Transcribed from "English, Monday 27/2/1978—Thursday AM, 2/3/1978: Interpreter Floor Tapes Used for the Consultative Meeting on Antarctica, Canberra" (NAA: A10734, 2).
3. Ibid.
4. Richard M. Laws, *Large Animals and Wide Horizons: Adventures of a Biologist; The Autobiography of Richard M. Laws*, 3 vols. (Cambridge, UK: Scott Polar Research Institute, 2012); and Jeff Schauer, "The Elephant Problem: Science, Bureaucracy, and Kenya's National Parks, 1955 to 1975," *African Studies Review* 58, no. 1 (2015): 184–91.
5. Transcribed from "English, Monday 27/2/1978–Thursday AM, 2/3/1978: Interpreter Floor Tapes Used for the Consultative Meeting on Antarctica, Canberra" (NAA: A10734, 2).
6. Ibid.
7. Carmel Finley, *All the Fish in the Sea: Maximum Sustainable Yield and the Failure of Fisheries Management* (Chicago: University of Chicago Press, 2011).
8. An early and standard account of the CCAMLR negotiations is James N. Barnes, "The Emerging Convention on the Conservation of Antarctic Marine Living Resources: An Attempt to Meet the New Realities of Resource Exploitation in the Southern Ocean," in *The New Nationalism and the Use of Common Spaces: Issues in Marine Pollution and the Exploitation of Antarctica*, ed. Jonathan I. Charney (Totowa, NJ: Allanheld, Osmun Publishers, 1982), 239–86. Another early legal and political interpretation is David M. Edwards and John A. Heap, "Convention on the Conservation of Antarctic Marine Living Resources: A Commentary," *Polar Record* 20, no. 127 (1981): 353–62.
9. Dean Bavington makes a similar point in his historical study of the Newfoundland cod fishery. In that case, he suggests that making the ecosystem a considerable factor in fisheries management shifted the emphasis from "manageable wild cod" to "manageable human beings and their relations with marine ecosystems"; as the fish become too complex and difficult to manage, the fishing people are simplified and therefore seen as easy to manage. Dean Bavington, *Managed Annihilation: An Unnatural History of the Newfoundland Cod Collapse* (Vancouver: University of British Columbia Press, 2010), chs. 4 and 5.
10. R. N. Burukovskiy, ed., *Soviet Fishery Research on the Antarctic Krill* (Washington, DC: Joint Publications Research Service, 1967); and R. R. Makarov, A. G. Naumov, and V. V. Shevtsov, "The Biology and the Distribution of the Antarctic Krill," in

Antarctic Ecology, ed. M. W. Holdgate (London and New York: Academic Press, 1970), 176.

11. Paul R. Josephson, *Industrialized Nature: Brute Force Technology and the Transformation of the Natural World* (Washington, DC: Island Press, 2002), 200–201.
12. James Marr, "The Natural History and Geography of the Antarctic Krill (*Euphausia Superba* Dana)," *Discovery Reports* 32 (1962): 33–464; and John Mauchline and Leonard R. Fisher, *The Biology of Euphausiids*, Advances in Marine Biology (London: Academic Press, 1969).
13. F. D. Ommanney, quoted in Marr, "The Natural History and Geography of the Antarctic Krill," 156; and David G. Campbell, *The Crystal Desert: Summers in Antarctica* (London: Minerva, [1992] 1993), ch. 5.
14. "One short link" is Campbell's phrase in *The Crystal Desert*, 97.
15. Marr, "The Natural History and Geography of the Antarctic Krill," 37; Alister Hardy, *Great Waters: A Voyage of Natural History to Study Whales, Plankton and the Waters of the Southern Ocean in the Old Royal Research Ship* Discovery *with the Results Brought up to Date by the Findings of the R.R.S.* Discovery II (London: Collins, 1967); N. A. Mackintosh, "The Work of the *Discovery* Committee," *Proceedings of the Royal Society B* 137, no. 887 (1950); D. Graham Burnett, *The Sounding of the Whale: Science and Cetaceans in the Twentieth Century* (Chicago: University of Chicago Press, 2012), ch. 2; and Peder Roberts, *The European Antarctic: Science and Strategy in Scandinavia and the British Empire* (New York: Palgrave Macmillan, 2011), ch. 1.
16. Burnett, *Sounding of the Whale*, 423–25.
17. Marr, "The Natural History and Geography of the Antarctic Krill." Marr had an interesting Antarctic history, for he was one of the two scouts who took part in Shackleton's Quest expedition of 1921–1922 (the expedition Shackelton died on), and he was also the leader of the British wartime operation Tabarin to secure British title to the Falkland Islands Dependencies.
18. Alister Hardy, "Oceans in 1984: New and Richer Marine Harvests Forecast," *New Scientist*, February 20, 1964, 483; and Alister Hardy, "The Krill—an Ocean Harvest of the Future?," *New Scientist*, July 1, 1965, 482–83.
19. Kenneth J. Carpenter, *Protein and Energy: A Study of Changing Ideas in Nutrition* (Cambridge, UK: Cambridge University Press, 1994), 161–68.
20. Alister Hardy, Letter to David Martin (Royal Society), October 12, 1965 (Royal Society: BNC Collection Roll 239).
21. Jacob Darwin Hamblin, *Oceanographers and the Cold War: Disciples of Marine Science* (Seattle: University of Washington Press, 2005), ch. 6.
22. Burukovskiy, *Soviet Fishery Research on the Antarctic Krill*.
23. A. T. Waterman, Letter to H. Brown, March 18, 1965 (NACP: RG 307, OAP, Central Subject Files, 1961–1969).

24. Vivian Fuchs (BAS), Letter to H. A. Cole (Fisheries Laboratory, Lowestoft), November 15, 1966 (BAS: AD3/1/AS/103/1(3)); so well-known were the Soviet fisheries interests that Sir Vivian's correspondent, H. A. Cole of the Lowestoft Fisheries Laboratory (Britain's principal fisheries research laboratory), proved to have very good information on the matter: Cole, Letter to Vivian Fuchs, November 16, 1966 (BAS: AD3/1/AS/103/1(3)).
25. *SCAR/SCOR/IAPO/IUBS Symposium on Antarctic Oceanography, Santiago, Chile, 13–16 September 1966*. (Cambridge, UK: [Scott Polar Research Institute], 1966).
26. Various Soviet contributions to M. W. Holdgate, ed., *Antarctic Ecology*, vol. 1 (London and New York: Academic Press, 1970); and Angela Croome, "Where Nations Do Co-Operate," *The Illustrated London News*, August 31, 1968, 15–17.
27. Brian Roberts, Minute to Atkinson, Anderson, Masefield, August 10, 1968 (TNA: FCO 7/1017); and Knowles Kerry, personal communication with author, January 2011.
28. Henry Francis (NSF), Memorandum to Louis Quam, November 10, 1970 (NACP: RG 307, OPP, Central Subject Files, 1969–1975); on information from overseas posts, see, for example, American Embassy, Mauritius, Airgram to Washington, April 26, 1969 (NACP: RG 59, Subject Numeric Files, 1970–1973).
29. See appendices to Charles Swithinbank (BAS), Letter to Richard Laws, November 22, 1971, and A. S. Ferguson (Base Commander, South Georgia), Report, April 1, 1973 (BAS: AD3/1/AS/107/5(1)).
30. Charles Swithinbank, Letter to Richard Laws, November 22, 1971 (BAS: AD3/1/AS/107/5(1)).
31. Brian Roberts, Minute to C. S. Rycroft, June 21, 1972 (BAS: AD3/1/AS/107/5(1)).
32. Ray Adie (BAS), Letter to Vivian Fuchs, May 26, 1970 (BAS: AD3/1/AS/107/5(1)).
33. G. J. Grantham, *The Utilization of Krill*, Southern Ocean Fisheries Survey Programme, GLO/SO/77/3 (Rome: Food and Agriculture Organization, 1977) is an exhaustive contemporaneous study of the uses of krill.
34. A. Banks (British Ministry of Agriculture, Fisheries and Food), Letter to T. M. Boyd (Boyd Line Ltd.), August 24, 1973 (BAS: AD3/1/AS/107/5(1)).
35. Josephson, *Industrialized Nature*, 226–27.
36. "Gift of the Ocean," *Evening Moscow*, August 12, 1978, advertising supp., sent by New Zealand Embassy, Moscow, Memorandum to Wellington, August 14, 1978 (ANZ: ABHS, 950, 208/1/10/1 Part 5).
37. D. K. Haskell (British Embassy, Santiago), Letter to John Heap, May 30, 1977; John Heap requested samples for the Polar Regions Section, Letter to D. K. Haskell, June 14, 1977; and finally, D. K. Haskell, Letter to John Heap, June 23, 1977 (TNA: FCO 7/3438).
38. New Zealand Embassy, Tokyo, Memorandum to Wellington, November 26, 1976 (ANZ: ABHS, 950, 208/1/10/1 Part 1).
39. Ibid.

40. For a discussion of subsidies, see New Zealand Embassy, Tokyo, Memorandum to Wellington, September 1, 1978 (ANZ: AATJ, 7428, 11/1/9 Part 1).
41. New Zealand Embassy, Tokyo, Memorandum to Wellington, December 9, 1976 (ANZ: ABHS, 950, 208/1/10/1 Part 1).
42. G. C. Eddie, *The Harvesting of Krill*, Southern Ocean Fisheries Survey Programme, GLO/SO/77/2 (Rome: Food and Agriculture Organization, 1977) outlines the environmental and technical issues associated with fishing in the Antarctic.
43. New Zealand Embassy, Tokyo, Memorandum to Wellington, December 9, 1976 (ANZ: ABHS, 950, 208/1/10/1 Part 1).
44. D. H. Cushing, *The Provident Sea* (Cambridge, UK: Cambridge University Press, 1988), ch. 13.
45. New Zealand Embassy, Tokyo, Memorandum to Wellington, November 18, 1977 (ANZ: ABHS, 950, 208/1/10/1 Part 2); a translated articled appended to this memorandum specifically noted the implications of "the era of 200 mile zones"; *Suisan Keizai Shimbun*, October 31, 1977.
46. Donald Worster, *Nature's Economy: A History of Ecological Ideas*, 2nd ed. (Cambridge, UK: Cambridge University Press, 1994); Frank Benjamin Golley, *A History of the Ecosystem Concept in Ecology: More Than the Sum of the Parts* (New Haven, CT: Yale University Press, 1993), 62–69; and Stephen Bocking, *Ecologists and Environmental Politics: A History of Contemporary Ecology* (New Haven, CT: Yale University Press, 1997).
47. Bocking, *Ecologists and Environmental Politics*, part 2; Chunglin Kwa, "Representations of Nature Mediating between Ecology and Science Policy: The Case of the International Biological Programme," *Social Studies of Science* 17, no. 3 (1987): 413–42; and Chunglin Kwa, "Modeling the Grasslands," *Historical Studies in the Physical and Biological Sciences* 24, no. 1 (1993): 125–55.
48. Chunglin Kwa, in "Representations of Nature," has investigated how metaphors and representations of nature were used in the context of the International Biological Program in the United States.
49. Commission on Marine Science, Engineering and Resources, *Our Nation and the Sea: A Plan for National Action* (Washington, DC: US Government Printing Office, 1969); and Edward Wenk Jr., *The Politics of the Ocean* (Seattle and London: University of Washington Press, 1972).
50. On the first four years, see K. G. Sandved, "USNS *Eltanin*: Four Years of Research," *Antarctic Journal of the United States* 1, no. 4 (1966): 164–74; Sayed Z. El-Sayed, "Biological Oceanography," *Antarctic Journal of the United States* 8, no. 3 (1973); and G. E. Fogg, *A History of Antarctic Science* (Cambridge, UK: Cambridge University Press, 1992), 214–17.
51. Sayed Z. El-Sayed, "Understanding the Antarctic Marine Ecosystem: A Prerequisite for Its Conservation," in *Proceedings of the Colloquium on Conservation Problems in Antarctica*, ed. Bruce C. Parker (Blacksburg, VA: Virginia Polytechnic Institute & State University, 1972), 136.

52. George Llano (OPP), Memorandum to Head, December 4, 1972 (NACP: RG 307, OPP, Records of the Head, Reading File, 1969–1975).
53. Sayed El-Sayed, Letter to Robert Rutford (DPP), December 17, 1976 (NACP: RG 307, NSF DPP Central Subject Files, 1976–1987).
54. Ibid.
55. Sayed El-Sayed, Letter to A. N. Fowler (NSF), March 5, 1975 (TNA: FCO 55/1335).
56. "Krill Position Paper" (NACP: RG 307, DPP, Records of the Program Manager for Biology and Medicine, Records Relating to the Polar Research Program, 1974–1977). When I say "featured all the hallmarks of thinking by El-Sayed and Green," I also want to suggest that they either wrote the first draft of this document or were closely involved in its early drafting. I offer one piece of evidence as suggesting this: the paper on which the first draft is typed has Texas A&M watermarks.
57. Katherine A. Green, "Simulation of the Pelagic Ecosystem of the Ross Sea, Antarctica: A Time Varying Compartmental Model" (PhD diss., Texas A&M University, 1975).
58. Katherine A. Green, "Conservation of Renewable Southern Ocean Resources: An Argument for an Ecosystem Approach," c. March 1977 (NACP: RG 307, DPP, Records of the Program Manager for Biology and Medicine, Records Relating to the Polar Research Program, 1974–1977); and Katherine A. Green, "Role of Krill in the Antarctic Marine Ecosystem," Final Report to the Department of State, Division of Ocean Affairs, Contract 1722-720248, December 1977 (ASOC).
59. US Department of State, "Final Environmental Impact Statement on the Negotiation of a Regime for Conservation of Antarctic Marine Living Resources" (1978).
60. Mary Alice McWhinnie, Letter to Robert Rutford (DPP), December 22, 1976 (NACP: RG 307, NSF DPP Central Subject Files, 1976–1987).
61. Ibid.
62. For information on the CEQ's creation, see the biography of its first chair: J. Brooks Flippen, *Conservative Conservationist: Russel E. Train and the Emergence of American Environmentalism* (Baton Rouge: Louisiana State University Press, 2006), especially ch. 5.
63. Lee Talbot (CEQ), Memorandum to S. Burton (Department of State), January 13, 1975 (NACP: RG 580, CEQ International Affairs Subject Files, 1970–1976).
64. Lee Talbot (CEQ), Memorandum for Bennsky, Gutting, Mandros, Bertrand, Bente, July 2, 1976 (NACP: RG 580, CEQ International Affairs Subject Files, 1970–1976).
65. Lee Talbot (CEQ), Letter to Patsy Mink (Department of State), August 23, 1977 (NACP: RG 580, CEQ Chairman's Subject Files, 1970–1981).
66. Martin Holdgate, Interview by John Heap, October 14, 2000 (SPRI Oral History Collection). Holdgate had known Talbot since the mid-1960s, along with other

prominent conservation scientists. Notably, John Heap corrected Holdgate in this oral history interview, stating that it was Richard Laws who brought the ecosystem approach into CCAMLR.

67. G. Carleton Ray and Frank M. Potter Jr., "The Making of the Marine Mammal Protection Act of 1972," *Aquatic Mammals* 37, no. 4 (2011): 522–53; Robert J. Hofman, "The Continuing Legacies of the Marine Mammal Commission and Its Committee of Scientific Advisors on Marine Mammals," *Aquatic Mammals* 35, no. 1 (2009): 94–129; and Etienne Benson, "Endangered Science: The Regulation of Research by the U.S. Marine Mammal Protection and Endangered Species Acts," *Historical Studies in the Natural Sciences* 42, no. 1 (2012): 30–61.
68. "United States: Marine Mammal Protection Act," *International Legal Materials* 12, no. 1 (1973): 164–81.
69. Hofman, "The Continuing Legacies of the Marine Mammal Commission," 94.
70. Katherine A. Green, *Antarctic Marine Ecosystem Modeling Revised Ross Sea Model, General Southern Ocean Budget, and Seal Model (MMC-76/03)* (Washington, DC: Marine Mammal Commission, 1977).
71. Finley, *All the Fish in the Sea*; and Helen M. Rozwadowski, *The Sea Knows No Boundaries: A Century of Marine Science under ICES* (Copenhagen, Seattle, and London: International Council for the Exploration of the Sea in association with University of Washington Press, 2002).
72. David C. Coleman, David M. Swift, and John E. Mitchell, "From the Frontier to the Biosphere: A Brief History of the USIBP Grasslands Biome Program and Its Impact on Scientific Research in North America," *Rangelands* 26, no. 4 (2004): 8–15.
73. Sidney J. Holt and Lee M. Talbot, "New Principles for the Conservation of Wild Living Resources," *Wildlife Monographs*, no. 59 (1978): 7.
74. Ibid., 14–15.
75. "English, Finish 10:00pm, Saturday 11/3/1978: Interpreter Floor Tapes Used for the Consultative Meeting on Antarctica, Canberra" (NAA: A10734, 5).
76. For example, the emphatic statements on the ecosystem in "Memorandum from the Director of the Office of Ocean Affairs (Busby) to the Deputy Assistant Secretary for Oceans and International and Scientific Affairs (Irving)," September 30, 1976, in US Department of State, *Foreign Relations of the United States, 1969–1976*, Vol. E-3, Documents on Global Issues, 1973–1976 (Washington, DC: US Government Printing Office, 2009), document 69, http://history.state.gov/historicaldocuments/frus1969-76ve03/d69.
77. "US Policy on Antarctic Resource Issues," a study by the Antarctic Policy Group for the National Security Council, August 25, 1977 (DDRS-268091-i1-26).
78. Ibid.
79. United States, Position Paper for International Coordination Group on the Southern Ocean, Intergovernmental Oceanographic Commission, First Session, Brussels, November 23–26, 1970 (NACP: RG 307, DPP, Central Subject Files,

1969–1975); see also SCAR Circular to Members of the SCAR Working Group on Biology, July 31, 1967 (SCAR Secretariat).

80. "SCAR Working Group on Oceanography: Tokyo, 22 September 1970," *SCAR Bulletin*, no. 39 (September 1971): 985–86.
81. "SCAR Executive Meeting: Moscow, 2–5 August, 1971," *SCAR Bulletin*, no. 40 (January 1972): 185.
82. Hamblin, *Oceanographers and the Cold War*, 178–80.
83. At a point unknown and unrecorded, this became the Subcommittee on Marine Living Resources.
84. "Twelfth Meeting of SCAR, Canberra: 14 to 19 August 1972," *SCAR Bulletin*, no. 43 (January 1973): 635.
85. "Thirteenth Meeting of SCAR, Jackson Hole: 3 to 7 September 1974," *SCAR Bulletin*, no. 49 (January 1975): 440–41.
86. "Report of the SCAR Executive Meeting, Cambridge: 25–26 June 1971," *SCAR Bulletin*, no. 51 (September 1975): 714.
87. Ibid.
88. George Hemmen, Letter to Richard Laws (BAS), May 30, 1975 (SCAR Secretariat); Hemmen wrote similarly to Tore Gjelsvik on June 11, 1975 (SCAR Secretariat).
89. Scientific Committee on Antarctic Research et al., *Biological Investigations of Marine Antarctic Systems and Stocks (BIOMASS)*, vol. 1, *Research Proposals* (Cambridge, UK: Scientific Committee on Antarctic Research and Scientific Committee on Oceanic Research, 1977); and "SCAR/SCOR Group on the Living Resources of the Southern Ocean (SCOR Working Group 54): Report of a meeting held at Woods Hold, USA, 23–24 August 1976," *SCAR Bulletin*, no. 55 (January 1977): 419–26.
90. "Fourteenth Meeting of SCAR, Mendoza: 18 to 23 October 1976," *SCAR Bulletin*, no. 56 (May 1977): 535.
91. "Report of the SCAR Executive Meeting, Cambridge, UK, 6–7 July 1977," *SCAR Bulletin*, no. 58 (January 1978): 98.
92. Simone Turchetti et al. have suggested that there was a decline in international scientific collaboration in Antarctica in the 1970s, owing especially to changes in US Antarctic policy that worked against such collaboration. They overlook BIOMASS (perhaps because of their focus on the geophysical sciences) and therefore also overlook the leading role of US scientists and government institutions in it. Simone Turchetti et al., "On Thick Ice: Scientific Internationalism and Antarctic Affairs, 1957–1980," *History and Technology* 24, no. 4 (2008): 365–67.
93. Scientific Committee on Antarctic Research et al., *Biological Investigations of Marine Antarctic Systems and Stocks*, 1:5.
94. Ibid.

95. Sayed El-Sayed, Letter to Richard Laws and Don Siniff (University of Minnesota), May 16, 1975 (SCAR Secretariat).
96. George Llano, Memorandum, September 17, 1976 (NACP: RG 307, DPP, Records of the Program Manager for Biology and Medicine, Memorandums, 1976).
97. Llano noted that Gulland tried to insert material into the Woods Hole meeting report that had not been agreed to; George Llano, Memorandum, September 17, 1976 (NACP: RG 307, DPP, Records of the Program Manager for Biology and Medicine, Memorandums, 1976).
98. Louis DeGoes (NAS), Letter to George Knox (University of Canterbury, New Zealand), August 11, 1978 (SCAR Secretariat); the SCAR-FAO tensions seemed real, and drawing on Llano's interpretation of the Woods Hole meeting, control of BIOMASS planning and intellectual direction would have had consequential effects on thinking about the Southern Ocean's resources. Hemmen seemed equally disturbed by the prospect of FAO leadership of BIOMASS in Letter to DeGoes, September 12, 1978 (SCAR Secretariat) and Letter to Basil Parrish (Department of Agriculture and Fisheries for Scotland), January 5, 1978 (BAS: 243/244/01 Vol. 1), in which he had more to say about Mario Ruivo and FAO jockeying—though Hemmen distinguished Gulland from other FAO officials.
99. John Gulland, Letter to Sayed El-Sayed, September 6, 1977 (BAS: 243/244/01 Vol. 1).
100. Mary Alice McWhinnie, Letter to Robert Rutford (DPP), November 23, 1976 (NACP: RG 307, NSF DPP Central Subject Files, 1976–1987).
101. Ibid.
102. George Llano (DPP), Memorandum, September 17, 1976 (NACP: RG 307, DPP, Records of the Program Manager for Biology and Medicine, Memorandums, 1976).
103. C. P. Scott (British Embassy, Oslo), Dispatch to Secretary of State for Foreign and Commonwealth Affairs, August 8, 1975 (TNA: FCO 7/2993).
104. See the senior Australian official, J. P. Lonergan's, notes on the Eighth Antarctic Treaty Consultative Meeting (NAA: B1387, 1991/688 Part 1).
105. Andrew Darby, *Harpoon: Into the Heart of Whaling* (Crows Nest, Australia: Allen & Unwin, 2007), 104; and Frank Zelko, *Make It a Green Peace! The Rise of Countercultural Environmentalism* (New York: Oxford University Press, 2013), ch. 9.
106. "Our Men in Oslo Fighting to Save the Krill," *The Evening Post* (Wellington), June 12, 1975 (ANZ: AATJ, 7428, 11/1/9 Part 1).
107. "Memorandum from the President's Assistant for National Security Affairs (Kissinger) to President Ford, Washington," March 14, 1975, in US Department of State, *Foreign Relations of the United States, 1969–1976*, Vol. E-3, Documents on Global Issues, 1973–1976 (Washington, DC: US Government Printing

Office, 2009), document 17, http://history.state.gov/historicaldocuments/frus1969-76ve03/d17.

108. *Report of the Ninth Consultative Meeting, London, 19 September—7 October 1977* (London: Foreign and Commonwealth Office, 1977), recommendation IX-2, 13–16.

109. John Heap, Letter to H. J. S. Pearce (British Embassy, Buenos Aires), January 9, 1978 (NAA: A1838, 1743/1/4 Part 2).

110. See, for example, J. A. Heap (FCO), Letter to G. C. Eddie, July 29, 1976 (BAS: 243/189/01); and American Embassy, London, Cable 4067 to Washington, March 10 1977 (NACP: RG 59, Central Foreign Policy Files, 1973–1979).

111. On the history of Soviet conservation and environmental protection, see Douglas R. Weiner, *Models of Nature: Ecology, Conservation, and Cultural Revolution in Soviet Russia* (Bloomington: Indiana University Press, 1988); and Douglas R. Weiner, *A Little Corner of Freedom: Russian Nature Protection from Stalin to Gorbachëv* (Berkeley: University of California Press, 1999).

112. Transcribed from "English, Monday 27/2/1978—Thursday AM, 2/3/1978: Interpreter Floor Tapes Used for the Consultative Meeting on Antarctica, Canberra" (NAA: A10734, 2).

113. Transcribed from "English, Thursday, 3:00pm, 2/3/1978–Thursday 4:30pm, 9/3/1978: Interpreter Floor Tapes Used for the Consultative Meeting on Antarctica, Canberra" (NAA: A10734, 4).

114. Transcribed from "English, Monday 27/2/1978—Thursday AM, 2/3/1978: Interpreter Floor Tapes Used for the Consultative Meeting on Antarctica, Canberra" (NAA: A10734, 2).

115. Finley, *All the Fish in the Sea*, ch. 7.

116. Ibid., 127. Graham Burnett also shows how the Chilean foreign minister articulated similar concepts at this meeting in *Sounding of the Whale*, 415–16.

117. D. G. Holborow (New Zealand Embassy, Santiago), Memorandum to Wellington, August 2, 1978 (ANZ: ABHS, 950, 208/1/10/1 Part 5).

118. Richard Laws, Letter to John Heap, April 11, 1979 (BAS: AD3/2/136/66/01).

119. Merwyn Norrish (New Zealand Embassy, Washington), Memorandum to Wellington, July 31, 1978 (ANZ: ABHS, 950, 208/1/10/1 Part 4).

120. Martin Holdgate also found it problematic; Letter to J. Ayres, April 15, 1980 (TNA: FCO7/3837). See also Richard Laws, "Difficulties and Ambiguities in the Wording of Article II," March 27, 1980 (TNA: FCO 7/3836); and the report and recommendations of the Southern Ocean Convention Workshop on Management of Antarctic Marine Living Organisms, held in Washington, DC, March 31–April 2, 1980, under the auspices of the Center for Law and Social Policy (James Barnes's organization), the Oceanic Society, IUCN, the Center for Environmental Education–the Whale Protection Fund, and the Carnegie Endowment for International Peace.

121. James C. Scott, *Seeing Like a State: How Certain Schemes to Improve the Human Condition Have Failed* (New Haven, CT: Yale University Press, 1998), 2–5.

CHAPTER 5

1. Charles S. Maier, *Once within Borders: Territories of Power, Wealth, and Belonging since 1500* (Cambridge, MA: The Belknap Press, 2016). A legally focused introduction to boundaries can be found in J. R. V. Prescott and Gillian D. Triggs, *International Frontiers and Boundaries: Law, Politics and Geography* (Leiden: Martinus Nijhoff, 2008), ch. 3.
2. Thomas F. Gieryn, "Boundaries of Science," in *Handbook of Science and Technology Studies*, ed. Sheila Jasanoff et al. (Thousand Oaks, CA: Sage, 1995), 393–443; and Thomas F. Gieryn, *Cultural Boundaries of Science: Credibility on the Line* (Chicago: University of Chicago Press, 1999).
3. Clyde Sanger, *Ordering the Oceans: The Making of the Law of the Sea* (Toronto: University of Toronto Press, 1987).
4. Niall Ferguson et al., eds., *The Shock of the Global: The 1970s in Perspective* (Cambridge, MA: Belknap Press, 2010); and Daniel J. Sargent, *A Superpower Transformed: The Remaking of American Foreign Relations in the 1970s* (New York: Oxford University Press, 2015).
5. New Zealand High Commission, London, Telegram 6144 to Wellington, September 22, 1977 (ANZ: ABHS, 7148, LONB 68/2 Part 10).
6. Transcribed from "English, Monday 27/2/1978–Thursday AM, 2/3/1978: Interpreter Floor Tapes Used for the Consultative Meeting on Antarctica, Canberra" (NAA: A10734, 2).
7. On India at the United Nations in the 1950s, see Adrian Howkins, "Defending Polar Empire: Opposition to India's Proposal to Raise the 'Antarctic Question' at the United Nations in 1956," *Polar Record* 44, no. 1 (2007): 35–44; and Klaus Dodds, *Geopolitics in Antarctica: Views from the Southern Ocean Rim* (Chichester, UK: John Wiley & Sons, 1997), 136–41. Peter Beck gives a brief description of these 1970s issues in Peter J. Beck, *The International Politics of Antarctica* (London: Croom Helm, 1986), 275–78. On Malaysia at the United Nations in the 1980s, see Rohan Tepper and Marcus Haward, "The Development of Malaysia's Position on Antarctica: 1982 to 2004," *Polar Record* 41, no. 217 (2005): 112–24.
8. The clearest and fullest account of the nine-year conference is Sanger, *Ordering the Oceans*, which deals both chronologically and thematically with the issues. Two other detailed and chronological accounts are James B. Morell, *The Law of the Sea: An Historical Analysis of the 1982 Treaty and Its Rejection by the United States* (Jefferson, NC: McFarland & Company, 1992), chs. 2 and 3; and Ann L. Hollick, *U.S. Foreign Policy and the Law of the Sea* (Princeton, NJ: Princeton University Press, 1981). An account of how international nongovernmental organizations tried to influence the negotiations is Ralph B. Levering and Miriam L. Levering, *Citizen Action for Global Change: The Neptune Group and Law of the Sea* (Syracuse, NY: Syracuse University Press, 1999). Some of these activists engaged with Antarctic matters in the late 1970s and 1980s.

9. See documents in US Department of State, *Foreign Relations of the United States, 1969–1976*, Vol. E-1, Documents on Global Issues, 1969–1972 (Washington, DC: US Government Printing Office, 2005), https://history.state.gov/historicaldocuments/frus1969-76ve01; and US Department of State, *Foreign Relations of the United States, 1969–1976*, Vol. E-3, Documents on Global Issues, 1973–1976 (Washington, DC: US Government Printing Office, 2005), http://history.state.gov/historicaldocuments/frus1969-76ve03/.
10. United Nations General Assembly, First Committee, Official Records, 22nd Session, November 1, 1967, A/C. 1/PV. 1516.
11. Detailed reporting of the last few years of the negotiations can be found in William Wertenbaker, "The Law of the Sea—I," *New Yorker*, August 1, 1983, 38–65; and William Wertenbaker, "The Law of the Sea—II," *New Yorker*, August 8, 1983, 56–83.
12. Christopher C. Joyner, "Legal Implications of the Concept of the Common Heritage of Mankind," *International and Comparative Law Quarterly* 35, no. 1 (1986): 190–99, details the broader basis for the common heritage of mankind in international law.
13. D. H. Anderson (British Delegation to UNCLOS, Caracas), Letter to John Heap, August 14, 1974 (TNA: FCO 7/2724).
14. See also US Mission, Geneva, Cable 5821 to Washington, April 18, 1978 (NACP: RG 59, Central Foreign Policy Files, 1973–1979).
15. New Zealand Delegation to the Third UN Conference on the Law of the Sea, Geneva, Memorandum to Wellington, April 19, 1978 (ANZ: ABHS, 950, 208/1/10/1 Part 4).
16. John Heap, Letter to J. C. Thomas (British Mission, United Nations), August 1, 1975, and New Zealand Mission, United Nations, Telegram 477 to Wellington, August 5, 1975 (ANZ: ABHS, 7148, LONB 68/2 Part 8).
17. New Zealand Mission, United Nations, Telegram 477 to Wellington, August 5, 1975 (ANZ: ABHS, 7148, LONB 68/2 Part 8).
18. New Zealand Ministry of Foreign Affairs, Telegram 668 to New York, August 21, 1975 (ANZ: ABHS, 7148, LONB 68/2 Part 8).
19. New Zealand High Commission, Canberra, Memorandum to Wellington, September 11, 1975 (ANZ: ABHS, 7148, LONB 68/2 Part 8).
20. New Zealand Ministry of Foreign Affairs, Telegram 668 to New York, August 21, 1975 (ANZ: ABHS, 7148, LONB 68/2 Part 8).
21. Ibid.
22. Australian Mission, United Nations, Cablegram UN5612 to Canberra, May 4, 1976 (NAA: A1838, 1743/1/2 Part 2).
23. Australian Mission, United Nations, Cablegram UN6141 to Canberra, August 6, 1976 (NAA: B1387, 1991/708 Part 3).
24. Australian Embassy, Buenos Aires, Memorandum and Record of Conversation, January 16, 1976 (NAA: B1387, 1991/708 Part 2).

25. This program produced three important studies: Inigo Everson, *The Living Resources of the Southern Ocean*, Southern Ocean Fisheries Survey Programme, GLO/SO/77/1 (Rome: Food and Agriculture Organization, 1977); G. C. Eddie, *The Harvesting of Krill*, Southern Ocean Fisheries Survey Programme, GLO/SO/77/2 (Rome: Food and Agriculture Organization, 1977); and G. J. Grantham, *The Utilization of Krill*, Southern Ocean Fisheries Survey Programme, GLO/SO/77/3 (Rome: Food and Agriculture Organization, 1977).
26. New Zealand Embassy, Rome, Memorandum, "FAO/UNDP: Southern Ocean Fisheries Survey Programme," to Wellington, May 20, 1976 (ANZ: ABHS, 950, 208/1/10/1 Part 1).
27. New Zealand Ministry of Foreign Affairs, Telegram 1058 to Rome, November 18, 1975 (ANZ: ABHS, 950, 208/1/10/1 Part 1).
28. New Zealand Ministry of Foreign Affairs, Telegram 297 to Rome, April 1, 1977 (ANZ: ABHS, 950, 208/1/10/1 Part 2).
29. Sergio Marchisio and Antonietta Di Blase, *The Food and Agriculture Organization (FAO)* (Dordrecht, Netherlands: Martinus Nijhoff Publishers, 1991), 128–42; and Ralph W. Phillips, *FAO: Its Origins, Formation and Evolution 1945–1981* (Rome: Food and Agriculture Organization, 1981), 134.
30. New Zealand Ministry of Foreign Affairs, Telegram 297 to Rome, April 1, 1977 (ANZ: ABHS, 950, 208/1/10/1 Part 2).
31. New Zealand High Commission, London, Telegram 7772 to Wellington, December 15, 1975 (ANZ: ABHS, 950, 208/1/10/1 Part 1).
32. New Zealand High Commission, Canberra, Telegram 2366 to Wellington, December 16, 1975 (ANZ: ABHS, 950, 208/1/10/1 Part 1).
33. New Zealand Embassy Rome, Memorandum, "UNDP/FAO Southern Ocean Fisheries Survey Programme," to Wellington, May 7, 1976 (ANZ: ABHS, 950, 208/1/10/1 Part 1).
34. Australian High Commission, London, Cablegram LH75012 to Canberra, April 19, 1977 (NAA: A1838, 738/1/1/1 Part 1).
35. New Zealand Embassy, Rome, Telegram 250 to Wellington, April 28, 1977 (ANZ: ABHS, 950, 208/1/10/1 Part 2).
36. New Zealand Embassy Rome, Telegram 250 to Wellington, April 28, 1977 (ANZ: ABHS, 950, 208/1/10/1 Part 2).
37. Australian High Commission, London, Cablegram LH85481 to Canberra, September 13, 1977 (NAA: B1387, 1976/33 Part 1).
38. Australian Mission, Geneva, Cablegram GE29465 to Canberra, April 19, 1978 (NAA: B1387, 1991/821 Part 5).
39. Australian High Commission, London, Cablegram LH86883 to Canberra, September 29, 1977 (NAA: B1387, 1976/33 Part 1).
40. New Zealand High Commission, Canberra, Telegram 611 to Wellington, March 16, 1978 (ANZ: ABHS, 950, 208/1/10/1 Part 3).

41. Australian Embassy, Rome, Cablegram RO6213 to Canberra, June 16, 1978 (NAA: B1387, 1996/877 Part 1).
42. New Zealand Embassy, Rome, Telegram 438 to Wellington, June 22, 1978 (ANZ: ABHS, 950, 208/1/10/1 Part 4).
43. Peter Bunyard and Robert Prescott-Allen, "Obituary: Ecologist Cartoonist Richard Willson," *The Ecologist*, November 30, 2011, https://theecologist.org/2011/nov/30/obituary-ecologist-cartoonist-richard-willson; and Mark Bryant, "Richard Willson: Political Cartoonist and Environmentalist," *The Independent*, December 26, 2011, https://www.independent.co.uk/news/obituaries/richard-willson-political-cartoonist-and-environmentalist-6281503.html.
44. *New Scientist*, January 13, 1977.
45. Lee Kimball, "The Role of Non-Governmental Organizations in Antarctic Affairs," in *The Antarctic Legal Regime*, ed. Christopher C. Joyner and Sudhir K. Chopra (Dordrecht, Netherlands: Martinus Nijhoff Publishers, 1988), 59n15.
46. Barbara Mitchell, "Antarctica: A Special Case?," *New Scientist*, January 13, 1977, 64–66.
47. D. J. Carter (New Zealand High Commissioner, UK), Letter to the Editor, *New Scientist*, January 31, 1977 (ANZ: ABHS, 7148, LONB 68/2 Part 9).
48. New Zealand High Commission, London, Memorandum to Wellington, January 31, 1977 (ANZ: ABHS, 7148, LONB 68/2 Part 9).
49. Kimball, "The Role of Non-Governmental Organizations in Antarctic Affairs," 46.
50. For example, the New Zealand High Commission in London organized a public briefing on CCAMLR in association with Earthscan: "Earthscan Press Briefing Seminar, Held at New Zealand House, London," July 25, 1977 (ANZ: ABHS, 7148, LONB 68/2 Part 10).
51. "Why Ice?" *Ice*, no. 1, February 29, 1978, 1. We do not know the individual authors of articles, though the creators and contributors are listed in the newsletter. The past issues of *Ice* and *Eco* have been digitized and are available on the ASOC website at http://www.asoc.org/.
52. "Ice Contributions," *Ice*, no. 4, June 1978, 4.
53. "Why Ice?" *Ice*, no. 1, February 29, 1978, 1.
54. *Ice*, no. 1, February 29, 1978; and *Ice*, no. 2, March 10, 1978.
55. A list of member organizations in 1982 can be found in James N. Barnes, *Let's Save Antarctica!* (Richmond, Australia: Greenhouse Publications, 1982).
56. James Barnes and J. L. Kleckner, Letter to John Negroponte, February 29, 1979 (ASOC); and James Barnes, Memorandum to US Antarctic Delegation, September 5, 1979 (ASOC).
57. P. G. F. Henderson, "Brennan, Keith Gabriel (1915–1985)," in *Australian Dictionary of Biography* (2007), http://adb.anu.edu.au/biography/brennan-keith-gabriel-12252; William Wertenbaker, *The Floor of the Sea: Maurice Ewing and the Search to Understand the Earth* (Boston: Little, Brown, 1974); and William Wertenbaker, "The Law of the Sea—I."

58. New Zealand Embassy, Paris, Telegram 717 to Wellington, July 6, 1976 (ANZ: ABHS, 7148, LONB 68/2 Part 8).
59. J. G. McArthur (New Zealand Ambassador, Paris), Letter to N. Mullins (New Zealand High Commission, Canberra), August 6, 1976 (ANZ: ABHS, 22310, PAR322/1/1 Part 10).
60. New Zealand Embassy, Paris, Memorandum to Wellington, August 5, 1976 (ANZ: ABHS, 7148, LONB 68/2 Part 8).
61. New Zealand High Commission, London, Saving 3 to Wellington (and Paris, Washington, Canberra, New York, Tokyo, Santiago, Moscow, Rome, and Bonn), October 10, 1977 (ANZ: ABHS, 950, 208/1/10/1 Part 2).
62. New Zealand High Commission, London, Telegram 4993 to Wellington, July 29, 1977 (ANZ: ABHS, 7148, LONB 68/2 Part 9).
63. Australian Mission, United Nations, Cablegram UN8444 to Canberra, June 10, 1977 (NAA: A1838, 738/1/1/1 Part 2).
64. Australian Embassy, Berne, Cablegram BU3609 to Canberra, October 10, 1977 (NAA: B1387, 1976/33 Part 1).
65. Keith Brennan, Minute to Minister, March 2, 1978 (NAA: M2641, 1978-5/5 Part 2).
66. Transcribed from "English, Thursday, 3: 00pm, 2/3/1978—Thursday 4: 30pm, 9/3/1978: Interpreter Floor Tapes Used for the Consultative Meeting on Antarctica, Canberra" (NAA: A10734, 4).
67. Ibid.
68. The New Zealand government had never been particularly attached to the Ross Dependency, and successive governments from both sides of politics had been basically committed to international solutions and approaches to Antarctic problems. Dodds, *Geopolitics in Antarctica*, ch. 7.
69. Transcribed from "English, Thursday, 3: 00pm, 2/3/1978–Thursday 4: 30pm, 9/3/1978: Interpreter Floor Tapes Used for the Consultative Meeting on Antarctica, Canberra" (NAA: A10734, 4).
70. Australian Embassy, Berne, Cablegram BU4948 to Canberra, February 15, 1979 (NAA: B1387, 1996/882 Part 3).
71. James N. Barnes, "The Emerging Convention on the Conservation of Antarctic Marine Living Resources: An Attempt to Meet the New Realities of Resource Exploitation in the Southern Ocean," in *The New Nationalism and the Use of Common Spaces: Issues in Marine Pollution and the Exploitation of Antarctica*, ed. Jonathan I. Charney (Totowa, NJ: Allanheld, Osmun Publishers, 1982), 265–66.
72. Australian Embassy, Moscow, Cablegram MS8136 to Canberra, May 29, 1978 (NAA: B1387, 1996/877 Part 1).
73. Ibid.
74. "Special Antarctic Consultative Meeting, Buenos Aires, 17–28 July 1978, Report of the Leader of the UK Delegation," August 1, 1978 (TNA: FCO 7/3555).

75. Ibid.
76. Sanger, *Ordering the Oceans*, 65.
77. Australian Embassy, Paris, Cablegram PA48332 to Canberra, October 2, 1978 (NAA: B1387, 1996/881 Part 1); and Australian Embassy, Paris, Cablegram PA53176 to Canberra, March 21, 1979 (NAA: A1838, 1743/1/5 Part 6).
78. Australian Embassy, Paris, Cablegram PA44608 to Canberra, June 8, 1978 (NAA: B1387, 1996/877 Part 1); Australian Embassy, Paris, Cablegram PA49413 to Canberra, November 6, 1978 (NAA: B1387, 1996/883 Part 2); and N. Gordon Lennox (British Embassy, Paris), Letter to J. B. Ure, April 30, 1979 (TNA: FCO 7/3713).
79. Australian Embassy, Paris, Cablegram PA49413 to Canberra, November 6, 1978 (NAA: B1387, 1996/883 Part 2). The French later did conduct bilateral negotiations with the Soviet Union regarding access to fisheries in the exclusive economic zones of the Kerguelen and Crozet island groups, which, according to diplomatic reports, was an important step to seeing it accept the CCAMLR proposals. Australian Embassy, Berne, Cablegram BU5273 to Canberra, July 10, 1979, and Australian Embassy, Paris, Cablegram PA67174 to Canberra, July 28, 1979 (NAA: B1387, 1996/884 Part 4).
80. Australian Embassy, Paris, Cablegram PA53176 to Canberra, March 21, 1979 (NAA: A1838, 1743/1/5 Part 6).
81. "Report of the United Kingdom Delegation to the Tenth Antarctic Treaty Consultative Meeting, Washington, 17 September–5 October 1979" (Royal Society: BNC Collection Roll 243).
82. New Zealand Embassy, Washington, Telegram 2490 to Wellington, July 9, 1979 (ANZ: ABHS, 950, 208/1/10/1 Part 7).
83. The chairman's statement is in the final act.
84. James J. Sheehan, "The Problem of Sovereignty in European History," *American Historical Review* 111, no. 1 (2006): 3.
85. Ibid., 4.
86. Australian Embassy, Berne, Cablegram BU3185 to Canberra, April 29, 1977 (NAA: A1838, 625/14/78 Part 1).
87. For related accounts of the changes in international politics in the 1970s, see Sargent, *A Superpower Transformed*, focusing on economics and globalization; Barbara J. Keys, *Reclaiming American Virtue: The Human Rights Revolution of the 1970s* (Cambridge, MA: Harvard University Press, 2014), on human rights; and Ferguson et al., *The Shock of the Global*, for other developments.
88. Charles S. Maier, "Consigning the Twentieth Century to History: Alternative Narratives for the Modern Era," *American Historical Review* 105, no. 3 (2000): 815.
89. Ibid., 824.

EPILOGUE

1. Stephen J. Pyne, *The Ice: A Journey to Antarctica* (Seattle: University of Washington Press, [1986] 1998), 68.
2. Tom Griffiths, "A Humanist on Thin Ice," *Griffith Review*, no. 29 (2010): 67–88.
3. Davor Vidas, "Entry into Force of the Environmental Protocol and Implementation Issues: An Overview," in *Implementing the Environmental Protection Regime for the Antarctic*, ed. Davor Vidas (Dordrecht, Netherlands: Kluwer Academic Publishers, 2000), 4.
4. Peter J. Beck, *The International Politics of Antarctica* (London: Croom Helm, 1986), 284–97; Rohan Tepper and Marcus Haward, "The Development of Malaysia's Position on Antarctica: 1982 to 2004," *Polar Record* 41, no. 217 (2005): 113–24; and Marcus Haward and David Mason, "Australia, the United Nations and the Question of Antarctica," in *Australia and the Antarctic Treaty System: 50 Years of Influence*, ed. Marcus Haward and Tom Griffiths (Sydney, Australia: University of New South Wales Press, 2011), 202–21.
5. Andrew Jackson and Peter Boyce, "Mining and 'World Park Antarctica', 1982–1991," in *Australia and the Antarctic Treaty System: 50 Years of Influence*, ed. Marcus Haward and Tom Griffiths (Sydney, Australia: University of New South Wales Press, 2011), 243–73.
6. I have explored ice as a contemporary space of Antarctic politics in Alessandro Antonello, "Life, Ice and Ocean: Contemporary Antarctic Spaces," in *Handbook on the Politics of Antarctica*, ed. Klaus Dodds, Alan D. Hemmings, and Peder Roberts (Cheltenham, UK: Edward Elgar, 2017), 172–75.
7. Tom Griffiths, *Slicing the Silence: Voyaging to Antarctica* (Sydney, Australia: University of New South Wales Press, 2007), 3.

Bibliography

ANTARCTIC TREATY SOURCES

Authentic texts in the four official languages of the Antarctic Treaty (1959), the Agreed Measures for the Conservation of Antarctic Fauna and Flora (1964), Convention for the Conservation of Antarctic Seals (1972), Convention on the Conservation of Antarctic Marine Living Resources (1980), and reports and recommendations of the Antarctic Treaty Consultative Meetings can be found on the website of the Antarctic Treaty Secretariat, www.ats.aq.

ARCHIVAL AND MANUSCRIPT SOURCES

Antarctic and Southern Ocean Coalition Secretariat, Washington, DC (ASOC)

Office files (uncataloged)

These files are kept in the ASOC office in filing cabinets without any particular order and have not been cataloged. They cover the full range of ASOC activities since 1978 and include files created by James Barnes at the Center for Legal and Social Policy (CLSP) in the year or so before ASOC's creation.

Archives New Zealand, Wellington (ANZ)

AAEG, Ministry of Foreign Affairs, Head Office

6956, Central Filing System: Tokyo Embassy

AATJ, Ministry of Economic Development, Head Office

7428, Central Filing System Records

ABHS, Ministry of External Relations and Trade, Head Office

950, Multiple number subject files

7148, Central Filing System: London High Commission

22310, Paris Embassy Central File Registry

ACIE, Department of External Affairs

8798, Registered Subject Files

British Antarctic Survey, Cambridge (BAS)
AD3/1, First Registry Filing System, 1950–1976
AD3/2, Second Registry Filing System, 1959–1984
2nd BAS Registry Filing System (files awaiting disposal decision)
Hoover Institution Archives, Stanford University, California
Dixy Lee Ray Papers
National Academy of Sciences, Washington, DC (NAS)
Committee on Polar Research Collection
National Archives and Records Administration, College Park, Maryland (NACP)
RG 43, Records of International Conferences, Commissions, and Expositions
US Delegation Antarctic Conference
RG 59, General Records of the Department of State
Central Decimal File, 1960–1963
Central Foreign Policy Files, 1963
Central Foreign Policy Files, 1964–1966
Central Foreign Policy Files, 1967–1969
Subject Numeric Files, 1970–1973
Central Foreign Policy Files, 1973–1979 (http://aad.archives.gov/aad/)
Subject Files of Francis O. Wilcox, Assistant Secretary of State for International Organization Affairs, 1958–1959
RG 307, National Science Foundation
Division of Polar Programs (DPP), Central Subject Files, 1976–1987
Division of Polar Programs (DPP), Office Files of Henry S. Francis
Division of Polar Programs (DPP), Records of the Program Manager for Biology and Medicine, Memorandums, 1976
Division of Polar Programs (DPP), Records of the Program Manager for Biology and Medicine, Records Relating to the Polar Research Program, 1974–1977
Office of Antarctic Programs (OAP), Central Subject Files, 1961–1969
Office of Polar Programs (OPP), Central Subject Files, 1969–1975
Office of Polar Programs (OPP), Records of the Head (Fletcher), Reading File, 1969–1975
RG 580, Executive Office of the President
Council on Environmental Quality, Office of the Chairman, Chairman's Subject Files 1970–1981
Council on Environmental Quality, International Affairs and Oceans Office, International Affairs Subject Files, 1970–76
National Archives of Australia (NAA)
A1838, Department of External Affairs/Department of Foreign Affairs, Correspondence Files
A9697, CSIRO, Division of Wildlife and Ecology—Wildlife Survey Section, Correspondence Files

A10734, Department of Foreign Affairs, Interpreter Floor Tapes used for the Consultative Meeting on Antarctica in Canberra, February to March 1978 and May 1980

B1387, Australian Antarctic Division, Correspondence Files

M2641, Minister for Foreign Affairs (Andrew Peacock), Correspondence Files

National Archives of the United Kingdom (TNA)

FO 371, Foreign Office: Political Departments: General Correspondence from 1906–1966

FCO 7, Foreign Office and Foreign and Commonwealth Office: American and Latin American Departments: Registered Files (A and AL Series)

National Library of Australia (NLA)

MS 6150, Casey Family Papers

The Royal Society, London

British National Committees Collection (microfilm)

Scientific Committee on Antarctic Research (SCAR) Secretariat

Office Files (uncataloged)

These files are the historical records of SCAR that are kept in the offices of the SCAR Secretariat, which is housed in the building of the Scott Polar Research Institute. Though they have now been transferred to the archives of the Scott Polar Research Institute, they have not been cataloged.

Scott Polar Research Institute, Thomas Manning Archives, University of Cambridge (SPRI)

MS 1308, Brian Roberts Collection

PUBLISHED SOURCES

Agar, Jon. *Science in the Twentieth Century and Beyond*. Cambridge, UK: Polity, 2012.

Amadon, Dean. "In Memoriam: Robert Cushman Murphy, April 29, 1887–March 20, 1973." *The Auk: A Quarterly Journal of Ornithology* 91, no. 1 (1974): 1–9.

Anderson, Ben, and Colin McFarlane. "Assemblage and Geography." *Area* 43, no. 2 (2011): 124–27.

Anderson, David. "The Conservation of Wildlife under the Antarctic Treaty." *Polar Record* 14, no. 88 (1968): 25–32.

Andrews, Richard N. L. *Managing the Environment, Managing Ourselves: A History of American Environmental Policy*. 2nd ed. New Haven, CT: Yale University Press, 2006.

"Antarctic Resources—Effects of Mineral Exploration: Initial Response by SCAR, Dated May 1976, to Antarctic Treaty Recommendation VIII-14." *SCAR Bulletin*, no. 57 (September 1977): 631–36.

Antonello, Alessandro. "Australia, the International Geophysical Year and the 1959 Antarctic Treaty." *Australian Journal of Politics and History* 59, no. 4 (2013): 532–46.

Antonello, Alessandro. "Finding Place in Antarctica." In *Antarctica and the Humanities*, edited by Peder Roberts, Lize-Marié van der Watt, and Adrian Howkins, 181–203. Houndmills, UK: Palgrave Macmillan, 2016.

Antonello, Alessandro. "The Greening of Antarctica: Environment, Science and Diplomacy, 1959–1980." PhD thesis, Australian National University, 2014.

Antonello, Alessandro. "Life, Ice and Ocean: Contemporary Antarctic Spaces." In *Handbook on the Politics of Antarctica*, edited by Klaus Dodds, Alan D. Hemmings, and Peder Roberts, 167–82. Cheltenham, UK: Edward Elgar, 2017.

Auburn, F. M. *Antarctic Law and Politics*. London: C. Hurst & Co., 1982.

Ayres, Philip. *Mawson: A Life*. Melbourne, Australia: Miegunyah Press, 1999.

Barnes, James N. "The Emerging Convention on the Conservation of Antarctic Marine Living Resources: An Attempt to Meet the New Realities of Resource Exploitation in the Southern Ocean." In *The New Nationalism and the Use of Common Spaces: Issues in Marine Pollution and the Exploitation of Antarctica*, edited by Jonathan I. Charney, 239–86. Totowa, NJ: Allanheld, Osmun Publishers, 1982.

Barnes, James N. *Let's Save Antarctica!* Richmond, Australia: Greenhouse Publications, 1982.

Barrow, Mark V., Jr. *Nature's Ghosts: Confronting Extinction from the Age of Jefferson to the Age of Ecology*. Chicago: University of Chicago Press, 2009.

Barrow, Mark V., Jr. *A Passion for Birds: American Ornithology after Audubon*. Princeton, NJ: Princeton University Press, 1998.

Basberg, Bjørn L., and Robert K. Headland. "The Economic Significance of the 19th Century Antarctic Sealing Industry." *Polar Record* 49, no. 4 (2013): 381–91.

Bashford, Alison. *Global Population: History, Geopolitics, and Life on Earth*. New York: Columbia University Press, 2014.

Bavington, Dean. *Managed Annihilation: An Unnatural History of the Newfoundland Cod Collapse*. Vancouver: University of British Columbia Press, 2010.

Beck, Peter J. *The International Politics of Antarctica*. London: Croom Helm, 1986.

Belanger, Dian Olson. *Deep Freeze: The United States, the International Geophysical Year, and the Origins of Antarctica's Age of Science*. Boulder: University Press of Colorado, 2006.

Bennett, Jane. "The Agency of Assemblages and the North American Blackout." *Public Culture* 17, no. 3 (2005): 445–65.

Benson, Etienne. "Endangered Science: The Regulation of Research by the U.S. Marine Mammal Protection and Endangered Species Acts." *Historical Studies in the Natural Sciences* 42, no. 1 (2012): 30–61.

Berkman, Paul Arthur. *Science into Policy: Global Lessons from Antarctica*. San Diego, CA: Academic Press, 2002.

Berkman, Paul Arthur, Michael A. Lang, David W. H. Walton, and Oran R. Young, eds. *Science Diplomacy: Antarctica, Science, and the Governance of International Spaces*. Washington, DC: Smithsonian Institution Scholarly Press, 2011.

Bertrand, Kenneth J. *Americans in Antarctica 1775–1948*. Special Publication No. 39. New York: American Geographical Society, 1971.

Bini, Elisabetta, Giuliano Garavini, and Federico Romero, eds. *Oil Shock: The 1973 Crisis and Its Economic Legacy*. London and New York: I. B. Tauris, 2016.

Black, Megan. "Interior's Exterior: The State, Mining Companies, and Resource Ideologies in the Point Four Program." *Diplomatic History* 40, no. 1 (2016): 81–110.

Boardman, Robert. *International Organization and the Conservation of Nature.* London: Macmillan, 1981.

Bocking, Stephen. *Ecologists and Environmental Politics: A History of Contemporary Ecology*. New Haven, CT: Yale University Press, 1997.

Bocking, Stephen. "Ecosystems, Ecologists, and the Atom: Environmental Research at Oak Ridge National Laboratory." *Journal of the History of Biology* 28, no. 1 (1995): 1–47.

Bocking, Stephen. "Nature on the Home Front: British Ecologists' Advocacy for Science and Conservation." *Environment and History* 18, no. 2 (2012): 261–81.

Bocking, Stephen. *Nature's Experts: Science, Politics, and the Environment.* New Brunswick, NJ: Rutgers University Press, 2004.

Bocking, Stephen. "Science and Spaces in the Northern Environment." *Environmental History* 12, no. 4 (2007): 867–94.

Bonner, W. Nigel, and Richard M. Laws. "Seals and Sealing." In *Antarctic Research: A Review of British Scientific Achievement in Antarctica*, edited by Raymond Priestley, Raymond J. Adie, and G. de Q. Robin, 163–90. London: Butterworths, 1964.

Bowden, Tim. *The Silence Calling: Australians in Antarctica 1947–97*. St. Leonards, Australia: Allen & Unwin, 1997.

Brady, Anne-Marie, ed. *The Emerging Politics of Antarctica.* Abingdon, UK: Routledge, 2013.

Bsumek, Erika Marie, David Kinkela, and Mark Atwood Lawrence, eds. *Nation-States and the Global Environment: New Approaches to International Environmental History*. New York: Oxford University Press, 2013.

Bull, Hedley. *The Anarchical Society*. New York: Columbia University Press, 1977.

Burnett, D. Graham. *The Sounding of the Whale: Science and Cetaceans in the Twentieth Century*. Chicago: University of Chicago Press, 2012.

Burukovskiy, R. N., ed. *Soviet Fishery Research on the Antarctic Krill.* Washington, DC: Joint Publications Research Service, 1967.

Busch, Briton Cooper. *The War against the Seals: A History of the North American Seal Fishery*. Kingston, ON: McGill-Queen's University Press, 1985.

Bush, W. M., ed. *Antarctica and International Law: A Collection of Inter-State and National Documents*. London: Oceana, 1982.

Buzan, Barry. *An Introduction to the English School of International Relations: The Societal Approach*. London: Polity, 2014.

Campbell, David G. *The Crystal Desert: Summers in Antarctica*. London: Minerva, (1992) 1993.

Campbell, R. J., ed. *The Discovery of the South Shetland Islands: The Voyages of the Brig* Williams *1819–1820 as Recorded in Contemporary Documents and the Journal of Midshipman C. W. Poynter*. London: Hakluyt Society, 2000.

Canada. Royal Commission on Seals and the Sealing Industry in Canada. *Seals and Sealing in Canada*. Vol. 2. Ottawa: Canadian Government Publishing Centre, 1986.

Canada. Royal Commission on Seals and the Sealing Industry in Canada. *Seals and Sealing in Canada*. Vol. 3. Ottawa: Canadian Government Publishing Centre, 1986.

Carey, Mark. *In the Shadow of Melting Glaciers: Climate Change and Andean Society*. New York: Oxford University Press, 2010.

Carey, Mark. "Science, Models, and Historians: Toward a Critical Climate History." *Environmental History* 19, no. 2 (2014): 354–64.

Carpenter, Kenneth J. *Protein and Energy: A Study of Changing Ideas in Nutrition*. Cambridge, UK: Cambridge University Press, 1994.

Carrick, Robert. "Conservation of Nature in the Antarctic." *SCAR Bulletin*, no. 6 (September 1960): 299–306.

Cioc, Mark. *The Game of Conservation: International Treaties to Protect the World's Migratory Animals*. Athens: Ohio University Press, 2009.

Cioc, Mark. *The Rhine: An Eco-Biography, 1815–2000*. Seattle: University of Washington Press, 2002.

Coates, Peter. *Trans-Alaska Pipeline Controversy: Technology, Conservation, and the Frontier*. Bethlehem, PA: Lehigh University Press, 1991.

Coleman, David C., David M. Swift, and John E. Mitchell. "From the Frontier to the Biosphere: A Brief History of the USIBP Grasslands Biome Program and Its Impact on Scientific Research in North America." *Rangelands* 26, no. 4 (2004): 8–15.

Collis, Christy, and Klaus Dodds. "Assault on the Unknown: The Historical and Political Geographies of the International Geophysical Year (1957–8)." *Journal of Historical Geography* 34, no. 4 (2008): 555–73.

Commission on Marine Science, Engineering and Resources. *Our Nation and the Sea: A Plan for National Action*. Washington, DC: US Government Printing Office, 1969.

Connelly, Matthew. "Future Shock: The End of the World as They Know It." In *The Shock of the Global: The 1970s in Perspective*, edited by Niall Ferguson, Charles S. Maier, Erez Manela, and Daniel J. Sargent, 337–50. Cambridge, MA: Belknap Press, 2010.

"Conservation of Nature in Antarctica." *SCAR Bulletin*, no. 8 (May 1961): 532–40.

Craddock, Campbell, et al. *Geologic Maps of Antarctica*. Antarctic Map Folio Series, folio 12. New York: American Geographical Society, 1969–1970.

Cumpston, J. S. *Macquarie Island*. ANARE Scientific Reports, Series A(1). Melbourne, Australia: Antarctic Division, Department of External Affairs, 1968.

Cushing, D. H. *The Provident Sea*. Cambridge, UK: Cambridge University Press, 1988.

Cushman, Gregory T. "'The Most Valuable Birds in the World': International Conservation Science and the Revival of Peru's Guano Industry, 1909–1965." *Environmental History* 10, no. 3 (2005): 477–509.

Darby, Andrew. *Harpoon: Into the Heart of Whaling*. Crows Nest, Australia: Allen & Unwin, 2007.

Day, David. *Antarctica: A Biography*. North Sydney, Australia: Knopf, 2012.

Dean, Arthur H. "The Geneva Conference on the Law of the Sea: What Was Accomplished." *American Journal of International Law* 52, no. 4 (1958): 607–28.

Deleuze, Gilles, and Félix Guattari. *A Thousand Plateaus: Capitalism and Schizophrenia*. Translated by Brian Massumi. Minneapolis: University of Minnesota Press, 1987.

Dickinson, A. B. *Seal Fisheries of the Falkland Islands and Dependencies: An Historical Review*. St. John's, NL: International Maritime Economic History Association, 2007.

Dodds, Klaus. "Assault on the Unknown: Geopolitics, Antarctic Science, and the International Geophysical Year (1957–8)." In *New Spaces of Exploration: Geographies of Discovery in the Twentieth Century*, edited by Simon Naylor and James R. Ryan, 148–72. London: I. B. Tauris, 2010.

Dodds, Klaus. *Geopolitics in Antarctica: Views from the Southern Ocean Rim*. Chichester, UK: John Wiley & Sons, 1997.

Dodds, Klaus. "The Great Game in Antarctica: Britain and the 1959 Antarctic Treaty." *Contemporary British History* 22, no. 1 (2008): 43–66.

Dodds, Klaus. "Guest Editorial—the 1959 Antarctic Treaty: Reflecting on the 50th Anniversary of a Landmark Agreement." *Polar Research* 29 (2010): 145–49.

Dodds, Klaus. *Pink Ice: Britain and the South Atlantic Empire*. London: I. B. Tauris, 2002.

Dodds, Klaus, and Alan D. Hemmings. "Britain and the British Antarctic Territory in the Wider Geopolitics of the Antarctic and the Southern Ocean." *International Affairs* 89, no. 6 (2013): 1429–44.

Doel, Ronald E. "Constituting the Postwar Earth Sciences: The Military's Influence on the Environmental Sciences in the USA after 1945." *Social Studies of Science* 33, no. 5 (2003): 635–66.

Dorsey, Kurkpatrick. *The Dawn of Conservation Diplomacy: U.S.-Canadian Wildlife Protection Treaties in the Progressive Era*. Seattle: University of Washington Press, 1998.

Dorsey, Kurkpatrick. *Whales and Nations: Environmental Diplomacy on the High Seas*. Seattle: University of Washington Press, 2013.

Drewry, David J. "Deep-Sea Drilling from Glomar Challenger in the Southern Ocean: The Results and Their Geophysical and Geological Implications." *Polar Record* 18, no. 112 (1976): 47–77.

Drewry, David J. "Gordon De Quetteville Robin." *Polar Record* 39, no. 208 (2003): 61–78.

Dunlap, Thomas. *Nature and the English Diaspora: Environment and History in the United States, Canada, Australia, and New Zealand*. Cambridge, UK: Cambridge University Press, 1999.

Dunnet, G. M. "Robert Carrick 1911–88." *Scottish Birds* 15, no. 2 (1988): 93.

Eddie, G. C. *The Harvesting of Krill*. Southern Ocean Fisheries Survey Programme, GLO/SO/77/2. Rome: Food and Agriculture Organization, 1977.

Edwards, David M., and John A. Heap. "Convention on the Conservation of Antarctic Marine Living Resources: A Commentary." *Polar Record* 20, no. 127 (1981): 353–62.

Eklund, Carl R., and Joan Beckman. *Antarctica: Polar Research and Discovery During the International Geophysical Year*. New York: Holt, Rinehart and Winston, 1963.

"Eleventh Meeting of SCAR, Oslo: 17 to 22 August 1970." *SCAR Bulletin*, no. 37 (January 1971): 619–49.

Elliot, Lorraine M. *International Environmental Politics: Protecting the Antarctic*. New York: St. Martin's Press, 1994.

El-Sayed, Sayed Z. "Biological Oceanography." *Antarctic Journal of the United States* 8, no. 3 (1973): 93–100.

El-Sayed, Sayed Z. "Understanding the Antarctic Marine Ecosystem: A Prerequisite for Its Conservation." In *Proceedings of the Colloquium on Conservation Problems in Antarctica*, edited by Bruce C. Parker, 131–41. Blacksburg, VA: Virginia Polytechnic Institute & State University, 1972.

Elzinga, Aant. "Antarctica: The Construction of a Continent by and for Science." In *Denationalizing Science: The Contexts of International Scientific Practice*, edited by Elisabeth Crawford, Terry Shinn, and Sverker Sörlin, 73–106. Dordrecht, Netherlands: Kluwer Academic Publishers, 1993.

Everson, Inigo. *The Living Resources of the Southern Ocean*. Southern Ocean Fisheries Survey Programme, GLO/SO/77/1. Rome: Food and Agriculture Organization, 1977.

Ferguson, Niall, Charles S. Maier, Erez Manela, and Daniel J. Sargent, eds. *The Shock of the Global: The 1970s in Perspective*. Cambridge, MA: Belknap Press, 2010.

Finley, Carmel. *All the Fish in the Sea: Maximum Sustainable Yield and the Failure of Fisheries Management*. Chicago: University of Chicago Press, 2011.

Finley, Carmel. "Global Borders and the Fish That Ignore Them: The Cold War Roots of Overfishing." In *Nation-States and the Global Environment: New Approaches to International Environmental History*, edited by Erika Marie Bsumek, David Kinkela, and Mark Atwood Lawrence, 62–75. New York: Oxford University Press, 2013.

"First meeting of S.C.A.R. held at The Hague, 3 to 5 February 1958." *SCAR Bulletin*, no. 1 (January 1959): 361–66.

Flippen, J. Brooks. *Conservative Conservationist: Russel E. Train and the Emergence of American Environmentalism*. Baton Rouge: Louisiana State University Press, 2006.

Flippen, J. Brooks. "Richard Nixon, Russell Train, and the Birth of Modern American Environmental Diplomacy." *Diplomatic History* 32, no. 4 (2008): 613–38.

Fogg, G. E. *A History of Antarctic Science*. Cambridge, UK: Cambridge University Press, 1992.

"Fourteenth Meeting of SCAR, Mendoza: 18 to 23 October 1976." *SCAR Bulletin*, no. 56 (May 1977): 531–53.

Gan, Irina. "Red Antarctica: Soviet Interests in the South Polar Region Prior to the Antarctic Treaty, 1946–1958." PhD thesis, University of Tasmania, 2009.

Gieryn, Thomas F. "Boundaries of Science." In *Handbook of Science and Technology Studies*, edited by Sheila Jasanoff, Gerald E. Markle, James C. Petersen, and Trevor Pinch, 393–443. Thousand Oaks, CA: Sage, 1995.

Gieryn, Thomas F. *Cultural Boundaries of Science: Credibility on the Line*. Chicago: University of Chicago Press, 1999.

Gissibl, Bernhard. "German Colonialism and the Beginnings of International Wildlife Preservation in Africa." *German Historical Institute Bulletin Supplement*, no. 3 (2006): 121–43.

Gissibl, Bernhard. *The Nature of German Imperialism: Conservation and the Politics of Wildlife in Colonial East Africa*. New York and Oxford: Berghahn, 2016.

Gissibl, Bernhard, Sabine Höhler, and Patrick Kupper, eds. *Civilizing Nature: National Parks in Global Historical Perspective*. New York: Berghahn, 2012.

Golley, Frank Benjamin. *A History of the Ecosystem Concept in Ecology: More Than the Sum of the Parts*. New Haven, CT: Yale University Press, 1993.

Gramling, Robert. *Oil on the Edge: Offshore Development, Conflict, Gridlock*. Albany: State University of New York Press, 1996.

Grantham, G. J. *The Utilization of Krill*. Southern Ocean Fisheries Survey Programme, GLO/SO/77/3. Rome: Food and Agriculture Organization, 1977.

Green, Katherine A. *Antarctic Marine Ecosystem Modeling Revised Ross Sea Model, General Southern Ocean Budget, and Seal Model (MMC-76/03)*. Washington, DC: Marine Mammal Commission, 1977.

Green, Katherine A. "Simulation of the Pelagic Ecosystem of the Ross Sea, Antarctica: A Time Varying Compartmental Model." PhD diss., Texas A&M University, 1975.

Griffiths, Tom. "A Humanist on Thin Ice." *Griffith Review*, no. 29 (2010): 67–88.

Griffiths, Tom. *Slicing the Silence: Voyaging to Antarctica*. Sydney, Australia: University of New South Wales Press, 2007.

Haas, Peter M., Robert O. Keohane, and Marc A. Levy, eds. *Institutions for the Earth: Sources of Effective International Environmental Protection*. Cambridge, MA: The MIT Press, 1993.

Hains, Brigid. *The Ice and the Inland: Mawson, Flynn, and the Myth of the Frontier*. Melbourne, Australia: Melbourne University Press, 2002.

Hall, H. Robert. "International Regime Formation and Leadership: The Origins of the Antarctic Treaty." PhD thesis, University of Tasmania, 1994.

Hall, Rob, and Marie Kawaja. "Australia and the Negotiation of the Antarctic Treaty." In *Australia and the Antarctic Treaty System: 50 Years of Influence*, edited by Marcus Haward and Tom Griffiths, 68–96. Sydney, Australia: University of New South Wales Press, 2011.

Hamblin, Jacob Darwin. *Arming Mother Nature: The Birth of Catastrophic Environmentalism*. Oxford: Oxford University Press, 2013.

Hamblin, Jacob Darwin. *Oceanographers and the Cold War: Disciples of Marine Science*. Seattle: University of Washington Press, 2005.

Hamblin, Jacob Darwin. *Poison in the Well: Radioactive Waste in the Oceans at the Dawn of the Nuclear Age*. New Brunswick, NJ, and London: Rutgers University Press, 2008.

Hanessian, John. "The Antarctic Treaty 1959." *International and Comparative Law Quarterly* 9, no. 3 (1960): 436–80.

Hardy, Alister. *Great Waters: A Voyage of Natural History to Study Whales, Plankton and the Waters of the Southern Ocean in the Old Royal Research Ship* Discovery *with the Results Brought up to Date by the Findings of the R.R.S.* Discovery II. London: Collins, 1967.

Hardy, Alister. "The Krill—an Ocean Harvest of the Future?" *New Scientist,* July 1, 1965, 41–43.

Hardy, Alister. "Oceans in 1984: New and Richer Marine Harvests Forecast." *New Scientist,* February 20, 1964, 482–83.

Hattersley-Smith, G. "Heap, John Arnfield (1932–2006)." In *Oxford Dictionary of National Biography.* Oxford: Oxford University Press, 2010. Online edition, January 2011, http://www.oxforddnb.com/view/article/97078.

Haward, Marcus, and Tom Griffiths, eds. *Australia and the Antarctic Treaty System: 50 Years of Influence.* Sydney, Australia: University of New South Wales Press, 2011.

Haward, Marcus, and David Mason. "Australia, the United Nations and the Question of Antarctica." In *Australia and the Antarctic Treaty System: 50 Years of Influence,* edited by Marcus Haward and Tom Griffiths, 202–21. Sydney, Australia: University of New South Wales Press, 2011.

Hayden, Sherman Strong. *The International Protection of Wild Life: An Examination of Treaties and Other Agreements for the Preservation of Birds and Mammals.* Studies in History, Economics and Public Law. New York: Columbia University Press, 1942.

Hayes, Dennis E., and Lawrence A. Frakes. "General Synthesis, Deep Sea Drilling Project Leg 28." *Initial Reports of the Deep Sea Drilling Project* 28 (1975): 919–42.

Hayes, J. Gordon. *The Conquest of the South Pole: Antarctic Exploration 1906–1931.* New York: Macmillan, 1933.

Hays, Samuel P. *Beauty, Health, and Permanence: Environmental Politics in the United States, 1955–1985.* Cambridge, UK: Cambridge University Press, 1987.

Hays, Samuel P. *Conservation and the Gospel of Efficiency: The Progressive Conservation Movement, 1890–1920.* Cambridge, MA: Harvard University Press, 1959.

Hayton, Robert D. "The Antarctic Settlement of 1959." *American Journal of International Law* 54, no. 2 (1960): 349–71.

Headland, Robert Keith. *A Chronology of Antarctic Exploration: A Synopsis of Events and Activities from the Earliest Times until the International Polar Years, 2007–09.* London: Quaritch, 2009.

Hemmings, Alan D., and Julia Jabour. "Already a Special Case? Australian Antarctic Policy in the First Decade of the Antarctic Treaty." In *Australia and the Antarctic Treaty System: 50 Years of Influence,* edited by Marcus Haward and Tom Griffiths, 118–37. Sydney, Australia: University of New South Wales Press, 2011.

Hemmings, Alan D., Donald R. Rothwell, and Karen N. Scott, eds. *Antarctic Security in the Twenty-First Century: Legal and Policy Perspectives.* London and New York: Routledge, 2012.

Henderson, P. G. F. "Brennan, Keith Gabriel (1915–1985)." In *Australian Dictionary of Biography* (2007). http://adb.anu.edu.au/biography/brennan-keith-gabriel-12252.

Hofman, Robert J. "The Continuing Legacies of the Marine Mammal Commission and Its Committee of Scientific Advisors on Marine Mammals." *Aquatic Mammals* 35, no. 1 (2009): 94–129.

Holdgate, M. W., ed. *Antarctic Ecology*. 2 vols. London and New York: Academic Press, 1970.

Holdgate, M. W. *Penguins and Mandarins: Memories of Natural and Unnatural History*. Whitworth Hall, Spennymoor, UK: The Memoir Club, 2003.

Hollick, Ann L. *U.S. Foreign Policy and the Law of the Sea*. Princeton, NJ: Princeton University Press, 1981.

Holt, Sidney J., and Lee M. Talbot. "New Principles for the Conservation of Wild Living Resources." *Wildlife Monographs*, no. 59 (1978): 1–33.

Howe, Joshua P. *Behind the Curve: Science and the Politics of Global Warming*. Seattle: University of Washington Press, 2014.

Howkins, Adrian. "Defending Polar Empire: Opposition to India's Proposal to Raise the 'Antarctic Question' at the United Nations in 1956." *Polar Record* 44, no. 1 (2007): 35–44.

Howkins, Adrian. *Frozen Empires: An Environmental History of the Antarctic Peninsula*. New York: Oxford University Press, 2017.

Howkins, Adrian. "Melting Empires? Climate Change and Politics in Antarctica since the International Geophysical Year." *Osiris* 26 (2011): 180–97.

Howkins, Adrian. *The Polar Regions: An Environmental History*. Cambridge, UK: Polity Press, 2016.

Howkins, Adrian. "Reluctant Collaborators: Argentina and Chile in Antarctica During the International Geophysical Year, 1957–58." *Journal of Historical Geography* 34, no. 4 (2008): 596–617.

Howkins, Adrian. "Science, Environment, and Sovereignty: The International Geophysical Year in the Antarctic Peninsula Region." In *Globalizing Polar Science: Reconsidering the International Polar and Geophysical Years*, edited by Roger D. Launius, James Rodger Fleming, and David H. DeVorkin, 245–64. Houndmills, UK: Palgrave Macmillan, 2010.

Howkins, Adrian. "The Significance of the Frontier in Antarctic History: How the US West Has Shaped the Geopolitics of the Far South." *The Polar Journal* 3, no. 1 (2013): 9–30.

"Ice Contributions." *Ice*, no. 4, June 1978, 4.

International Union of Geodesy and Geophysics. *Antarctic Symposium, Buenos Aires 17–25 Novembre 1959*. Monograph No. 5. Paris: Institut Géographique National, 1960.

Jackson, Andrew, and Peter Boyce. "Mining and 'World Park Antarctica', 1982–1991." In *Australia and the Antarctic Treaty System: 50 Years of Influence*, edited by Marcus Haward and Tom Griffiths, 243–73. Sydney, Australia: University of New South Wales Press, 2011.

Jenkins, J. J. "Obituary Dr. Robert Carrick." *Aurora: ANARE Club Journal* 8, no. 3 (March 1989): 13–14.

Jones, A. G. E. "British Sealing on New South Shetland, 1819–1826, Part I." *The Great Circle* 7, no. 1 (1985): 9–20.

Jones, A. G. E. "British Sealing on New South Shetland, 1819–1826, Part II." *The Great Circle* 7, no. 2 (1985): 74–85.

Jones, Max. *The Last Great Quest: Captain Scott's Antarctic Sacrifice*. Oxford: Oxford University Press, 2003.

Josephson, Paul R. *Industrialized Nature: Brute Force Technology and the Transformation of the Natural World*. Washington, DC: Island Press, 2002.

Joyner, Christopher C. *Antarctica and the Law of the Sea*. Publications on Ocean Development. Dordrecht, Netherlands: Martinus Nijhoff Publishers, 1992.

Joyner, Christopher C. *Governing the Frozen Commons: The Antarctic Regime and Environmental Protection*. Columbia: University of South Carolina Press, 1998.

Joyner, Christopher C. "Legal Implications of the Concept of the Common Heritage of Mankind." *International and Comparative Law Quarterly* 35, no. 1 (1986): 190–99.

Kaiser, Wolfram, and Jan-Henrik Meyer, eds. *International Organizations and Environmental Protection: Conservation and Globalization in the Twentieth Century*. New York and Oxford: Berghahn, 2016.

Kawaja, Marie. "The Politics and Diplomacy of the Australian Antarctic, 1901–1945." PhD thesis, Australian National University, 2010.

Keys, Barbara J. *Reclaiming American Virtue: The Human Rights Revolution of the 1970s*. Cambridge, MA: Harvard University Press, 2014.

Kimball, Lee. "The Role of Non-Governmental Organizations in Antarctic Affairs." In *The Antarctic Legal Regime*, edited by Christopher C. Joyner and Sudhir K. Chopra, 33–64. Dordrecht, Netherlands: Martinus Nijhoff Publishers, 1988.

King, H. G. R., and Ann Savours, eds. *Polar Pundit: Reminiscences about Brian Birley Roberts*. Cambridge, UK: Scott Polar Research Institute, 1995.

Kooyman, Gerald L. *Weddell Seal: Consummate Diver*. Cambridge, UK: Cambridge University Press, 1981.

Krasner, Stephen D. "Structural Causes and Regime Consequences: Regimes as Intervening Variables." *International Organization* 36, no. 2 (1982): 185–205.

Kroll, Gary. *America's Ocean Wilderness: A Cultural History of Twentieth-Century Exploration*. Lawrence: University Press of Kansas, 2008.

Kupper, Patrick. "Science and the National Parks: A Transatlantic Perspective on the Interwar Years." *Environmental History* 14, no. 1 (2009): 58–81.

Kwa, Chunglin. "Modeling the Grasslands." *Historical Studies in the Physical and Biological Sciences* 24, no. 1 (1993): 125–55.

Kwa, Chunglin. "Representations of Nature Mediating between Ecology and Science Policy: The Case of the International Biological Programme." *Social Studies of Science* 17, no. 3 (1987): 413–42.

Larson, Edward R. *An Empire of Ice: Scott, Shackleton, and the Heroic Age of Antarctic Science*. New Haven, CT: Yale University Press, 2011.

Latour, Bruno. *Reassembling the Social: An Introduction to Actor-Network-Theory*. Oxford: Oxford University Press, 2005.

Lavigne, David M., Victor B. Scheffer, and Stephen R. Kellert. "The Evolution of North American Attitudes toward Marine Mammals." In *Conservation and Management of Marine Mammals*, edited by John R. Twiss Jr. and Randall R. Reeves, 10–47. Washington, DC: Smithsonian Institution Press, 1998.

Law, Phillip. *Antarctica—1984: Sir John Morris Memorial Lecture*. Hobart: The Adult Education Board of Tasmania; D. E. Wilkinson, Government Printer, 1964.

Lawrence, Mark Atwood, David Kinkela, and Erika Marie Bsumek. "Introduction." In *Nation-States and the Global Environment: New Approaches to International Environmental History*, edited by Erika Marie Bsumek, David Kinkela, and Mark Atwood Lawrence, 1–21. New York: Oxford University Press, 2013.

Laws, Richard M. *The Elephant Seal (*Mirounga Leonina *Linn.): II, General, Social and Reproductive Behaviour*. Falkland Islands Dependencies Survey, Scientific Reports, no. 13. London: Her Majesty's Stationery Office, 1956.

Laws, Richard M. *Large Animals and Wide Horizons: Adventures of a Biologist; The Autobiography of Richard M. Laws*. 3 vols. Cambridge, UK: Scott Polar Research Institute, 2012.

Laws, Richard M. "The Seals of the Falkland Islands and Dependencies." *Oryx* 2, no. 2 (1953): 87–97.

Levering, Ralph B., and Miriam L. Levering. *Citizen Action for Global Change: The Neptune Group and Law of the Sea*. Syracuse, NY: Syracuse University Press, 1999.

Lifset, Robert D. "A New Understanding of the American Energy Crisis of the 1970s." *Historical Social Research/Historische Sozialforschung* 39, no. 4 (2014): 22–42.

Lindstrom, Matthew J., and Zachary A. Smith. *The National Environmental Policy Act: Judicial Misconstruction, Legislative Indifference, and Executive Neglect*. College Station: Texas A&M University Press, 2001.

Logevall, Frederik, and Andrew Preston, eds. *Nixon in the World: American Foreign Relations, 1969–1977*. Oxford: Oxford University Press, 2008.

Loo, Tina. *States of Nature: Conserving Canada's Wildlife in the Twentieth Century*. Vancouver: University of British Columbia Press, 2006.

Lyster, Simon. *International Wildlife Law*. Cambridge, UK: Grotius Publications, 1985.

Macekura, Stephen. "The Limits of the Global Community: The Nixon Administration and Global Environmental Politics." *Cold War History* 11, no. 4 (2011): 489–518.

Macekura, Stephen J. *Of Limits and Growth: The Rise of Global Sustainable Development in the Twentieth Century*. New York: Cambridge University Press, 2015.

MacKenzie, John M. *The Empire of Nature: Hunting, Conservation and British Imperialism*. Manchester, UK: Manchester University Press, 1988.

Mackintosh, N. A. "The Work of the Discovery Committee." *Proceedings of the Royal Society B* 137, no. 887 (1950): 137–52.

Maier, Charles S. "Consigning the Twentieth Century to History: Alternative Narratives for the Modern Era." *American Historical Review* 105, no. 3 (2000): 807–31.

Maier, Charles S. *Once within Borders: Territories of Power, Wealth, and Belonging since 1500*. Cambridge, MA: The Belknap Press, 2016.

Main, George, ed. *Of Beauty Rich and Rare: Fifty Years of CSIRO Wildlife and Ecology*. Canberra, Australia: CSIRO Division of Wildlife and Ecology, 1999.

Makarov, R. R., A. G. Naumov, and V. V. Shevtsov. "The Biology and the Distribution of the Antarctic Krill." In *Antarctic Ecology*, edited by M. W. Holdgate, 173–76. London and New York: Academic Press, 1970.

Marchisio, Sergio, and Antonietta Di Blase. *The Food and Agriculture Organization (FAO)*. Dordrecht, Netherlands: Martinus Nijhoff Publishers, 1991.

Marr, James. "The Natural History and Geography of the Antarctic Krill (*Euphausia Superba* Dana)." *Discovery Reports* 32 (1962): 33–464.

Matthews, L. Harrison. "The Natural History of the Elephant Seal with Notes on Other Seals Found at South Georgia." *Discovery Reports* 1 (1929): 233–56.

Matthews, L. Harrison. *Sea Elephant: The Life and Death of the Elephant Seal*. London: MacGibbon & Kee, 1952.

Mauchline, John, and Leonard R. Fisher. *The Biology of Euphausiids*. Advances in Marine Biology. London: Academic Press, 1969.

Mawson, Douglas. "The Proposed Australasian Antarctic Expedition, 1911–1914." *Report of the ANZAAS Congress* 13 (1912): 398–400.

McCormick, John. *Reclaiming Paradise: The Global Environmental Movement*. Bloomington: Indiana University Press, 1989.

McNeill, J. R., and Corinna R. Unger, eds. *Environmental Histories of the Cold War*. Washington, DC, and New York: German Historical Institute and Cambridge University Press, 2010.

Miller, Clark A., and Paul N. Edwards, eds. *Changing the Atmosphere: Expert Knowledge and Environmental Governance*. Cambridge, MA: The MIT Press, 2001.

Mitchell, Barbara. "Antarctica: A Special Case?" *New Scientist*, January 13, 1977, 64–66.

Mitchell, Timothy. *Carbon Democracy: Political Power in the Age of Oil*. London and New York: Verso, 2011.

Morell, James B. *The Law of the Sea: An Historical Analysis of the 1982 Treaty and Its Rejection by the United States*. Jefferson, NC: McFarland & Company, 1992.

Mueggler, Erik. *The Paper Road: Archive and Experience in the Botanical Exploration of West China and Tibet*. Berkeley: University of California Press, 2011.

Muir, Cameron. *The Broken Promise of Agricultural Progress: An Environmental History*. Abingdon, UK, and New York: Routledge, 2014.

Müller, Martin. "Text, Discourse, Affect and Things." In *The Ashgate Companion to Critical Geopolitics*, edited by Klaus Dodds, M. Kuus, and J. Sharp, 49–68. Farnham, UK: Ashgate, 2012.

Munn, R. E., ed. *Environmental Impact Assessment: Principles and Procedures*. 2nd ed. Chichester, UK: Scientific Committee on Problems of the Environment (SCOPE) and John Wiley & Sons, 1979.

Munn, R. E., and SCOPE Workshop on Impact Studies in the Environment, eds. *Environmental Impact Assessment: Principles and Procedures*. Toronto: Scientific Committee on Problems of the Environment (SCOPE), 1975.

Murphy, Robert Cushman. "Antarctic Conservation." *Science* 135, no. 3499 (1962): 194–97.

Murphy, Robert Cushman. *Logbook for Grace: Whaling Brig* Daisy, *1912–1913*. New York: Macmillan, 1947.

Nash, Roderick Frazier. *Wilderness and the American Mind*. 5th ed. New Haven, CT: Yale University Press, 2014.

Needell, Allan A. *Science, Cold War and the American State: Lloyd V. Berkner and the Balance of Professional Ideals*. Amsterdam: Harwood Academic Publishers in association with the National Air and Space Museum Smithsonian Institution, 2000.

Neumann, Roderick P. *Imposing Wilderness: Struggles over Livelihood and Nature Preservation in Africa*. Berkeley: University of California Press, 1998.

Nye, David E. *Consuming Power: A Social History of American Energies*. Cambridge, MA: The MIT Press, 1998.

O'Reilly, Jessica. *The Technocratic Antarctic: An Ethnography of Scientific Expertise and Environmental Governance*. Ithaca, NY: Cornell University Press, 2017.

Ó Tuathail, Gearóid. *Critical Geopolitics: The Politics of Writing Global Space*. Minneapolis: University of Minnesota Press, 1996.

Ó Tuathail, Gearóid, and John Agnew. "Geopolitics and Discourse: Practical Geopolitical Reasoning in American Foreign Policy." *Political Geography* 11, no. 2 (1992): 190–204.

Øritsland, T. "Sealing and Seal Research in the South-West Atlantic Pack Ice, Sept.–Oct.1964." In *Antarctic Ecology*, edited by M. W. Holdgate, 367–76. London and New York: Academic Press, 1970.

Orrego Vicuña, Francisco. *Antarctic Mineral Exploitation: The Emerging Legal Framework*. Cambridge, UK: Cambridge University Press, 1988.

Phillips, Ralph W. *FAO: Its Origins, Formation and Evolution 1945–1981*. Rome: Food and Agriculture Organization, 1981.

Potter, Neal. "The Antarctic: Any Economic Future?" *Bulletin of the Atomic Scientists* 26, no. 10 (1970): 94–99.

Potter, Neal. "Economic Potentials of the Antarctic." *Antarctic Journal of the United States* 4, no. 3 (1969): 61–72.

Potter, Neal. *Natural Resource Potentials of the Antarctic*. New York: American Geographical Society, 1969.

Prescott, J. R. V., and Gillian D. Triggs. *International Frontiers and Boundaries: Law, Politics and Geography*. Leiden, Netherlands: Martinus Nijhoff, 2008.

Priest, Tyler. *The Offshore Imperative: Shell Oil's Search for Petroleum in Postwar America*. College Station: Texas A&M University Press, 2007.

Pyne, Stephen J. *The Ice: A Journey to Antarctica*. Seattle: University of Washington Press, (1986) 1998.

Ray, G. Carleton, and Frank M. Potter Jr. "The Making of the Marine Mammal Protection Act of 1972." *Aquatic Mammals* 37, no. 4 (2011): 522–52.

Report of the Ninth Consultative Meeting, London, 19 September—7 October 1977. London: Foreign and Commonwealth Office, 1977.

"Report of the SCAR Executive Meeting: Cambridge, UK, 6–7 July 1977." *SCAR Bulletin*, no. 58 (January 1978): 97–102.

"Report of the SCAR Executive Meeting, Cambridge: 25–26 June 1971." *SCAR Bulletin*, no. 51 (September 1975): 711–17.

Richards, Rhys. *Sealing in the Southern Oceans 1788–1833*. Wellington, New Zealand: Paremata Press, 2010.

Riddle, Martin J., and Paul M. Goldsworthy. "Environmental Science and the Environmental Ethos of ANARE." In *Australian Antarctic Science: The First 50 Years of ANARE*, edited by Harvey J. Marchant, Desmond J. Lugg, and Patrick G. Quilty, 561–71. Kingston, Tasmania: Australian Antarctic Division, 2002.

Roberts, Peder. *The European Antarctic: Science and Strategy in Scandinavia and the British Empire*. New York: Palgrave Macmillan, 2011.

Roberts, Peder, Lize-Marié van der Watt, and Adrian Howkins, eds. *Antarctica and the Humanities*. London: Palgrave Macmillan, 2016.

Robertson, Thomas. *The Malthusian Moment: Global Population Growth and the Birth of American Environmentalism*. New Brunswick, NJ: Rutgers University Press, 2012.

Robin, Libby. *Defending the Little Desert: The Rise of Ecological Consciousness*. Melbourne, Australia: Melbourne University Press, 1998.

Robin, Libby. *The Flight of the Emu: A Hundred Years of Australian Ornithology 1901–2001*. Melbourne, Australia: Melbourne University Press, 2001.

Robin, Libby. *How a Continent Created a Nation*. Sydney, Australia: University of New South Wales Press, 2007.

Robin, Libby. "Nature Conservation as a National Concern: The Role of the Australian Academy of Science." *Historical Records of Australian Science* 10, no. 1 (1994): 1–24.

Robin, Libby, Sverker Sörlin, and Paul Warde. *The Future of Nature: Documents of Global Change*. New Haven, CT: Yale University Press, 2013.

Rose, Lisle A. *Explorer: The Life of Richard E. Byrd*. Columbia: University of Missouri Press, 2008.

Rothwell, Donald R. *The Polar Regions and the Development of International Law*. Cambridge, UK: Cambridge University Press, 1996.

Rozwadowski, Helen M. *The Sea Knows No Boundaries: A Century of Marine Science under ICES*. Copenhagen, Seattle, and London: International Council for the Exploration of the Sea in association with University of Washington Press, 2002.

Sandved, K. G. "USNS *Eltanin*: Four Years of Research." *Antarctic Journal of the United States* 1, no. 4 (1966): 164–74.

Sanger, Clyde. *Ordering the Oceans: The Making of the Law of the Sea*. Toronto: University of Toronto Press, 1987.

Sargent, Daniel J. *A Superpower Transformed: The Remaking of American Foreign Relations in the 1970s*. New York: Oxford University Press, 2015.

"SCAR Executive Meeting: Moscow, 2–5 August, 1971." *SCAR Bulletin*, no. 40 (January 1972): 179–90.

"SCAR/SCOR Group on the Living Resources of the Southern Ocean (SCOR Working Group 54): Report of a meeting held at Woods Hold, USA, 23–24 August 1976." *SCAR Bulletin*, no. 55 (January 1977): 419–26.

SCAR/SCOR/IAPO/IUBS Symposium on Antarctic Oceanography, Santiago, Chile, 13–16 September 1966. Cambridge, UK: [Scott Polar Research Institute], 1966.

"SCAR Working Group on Biology, Meeting Held in 1968." *SCAR Bulletin*, no. 32 (May 1969): 748–60.

"SCAR Working Group on Oceanography: Tokyo, 22 September 1970." *SCAR Bulletin*, no. 39 (September 1971): 985–87.

Schauer, Jeff. "The Elephant Problem: Science, Bureaucracy, and Kenya's National Parks, 1955 to 1975." *African Studies Review* 58, no. 1 (2015): 177–98.

Scheffer, Victor B. *Adventures of a Zoologist*. New York: Charles Scribner's Sons, 1980.

Scientific Committee on Antarctic Research, Scientific Committee on Oceanic Research, Group of Specialists on Living Resources of the Southern Ocean, SCOR Working Group 54, and Sayed Z. El-Sayed. *Biological Investigations of Marine Antarctic Systems and Stocks (BIOMASS)*. Volume 1, *Research Proposals*. Cambridge, UK: Scientific Committee on Antarctic Research and Scientific Committee on Oceanic Research, 1977.

Scott, James C. *Seeing Like a State: How Certain Schemes to Improve the Human Condition Have Failed*. New Haven, CT: Yale University Press, 1998.

Shapley, Deborah. "Antarctica's Future: Will Oslo Talks on Resources Mean That Scientists Have to Move Over?" *Science* 187, no. 4179 (1975): 820–21.

Sheail, John. *Nature in Trust: The History of Nature Conservation in Britain*. Glasgow, UK: Blackie, 1976.

Sheehan, James J. "The Problem of Sovereignty in European History." *American Historical Review* 111, no. 1 (2006): 1–15.

Shortis, Emma. "'Who Can Resist This Guy?' Jacques Cousteau, Celebrity Diplomacy, and the Environmental Protection of the Antarctic." *Australian Journal of Politics and History* 61, no. 3 (2015): 366–80.

Siple, Paul A. "Geographic Basis for Antarctic Scientific Observations." *Proceedings of the National Academy of Sciences* 40, no. 10 (1954): 978–82.

Smith, A. Gilbert, and A. Hallam. "The Fit of the Southern Continents." *Nature* 225, no. 5228 (1970): 139–44.

"Soviet Exploitation of Seals in the Bering Sea." *Polar Record* 13, no. 87 (1967): 793–94.

"Soviet Sealing in the North Pacific Ocean." *Polar Record* 13, no. 84 (1966): 342.

Spiller, James. *Frontiers for the American Century: Outer Space, Antarctica, and Cold War Nationalism*. Houndmills, UK: Palgrave Macmillan, 2015.

Staerck, Gillian, ed. *The Development of North Sea Oil and Gas*. London: Institute of Contemporary British History, 2002.

Stewart, Duncan. "Antarctic Minerals." *Bulletin of the US Antarctic Projects Officer* 5, no. 4 (December 1963): 12–14.

Stokke, Olav Schram, and Davor Vidas, eds. *Governing the Antarctic: The Effectiveness and Legitimacy of the Antarctic Treaty System*. Cambridge, UK: Cambridge University Press, 1996.

Sullivan, Walter. *Assault on the Unknown: The International Geophysical Year*. New York: McGraw-Hill, 1961.

Summerhayes, Colin P. "International Collaboration in Antarctica: The International Polar Years, the International Geophysical Year, and the Scientific Committee on Antarctic Research." *Polar Record* 44, no. 231 (2008): 321–34.

Taylor, Joseph E., III. "Boundary Terminology." *Environmental History* 13, no. 3 (2008): 454–81.

Templeton, Malcolm. *A Wise Adventure: New Zealand in Antarctica 1920–1960*. Wellington: Victoria University Press in association with the New Zealand Institute of International Affairs, 2000.

Tepper, Rohan, and Marcus Haward. "The Development of Malaysia's Position on Antarctica: 1982 to 2004." *Polar Record* 41, no. 217 (2005): 113–24.

"Third meeting of S.C.A.R. Held in Canberra, 2 to 6 March 1959." *SCAR Bulletin*, no. 3 (September 1959): 589–603.

"Thirteenth Meeting of SCAR, Jackson Hole: 3 to 7 September 1974." *SCAR Bulletin*, no. 49 (January 1975): 429–51.

Tønnessen, J. N., and A. O. Johnsen. *The History of Modern Whaling*. London and Canberra: C. Hurst & Co. and Australian National University Press, 1982.

Turchetti, Simone, Katrina Dean, Simon Naylor, and Martin Siegert. "Accidents and Opportunities: A History of the Radio Echo-Sounding of Antarctica, 1958–79." *British Journal of the History of Science* 41, no. 3 (2008): 417–44.

Turchetti, Simone, Simon Naylor, Katrina Dean, and Martin Siegert. "On Thick Ice: Scientific Internationalism and Antarctic Affairs, 1957–1980." *History and Technology* 24, no. 4 (2008): 351–76.

Turney, Chris. *1912: The Year the World Discovered Antarctica*. Melbourne, Australia: Text, 2012.

"Twelfth Meeting of SCAR, Canberra: 14 to 19 August 1972." *SCAR Bulletin*, no. 43 (January 1973): 621–55.

Tyrrell, Ian. *Crisis of the Wasteful Nation: Empire and Conservation in Theodore Roosevelt's America*. Chicago: University of Chicago Press, 2015.

"United States: Marine Mammal Protection Act." *International Legal Materials* 12, no. 1 (1973): 165–81.

US Department of State. *The Conference on Antarctica, Washington, October 15–December 1, 1959: Conference Documents, the Antarctic Treaty and Related Papers*. Washington, DC: US Department of State, 1959.

US Department of State. "Final Environmental Impact Statement on the Negotiation of a Regime for Conservation of Antarctic Marine Living Resources." 1978.

US Department of State. *Foreign Relations of the United States, 1949*. Vol. 1, *National Security Affairs, Foreign Economic Policy*. Washington, DC: US Government Printing Office, 1976.

US Department of State. *Foreign Relations of the United States, 1950*. Vol. 1, *National Security Affairs; Foreign Economic Policy*. Washington, DC: US Government Printing Office, 1977.

US Department of State. *Foreign Relations of the United States, 1958–1960*. Vol. 2, *United Nations and General International Matters*. Washington, DC: US Government Printing Office, 1991.

US Department of State. *Foreign Relations of the United States, 1969–1976*. Vol. E-1, *Documents on Global Issues, 1969–1972*. Washington, DC: US Government Printing Office, 2005. https://history.state.gov/historicaldocuments/frus1969-76ve01.

US Department of State. *Foreign Relations of the United States, 1969–1976*. Vol. E-3, *Documents on Global Issues, 1973–1976*. Washington, DC: US Government Printing Office, 2009. https://history.state.gov/historicaldocuments/frus1969-76ve03.

van der Watt, Lize-Marié. "Return to Gondwanaland: South Africa, Antarctica, Minerals and Apartheid." *The Polar Journal* 3, no. 1 (2013): 72–93.

Vidas, Davor. "Entry into Force of the Environmental Protocol and Implementation Issues: An Overview." In *Implementing the Environmental Protection Regime for the Antarctic*, edited by Davor Vidas, 1–17. Dordrecht, Netherlands: Kluwer Academic Publishers, 2000.

Wakild, Emily. *Revolutionary Parks: Conservation, Social Justice, and Mexico's National Parks, 1910–1940*. Tucson: University of Arizona Press, 2011.

Walton, David W. H., Peter D. Clarkson, and Colin P. Summerhayes. *Science in the Snow: Fifty Years of International Collaboration through the Scientific Committee on Antarctic Research*. Cambridge, UK: Scientific Committee on Antarctic Research, 2011.

Warde, Paul, Libby Robin, and Sverker Sörlin. *The Environment: A History*. Baltimore, MD: Johns Hopkins University Press, 2018.

Watts, Arthur. *International Law and the Antarctic Treaty System*. Cambridge, UK: Grotius Publications, 1992.

Weiner, Douglas R. *A Little Corner of Freedom: Russian Nature Protection from Stalin to Gorbachëv*. Berkeley: University of California Press, 1999.

Weiner, Douglas R. *Models of Nature: Ecology, Conservation, and Cultural Revolution in Soviet Russia*. Bloomington: Indiana University Press, 1988.

Wenk, Edward, Jr. *The Politics of the Ocean*. Seattle and London: University of Washington Press, 1972.

Wertenbaker, William. *The Floor of the Sea: Maurice Ewing and the Search to Understand the Earth*. Boston: Little, Brown, 1974.

Wertenbaker, William. "The Law of the Sea—I." *New Yorker*, August 1, 1983, 38–65.

Wertenbaker, William. "The Law of the Sea—II." *New Yorker*, August 8, 1983, 56–83.

"Why Ice?" *Ice*, no. 1, February 29, 1978, 1.

Wise, J. Macgregor. "Assemblage." In *Gilles Deleuze: Key Concepts*, edited by Charles J. Stivale, 77–87. Montreal and Kingston, ON: McGill-Queen's University Press, 2005.

Wöbse, Anna-Katharina. "'The World after All Was One': The International Environmental Network of UNESCO and IUPN, 1945–1950." *Contemporary European History* 20, no. 3 (2011): 331–48.

Wolfrum, Rüdiger. *The Convention on the Regulation of Antarctic Mineral Resource Activities: An Attempt to Break New Ground*. Berlin: Springer-Verlag, 1991.

Worster, Donald. *Nature's Economy: A History of Ecological Ideas*. 2nd ed. Cambridge, UK: Cambridge University Press, 1994.

Wright, N. A., and P. L. Williams, eds. *Mineral Resources of Antarctica*. Geological Survey Circular 705. Reston, VA: US Geological Survey, 1974.

Yergin, Daniel. *The Prize: The Epic Quest for Oil, Money & Power*. New York: Touchstone, 1991.

Youatt, Rafi. *Counting Species: Biodiversity in Global Environmental Politics*. Minneapolis: University of Minnesota Press, 2015.

Young, Oran R., ed. *The Effectiveness of International Environmental Regimes: Causal Connections and Behavioral Mechanisms*. Cambridge, MA: The MIT Press, 1999.

Young, Oran R. "The Politics of International Regime Formation: Managing Natural Resources and the Environment." *International Organization* 43, no. 3 (1989): 349–75.

Young, Oran R., and Gail Osherenko, eds. *Polar Politics: Creating International Environmental Regimes*. Ithaca, NY, and London: Cornell University Press, 1993.

Zelko, Frank. *Make It a Green Peace! The Rise of Countercultural Environmentalism*. New York: Oxford University Press, 2013.

Index